Hinduism in Middle India

Also Available from Bloomsbury:

Hinduism in America
Jeffery D. Long

Material Devotion in a South Indian Poetic World
Leah Elizabeth Comeau

Modern Hinduism in Text and Context
Edited by Lavanya Vemsani

Hinduism in Middle India

Narasimha, The Lord of the Middle

Lavanya Vemsani

BLOOMSBURY ACADEMIC
LONDON • NEW YORK • OXFORD • NEW DELHI • SYDNEY

BLOOMSBURY ACADEMIC
Bloomsbury Publishing Plc
50 Bedford Square, London, WC1B 3DP, UK
1385 Broadway, New York, NY 10018, USA
29 Earlsfort Terrace, Dublin 2, Ireland

BLOOMSBURY, BLOOMSBURY ACADEMIC and the Diana logo are trademarks of
Bloomsbury Publishing Plc

First published in Great Britain 2023
This edition published 2024

Copyright © Lavanya Vemsani, 2023

Lavanya Vemsani has asserted her right under the Copyright, Designs and Patents Act, 1988, to be identified as Author of this work.

For legal purposes the Acknowledgments on p. ix constitute an extension of this copyright page.

Cover design: Tjasa Krivec
Cover image © Raghupathi K.V. / Getty Images

All rights reserved. No part of this publication may be reproduced or transmitted in any form or by any means, electronic or mechanical, including photocopying, recording, or any information storage or retrieval system, without prior permission in writing from the publishers.

Bloomsbury Publishing Plc does not have any control over, or responsibility for, any third-party websites referred to or in this book. All internet addresses given in this book were correct at the time of going to press. The author and publisher regret any inconvenience caused if addresses have changed or sites have ceased to exist, but can accept no responsibility for any such changes.

A catalogue record for this book is available from the British Library.

Library of Congress Control Number: 2022936789

ISBN: HB: 978-1-3501-3851-3
PB: 978-1-3503-4386-3
ePDF: 978-1-3501-3852-0
eBook: 978-1-3501-3853-7

Typeset by Deanta Global Publishing Services, Chennai, India

To find out more about our authors and books visit www.bloomsbury.com and sign up for our newsletters

My parents Ramaseetha Devi and Vijaya Bhaskara Rao Mandalapu

Contents

List of Figures	viii
Acknowledgments	ix
Transliteration Conventions	xi
1 Introduction: Narasimha, the Lord of the Middle in Middle India	1
2 Classical Sources of Narasimha: Symbolism of the Middle	29
3 Historical Narasimha from Prehistory to Present	59
4 Narasimha in Middle India: From Rigveda to Oggukatha	81
5 Lakshmi in the Classical and Regional Tales of Narasimha: Gender and Family	101
6 Narasimha in the Eastern Region: Odisha and Andhra Pradesh	127
7 Narasimha in the Central Region: Madhya Pradesh, Chhattisgarh, and Telangana	151
8 Narasimha in the Western Region: Maharashtra and Karnataka	167
9 Narasimha in Popular Culture, Performing Arts, and Devotional Practice	183
10 Conclusion: Narasimha in Totality	201
Glossary	217
Notes	219
References	224
Index	237

Figures

1	Yoga Narasimha (first to third century CE), Nagarjunakonda in Guntur, Andhra Pradesh	4
2	Narasimha slaying Hiranyakashipu, lithograph from Calcutta (eighteenth century CE)	16
3	Narasimha slaying Hiranyakashipu with gods in attendance, lithograph from Calcutta (eighteenth century CE)	38
4	Yoga Narasimha, wood carving (fifteenth century CE), Kerala	43
5	Appearance of Narasimha, wooden image (seventeenth to eighteenth century CE)	66
6	Yoga Narasimha, largest known image of Narasimha (fifteenth century CE), Hampi	91
7	Lakshmi Narasimha (Narasimha seated with Lakshmi)	103
8	Narasimha seated with Lakshmi (Hoyasala Era twelfth century CE), Somanathapura, Mysore	106
9	Yoga Narasimha (third century CE), Srinagar Museum	154
10	Yoga Narasimha (twelfth century CE)	176
11	Yoga Narasimha, Chola Panchaloha image (tenth to twelfth century CE)	197

Acknowledgments

The subject of Narasimha has stayed with me since I visited the Narasimha temple at Simhachalam many years ago. Over the years I have visited many more centers of Narasimha in Middle India. I have also met practitioners of yoga based on the tradition of Narasimha yoga. I have also met performance artists of Oggukatha and Harikatha based on Narasimha as the central deity. I have also conducted research on the religion of Middle India examining the specific traditions and practices associated with Narasimha. This book represents my attempt to bring most of this disparate information together to comprehend the true depth of the god Narasimha felt in regional practice, which is presented in the regional texts and practices.

First of all, I would like to thank my editors at Bloomsbury, Lalle Purseglove, Camilla Erskine, and Lily McMahon.

I would like to thank Dr. Susan Huntington, distinguished professor (emerita), and Dr. John Huntington, professor (emeritus), Ohio State University, for developing the wonderful resource of photos hosted at https://www.huntingtonarchive.org/ and making them available to researchers freely. I thank them for readily giving me permission to publish a number of photographs of Narasimha included in this book. I would like to thank Dr. Cathleen Cummings, professor and director of the Cultural Studies Program at the University of Alabama, for the great picture of Narasimha at Hampi and for permitting me to publish the picture in this book.

I would like to thank the director and staff at the Napier Museum of Art, Trivandrum, Kerala, India, for permitting me to publish the photograph of Narasimha from their collection. I would like to thank the Metropolitan Museum of Art, New York, and Brooklyn Museum of Art, Brooklyn, New York, for permission to publish the photographs of Narasimha from their open museum collections. I would like to thank the Cleveland Museum of Art, Cleveland, Ohio, for permitting me to publish the photograph of Narasimha from their collection.

I would like to thank our Chair Dr. Chip Poirot and my colleagues in the Department of Social Sciences at Shawnee State University, for their support throughout the process of writing this book. I would like to thank our Dean Dr. Jennifer Pauley for supporting my research.

I thank the staff at our campus library, especially Suzanne Johnson-Varney, Director of Library Services, and Marla Beebe, Research and Instruction librarian, for acquiring the books I needed quickly and supporting me throughout the process of writing this book.

I thank Shawnee State University, especially our President Dr. Jeff Bauer and Provost Dr. Sunil Ahuja, for supporting my research and travel through funding and a sabbatical in 2021. I have presented a number of papers based on the subject of this book at the American Academy of Religion (AAR), Association of Asian Studies (AAS), and Canadian Society for the Study of Religion (CSSR). I thank my fellow researchers and friends for attending the presentations and for their insightful remarks.

I thank the Fulbright for awarding me the Fulbright Global Fellow Award (2021–22) during which I conducted my research for this book.

I would like to thank my friend R. L. Mohl for his animated discussions on goddesses and for reading parts of the manuscript.

My deepest gratitude is reserved for my family even though I feel words are not enough to express everything I owe to the support of my husband Venkata Ramana Vemsani and my son Aashish S. Vemsani.

Transliteration Conventions

No transliteration conventions were followed in this book as different Indian language words, including, but not limited to, Tamil, Telugu, Oriya, Kannada, and Marathi, are spelled in the mode of spelling commonly used. However, if a name appears in male and female genders, the female name is indicated by double vowels. For example, the daughter of the god Surya, as a female name, is spelled as Suryaa.

1

Introduction

Narasimha, the Lord of the Middle in Middle India

Hiranyakashipu, the lord of Daityas, has such prowess; in ancient times Vishnu, in the form of Narasimha, became death onto him.

Vayu Purana II.6.66

India is a rich storehouse of human experience on Earth. Each region of India preserves unique variations in language, religion, and culture deriving from its distinct historical path. The history of Hinduism in the middle region of India, Madhya Desha, can be learned from widely practiced religion represented in oral tales and temple traditions in addition to the classical texts, which preserve core narratives popularly known in Middle India. Classical stories fuse the theology of Vishnu with the land through adoption in practice and performance. Therefore, the middle avatara Narasimha is most closely linked to Middle India (Telangana, Andhra Pradesh, Maharashtra, Karnataka, Odisha, Madhya Pradesh, and Chhattisgarh). This is not to indicate that temples and practices associated with Narasimha are not found in other areas of India, but that deeper practices and literary sources emphatically connect it to Middle India, which will be examined in the following pages. This chapter is divided into four sections for the sake of convenience of study. The first section introduces the subject and hypothesis. The second section considers the sacred geography and the nature of Narasimha's association with the middle and the land of the middle. The third section examines the classical accounts of Narasimha to understand the symbolism of the middle in connection with Narasimha. Section four discusses the method and plan of study along with the significance of the project and its contribution to the academic study of Hinduism.

Introduction to the Subject and Scope of Study: Hinduism in Middle India

The middle region of India is the *leelasthali* (land of divine play) of the deity Narasimha widely represented in popular tales and practices of Middle India in conjunction with the classical texts, and therefore a study focused on Narasimha will illuminate the necessary aspects of the history of Hinduism, which have not become part of the academic understanding of the Hinduism of this region. Special features of Narasimha are symbolized in the middle, and transitions are also represented in local stories, practices, and even the location of temples. Hence, the profusion of Narasimha temples, tales, and practices in Middle India enlivens the theology of the middle juxtaposed with the sacred geography of Middle India resulting in a spirited practice. Therefore, my research in this book has the dual objectives of analyzing the classical texts and oral texts in addition to also examining the symbolic representation of texts in arts as well as cultural practices associated with the texts. Therefore, my work in this book focuses on two aspects of understanding of the god Narasimha. First, the classical, historical, and regional representations of Narasimha in texts, history, and folk stories are studied. Second, I will analyze the regional representations of Narasimha by examining the most important strands of religious practice from well-known temples of the middle region (central, eastern, and western parts of Middle India), understanding the sacred geography as well as the imprints of Narasimha's *leela* on the culture of the region.

Even though Narasimha temples and traditions are spread across the subcontinent I decided to focus on the core area of the Narasimha tradition in this book, since this region preserves crucial information for realizing the immensity of religious practice centered on Narasimha. Unless the core area and belief system are examined closely any studies focusing on the larger area might not be able to lead to a fruitful understanding of Indian religion. Hence, my study of Hinduism in Middle India contributes in multiple ways to gaining a deeper understanding of the religion in India and especially religion in Middle India and the traditions of Narasimha, which have been only superficially explored.

Consequently, in this book, *History of Hinduism in Middle India: Narasimha the Lord of the Middle*, I examine the classical and oral traditions of Madhya Desha (Middle India) along with practice. Specifically, I examine the popular texts and traditions of Narasimha in conjunction with the classical texts, but will also help elucidate the historical religion of one of the sparsely studied deities of Hinduism,

Narasimha; in addition, this book will help illustrate the Hindu religious practice of one of the least comprehensively studied regions of India. Three aspects of society, life, the land, and practice (religion), are interwoven forming a unitary thread in the stories and practices associated with the deity Narasimha.

The symbolism of the Simha/lion is ubiquitous in Indian culture and art. The lion is not merely an animal, but the most important symbol of great strength and courage in India. Buddha is referred to as Shakyasimha (Coomaraswamy 1929: 287–317). Numerous social groups in India use Singh, a derivative of Simha/Singha (lion), as a surname. Hence, the lion has played a significant role in the life of Indians for millennia, probably from the Upper Paleolithic period onwards as seen in the Bhimbetka cave paintings.[1] Prehistoric depictions of lions have been found across India including the oldest rock painting of the world at Bhimbedka, with the early phase datable between 150,000 years ago and 80,000 years ago (Badam and Sathe 1991: 196–208). The frequency of the occurrence of the lion in prehistoric symbols and paintings as well as later totemic symbols led to speculations about the origin of the Narasimha tradition in tribal religion (Jaiswal 1973: 140–151). On the contrary, it might only be an indication of the early origin of the worship of a lion-formed deity probably during the prehistoric era. Historical depictions of Narasimha are noted in classical texts including the Vedas. Sculptural representations are noted in the early art of India including the Ashokan capitals which depict single as well as multiple lions simultaneously: While the Sarnath and Sanchi capitals depict four seated lions, Vaishali capitals depict a single seated lion (300 BCE). Excavations at Basrah near Vaishali brought to light the earliest depiction of Kevala Narasimha, Narasimha seated on a high seat, which can be dated to at least about 300 BCE if not earlier, since this could be coeval with the other historical material excavated at Vaishali which ranges between 600 and 300 BCE. Sculptures of seated Narasimha datable between 1 and 300 CE were found in ruins among the excavations at Motadaka, Nagarjunakonda (see Figure 1), and Kondamotu (now preserved in the State Museum, Hyderabad) revealed unique early sculptures of Narasimha (see Chapter 3 for more historical information on Narasimha). Lion sculptures predominate and appear most commonly among temple sculptures, representing transitions and crossings as well as security from evil by sanctifying the transitions and crossings (see Chapter 4). Narasimha stories preserved in popular traditions provide far more information on popular practices and beliefs associated with Narasimha than the classical stories of Narasimha in the Purana texts, which provide theological and ritual aspects.

Figure 1 Yoga Narasimha (first to third century CE), Nagarjunakonda in Guntur, Andhra Pradesh. Photo by Susan C. Huntington. Courtesy of the John C. and Susan L. Huntington Photographic Archive of Buddhist and Asian Art.

In the middle region of India, especially in Andhra Pradesh, Telangana, and Karnataka, the Narasimha tradition abounds. Personal names of Narasimha, as well as names after sacred sites associated with Narasimha such as Ahobalam (Ahobala, Aubala, Obula, Obayya/Obamma), Simhachalam (Simhadri, Simhachalam, Chalam/Chalamayya), and Yadagiri (Yadadri, Yadayya/ Yadamma, Yadagiri), are frequent. If a random group of ten people is selected from any part of the Telugu states of Andhra Pradesh and Telangana, I am sure at least one would be named either Narasimha or some variation of it. It is also not a coincidence that the first Telugu Prime Minister of India was named after Narasimha too, P.V. Narasimha Rao. Therefore, although temples and practices associated with Narasimha are found widely across India, I decided to focus on the middle region of India for its close association with him as his *leelasthali* and his widespread popularity among the common people of Middle India, in addition to the abundance of multiple sources.

The popular nature of the deity Narasimha, the association with the prehistoric symbolism of lions, and the association with vanavasi social groups (an encompassing term for tribes, which are incorporated into the constitution of India as the Scheduled Tribes) and groups such as Khonds, Chenchus, and Sabaras confused earlier understandings of Narasimha categorizing him as a folk deity and refusing to accord him the status of Hindu deity (Sontheimer; Murty; Eschmann).

In this book the term vanavasi (forest-dwellers) is preferred to denote the communities commonly referred to as tribes or Scheduled Tribes, or more derogatorily as primitive or aborigines, since the term tribe does not fully encompass the social experience of the numerous social groups within Hinduism. The distinctions of social groups as tribes and castes within the spectrum of Indian social groupings are misleading as the distinctions between the tribes and castes were developed for administrative convenience under the British, without taking into account their social or cultural practices. Within the Narasimha tradition no distinction is noticed between the social groups as the simplest folks, the vanavasis, are frequently central to the tradition.

When one is examining a traditional religious practice more than 2,500–3,000 years old, it is important to bring together all the available evidence for the benefit of understanding the longstanding practice, its evolution, and continuity rather than juxtaposing texts with practice (folk tradition) or vice versa, which only leads to a partial understanding of the subject under study.

The land and religion fuse together in the concepts of cosmology, theology, and the personality of Narasimha, which also transposes onto the rituals and arts associated with Narasimha. Hence, it is important to analyze the multiple sources together to arrive at a comprehensive understanding of the religion and practice of the middle region of India in association with Narasimha.

This central aspect of Narasimha roaming the land is also embedded in the Rigvedic verse (I.154.2), which mentions that "In this way Vishnu will be praised for his heroic deed—(he who is) *like a fearsome wild beast, living in the mountains, and roaming wherever he wants*, in whose three wide strides dwell all living beings" (emphasis mine). Although not indicated directly, the words "fearsome wild beast, living in the mountains, and roaming wherever he wants," bring Narasimha to mind immediately. This is the central aspect of Narasimha incorporated into the practice and Sthalapuranas of Narasimha besides the classical texts. The Rigvedic verses I.154 and I.156 cryptically highlight the avataras of Vishnu and his divine deeds (*leela*) on the Earth as well as the celestial world and underworld (the triloka/three worlds). Thus, the cryptic Rigvedic verses and symbolism of prehistoric wanderings preserved in the popular local tales help us to understand the sacred geography of Middle India, which is also the *leelasthali* (region of divine deeds) of Narasimha.

However, a comprehensive study of classical stories, folk tales, and practice helps bring out the immensity of Narasimha tradition in the middle region and the impact on the history and cultural life of the region. Narasimha could gain his rightful place as a major god rather than a folk deity or demigod due to the fact of his representation as an anthropomorphic form along with non-traditional practice as interpreted in the previous scholarship.

Texts represent the past culture and history of society and simultaneously provide the basis for current practice as well as inspiration for the future. Hence, a comprehensive study of texts within the context of cultural practice is very important in order to gain a comprehensive understanding of historical society.

This book focuses on accounts of Narasimha from textual sources both in classical and regional records as well as performance traditions in order to understand historical Hinduism in text and practice. Theological aspects of representation, ritual, and worship practice associated with the sacred centers of the god Narasimha are included where necessary. Hence the present study represents a comprehensive historical understanding of text and practice.

Sacred Geography: Narasimha in the Land of the Middle

The middle region of India, especially Andhra Pradesh, now divided into two states: Andhra Pradesh and Telangana, forms the *leelasthali* (land of divine play) of Narasimha. Similar to the region of Braj (Braj Mandala) for Krishna, Ahobilam and a number of places located within a 100-mile radius of this region are linked to the appearance and *leela* of Narasimha. Other sacred sites beyond this region have links to Narasimha as he visits these places to vanquish demons and protect the folks of the region (e.g., Narasimha temple in Sholingur, Tamil Nadu) or appeared in the dream vision of a devotee (e.g., Narasimhanatha temple in Padampur, Odisha) informing him of his sacred appearance and instructing him to build a temple and perform pujas and sevas (worship and services). The sacred geography of the region is traced by the steps of Narasimha, which continue to be traced by the devotees. Similar to Krishna, who blessed the Gopis, cowherdesses, of Brajbhumi, Narasimha blessed the most simple folk of this region, the Chenchus, with his presence among them. Narasimha lived among the Chenchus, becoming one among them by marrying their daughter and becoming their son-in-law. Hence, historical, artistic, and cultural symbols marking their tryst with the divine, the deity Narasimha, are marked on the land of this region, while the stories are etched on the memory recollected through local folk tales and performance practices. Hence, the sacred geography connected with Narasimha recollects the significant events from the legend of Narasimha, noting each step of his divine descent and reflects his presence symbolical incorporating the symbolic features associated with the deity Narasimha. Events such as Narasimha vanquishing the demon, blessing the devotee Prahlada, practicing yoga, and marrying Chenchulakshmi, all form an integral part of the sacred landscape, and celebrating the people and land of Middle India. Middle India represents the symbolic nature of Narasimha as the god of the middle/transitions, thus becoming the spiritual land, the *leelasthali*. His imprint is sealed on the land through his sacred interactions with the land and the people.

Krishna is recognized as the *purna avatara* (full incarnation) of Vishnu. Similarly, textual sources depict Narasimha as another full form of Vishnu, since Narasimha is present within the universe and outside of the universe simultaneously, as Vishnu, but in his form as Narasimha. This similarity of Narasimha to Krishna is noticed as Narasimha is offered prayers in Krishna temples and Narasimha temples and Krishna temples are established next to each other in a number of temple centers in India. The most important example is the incorporation of Narasimha into the temple complex and ritual of Jagannatha at Jagannatha temple in Puri. Similar to Krishna Vasudeva, Narasimha is also represented as the *vyuha* indicating his presence within and outside of creation simultaneously. Examples of practice also show Krishna devotees realizing their enlightenment through worship of Narasimha (Vemsani 2016a: 147–61). Narayana Tirtha devoted his meditation to Narasimha to obtain a cure. He created the dance tradition of worshipping Krishna through *Krishna Leela Tharangini* after his cure, depicting the identity of Narasimha as Krishna, the purna avatara (full avatara) of Vishnu.

Regional boundaries or fixed boundaries that limit the movement of people are not traditionally known in historical India in the classical era. Hence, even though the sacred centers of Narasimha are spread over a large area belonging to different kingdoms at different points of time, the devotees and monks were not prevented from traveling, so their connection within sacred geography, as well as networks of Narasimha temples, was not disrupted over the millennia. Regional disruptions only become obvious in later history as borders limiting travel were gradually imposed on India beginning with Islamic rule as Hindu pilgrimages were gradually banned. Therefore, even though the Narasimha temples are located in areas separated by regional borders they frequently formed part of a unique networked practice, not hampered by regional borders. Geography is defined by theological connections, which is very clear with the spread of Narasimha temples in the middle region of India. The modern states formed on a linguistic basis redraw the historical borders of India, but do not disturb from devotional pilgrimage circuits but continue the historical connections. The theology of Narasimha has been expressed throughout the region in the landscape of the temples as well as the deep symbolism it represented.

While studying religion in Middle India, previous works focused on aspects of religion other than theology such as ethnology (Sontheimer 1978), pilgrimage (Feldhause 2003; 1995), and devotion (Debicka-Borek 2019: 159–85). However, it has been shown in the case of Narasimha temples that the geographical connectivity might have less to do with mere external factors than with theological aspects connected with the deity. Previous works have noted yoga, in connection with Yoga Narasimha, as one of the aspects of the concentration of Narasimha kshetras (sacred geography) in certain unique sites such as Mattapalli, Vadapalli, and Vedadri (Vedagiri 2004). However, my examination of classical stories of Narasimha in conjunction with local tales and practices helps reveal that it is the special theological features associated with Narasimha which help determine the specific geographical locations. External factors such as ethnological aspects of pilgrimage and devotion only form secondary aspects of the emergence of certain regions in connection with Narasimha's sacred geography. Therefore, in this book, the focus is on exploring the predominant features associated with Narasimha as part of his divine incarnation and how these features might find expression in local tales as well as the temples and their practices. The sacred geography represents the theological and metaphysical notions of the temple sites concerning the god. The origin and development of many sites of Narasimha temples are expressed in classical texts as well as the landscape in which they are located. The local tales preserved in regional language compositions, known as the Sthalapuranas and the Mahatmyas, represent the origin and connection of the sacred site with the deity while the geographical features, as well as the practices, demonstrate the direct connection with the central feature of the deity, the middle and/or the transitional nature.

Partial examination of stories of Narasimha and religious practice has also prompted historical presuppositions, which have occupied Indological scholarship for the past century (Sontheimer 1985; 2004; Debicka-Borek 2019: 167; Eschmann 1978: 79). Aryanization or many of its varied names, Sanskritization, or Hinduization, forms the central aspect of these studies rather than analyzing the available historical data on its own merit. The Chenchus are one of the living groups of this area maintaining a prehistoric lifestyle and social groups living within the area of Ahobilam. They might have protected the temples of Narasimha historically, and they also form the central part of temple stories, which indicates that prehistoric elements of culture are part of Hinduism during its early phase indicated by the Narasimha tradition rather than the Hinduization of a tribal group through the assimilation of Narasimha. The tribal groups are as much part of the early religion of India as the sages and saints, with other social groups located at various spots on the spectrum of the evolving religious life of India. Hinduism is the living religion of India, as the streams of practice and thought joined and evolved forming the unique religion of India, which is indigenous and incorporates the life of the land in multiple forms.

Genetic research conducted on the population groups of this region has revealed that all of the social groups, regardless of any social distinction such as the numerous castes or tribes in administrative terms, including the Chenchus, are autochthonous living groups and do not include any invaders. No sudden genetic or historical changes datable to 1900–1000 BCE were notable either in genetic heritage or archaeological data, even though that date is projected for the arrival of Aryans followed by their conquests and occupations across India (Vemsani 2014: 594–620; Shinde et al. 2019). During prehistory, all human groups lived a Paleolithic lifestyle before adapting to other modes of life. Hence, it is possible that some of the social groups following the Paleolithic lifestyle also preserved the elements of religion prevalent in the prehistoric period, while the other social groups gradually adapted to changes in lifestyles and other aspects of culture. It is, therefore, plausible that folks that have similar genetic heritage and cultural practices may not have been historically antagonistic groups, but allied with each other. Evidence is too scanty to support the theory that an invading group of foreigners could have brought the deity Narasimha about 3,000–3,500 years ago and imposed the religion on the indigenous populations of Andhra Pradesh through marriage stories. The dichotomy of "invaders vs. indigenous" is not plausible, especially when it is not possible to distinguish them based on their genetic heritage or religious practice either in a historical period or currently.

The worship of Narasimha preserves many prehistoric sentiments in the symbolic elements of life as hunter-gatherers, and the lion—symbolized as the best hunter of the forest—might have represented the sentiments of the population of this earlier era. However, the groups that adapted to new lifestyles might still have kept their religious traditions alive as did their social compatriots that remained with the prehistoric lifestyle. Hence, the traditions associated with Narasimha represent prehistoric traditions, which carried forward as many historical changes followed in society and culture. These historical changes might have happened gradually over many centuries, even millennia, since Narasimha-related religion and traditions are noticed in Andhra Pradesh from the first century CE. Such gradual historical change preserves original elements, preserving them as the core while accumulating later changes around this core. In contrast, sudden changes brought about by conquests or superimpositions from an alien population show complete erasure of the early core leaving it as an appendage to the new core that the invaders might introduce. On the contrary, the natural order of stories, the retention of the core story, gradual assimilation, and the adaption of regional tales demonstrate no sudden imposition, but the gradual evolution of the indigenous religious tradition, especially in the case of the religious tradition and practice associated with Narasimha.

The sages, monks, and ascetics that composed the texts and wandered across the land of India might have come from the same population that formed the larger population of the early society. An important example of the humble beginnings of the composer of texts is preserved in the Ramayana. Valmiki, the composer of Ramayana, had been a hunter before he decided to practice asceticism and compose the Ramayana. In addition, there is an abundance of inscriptions listing the names of monks at monasteries such as Nagarjunakonda (Vogel 1929–30), which include a variety of names, professions, and places, demonstrating that the traditional priests (learned class) of India were derived from many sections of society in the first millennium BCE when the classical texts first appeared in written form, probably derived from the long-known oral traditions. The later Vaishnava and Shaiva traditions of Middle India, especially Andhra Pradesh and Karnataka, continued this tradition of deriving their ascetic and learned followers from all sections of society. The Shaiva schools of thought, as well as the Vaishnava schools of thought, erased all distinctions, placing Shiva at the center of devotion from the sixth century CE onwards. One such important piece of evidence of accepting followers from all sections of society is preserved in the lives of Shankara[2] and Ramanuja[3] as well as Basavanna.[4] It is a common saying that the origin of sages cannot be known.[5]

The evidence within Narasimha tradition supports the idea that the historical changes might not have happened suddenly due to conquest and occupation. Elements of Narasimha tradition are tightly woven into the social and cultural fabric of India along with the strong symbolic imprint on the land. Religious elements of Narasimha contain the primal religious consciousness of prehistoric inhabitants of the region and demonstrate continuous evolution. The invader vs. indigenous paradigm has misled early studies, which didn't analyze the original core of the story and its growth through the assimilation of theogonic and theological features associated with Narasimha. Careful analysis of Narasimha stories reveals the original core of the religious practices, which represents the practices of prehistoric autochthonous inhabitants of India. This is the reason the central characteristic of Narasimha is all-encompassing and found in almost all the features associated with Middle India in the stories, practices, and religious traditions.

Importance of Sacred Geography within the Narasimha Stories

The concept of Time and Space is important in the stories of Narasimha. According to Hindu cosmogony, the universe revolves in relation to numerous worlds. The world of humans, the Earth, revolves in concert with the celestial worlds of the Devas (gods) and the underworld of the Asuras (demons). The story of Narasimha brings forward a reversal of this order, which pushed the universe into chaos. It is this time of chaos, which is represented by the reversals noted in the course of the universe, that necessitated the incarnation of Narasimha. As an incarnation marking the period of chaos, Narasimha represents the Time of Transition (Yuganta). Since the universe is in the reverse course due to the actions of Hiranyakashipu, Narasimha epitomizes the transitional phase of the reverse course of Time, and his killing of Hiranyakashipu marks the return of the world to its usual right course of direction. This also brings an end to the incarnation of Narasimha. The concepts of Time and Space are symbolically represented in the stories of Narasimha. Time is represented in the transitional qualities of Narasimha, and these features are also represented in space in the geographical features. For a discussion of the Time and Space continuum and the concept of Time in Hinduism, see Chapters 2 and 4.

Narasimha and the Geographical Affiliation

Vishnu and Lakshmi are the deities displaying the most affiliation with the Earth. The earthly nature and land affiliation of Vishnu are emblematic of his divine character. As Purusha, he represents creation including the Earth, and as Narayana, he represents the waters of the world (Dasgupta 1981; Bharadwaja 1981). His wife Lakshmi represents the wealth of the world (see Chapter 5). Therefore, Vishnu through his incarnations strides the world and the universe as noted in the accounts of his incarnations (Glucklick 2008).

Hindu tradition preserves the understanding of the Earth as originating from the divine body of the god, and hence preserves the identity of the divine within the land, which is expressed through special features that are also closely represented within the divine (see Chapter 4 for a discussion of the geography and symbolism of the middle).

Hence, in the popular practice the god Narasimha is not merely an incarnation of Vishnu but also symbolically represented in the sacred geography of the middle region of India, appears represented as the most important landscapes, including the hills, bounders, and caves across the land of the middle region of India. Numerous temples are dedicated to Narasimha. Some temples of Vishnu, representing other incarnations, also incorporate the worship of Narasimha even though the temple might have been dedicated to another deity. For example, Narasimha is one of the major deities at the sacred center of Tirupati even though the central temple is dedicated to Venkateshwara (Pidatala 2001 [1933]). At Jagannatha temple in Puri, the Narasimha temple is one the major temples and the Narasimha mantra is incorporated into the daily rituals of Jagannatha (Tripathi 1987: 83–93).

The Symbolism of Transitional Middle in the God Narasimha as the Geographical Middle

Being middle and transitional is a notable feature of Vishnu (Kuiper 1962: 143–5; Soifer 1991: 155), even though it is the most unique feature of the Narasimha avatara. The middle and the transitional phase are characteristically represented in the avatara Narasimha. Indeed, the centrality of the transitional middle is personified in the avatara of Narasimha (see Chapter 2 for more information on how the transitional middle is personified in the avatara of Narasimha). Unfortunately, this feature is misinterpreted with negative connotations in earlier studies, as a "loophole in the law" (Soifer 8–9; 13 Note 21).[6] This central characteristic of Narasimha is lost, through adaption of this motif of a "loophole in the law." In using this term, "loophole in the law," the analysis of the story shifts focus to the demon as the central character on whose law the world was supposed to be based rather than Vishnu. Fortunately, Soifer recognized that this motif is not quite useful or representative of Narasimha, admitting, "At the conclusion of the motific analysis it was evident that, although motifs had headed us down the right track, the cart was before the horse . . . brought the realization that the avatara was not the *creator* of this liminality, but relied on that quality inherent in the cosmological structures to *appear* liminal." However, through indicating a liminal state here, in another remote interpretation imposed on the incarnation of Narasimha, she further compares it to the liminality and communitas noted in the ritual process of Rite of Passage, noted in the anthropological research of

Turner (1969), which is also not applicable to this account of Narasimha. Soifer alludes to the communitas characteristic of the Bhakti movement[7] (Soifer 9), even though Bhakti is not a major part of the story of Narasimha in most of the available versions of the story. It is important to rescue the understanding of Narasimha from such disconnected comparisons to bring clarity to the practices associated with Narasimha in particular and to understand the cultural evolution of Indians in general.

However, as the story makes clear, from the beginning Hiranyakashipu wrested the power of law (dharma) into his hands away from those to whom it belonged through tricking one of the gods through his severe penances. Hence, the fact that Narasimha acquired the form representing the middle and not belonging to any known categorizations is not a "loophole in the law," but represents the enormous symbolism of events that conspired in this story to recover balance in the world. However, as shown in the story of Narasimha, the feature of transitions, or the middle and not belonging, is a strength rather than a shortcoming unless you are consciously deciding not to use that traditional form. Contrary to the explanations of a loophole, the centrality of transitions in the character of Narasimha proves the power of embracing a transitory nature, the strength of being the middle. I will discuss in the following chapters how the cultural aspects of Middle India as the region embraces this special characteristic of the middle or transitory nature as a central aspect and adapt Narasimha as the central deity in this region. A clear understanding of the stories is necessary as they are bearers of historical evidence to the cultural evolution of society and incorporation the divine within the sacred geography and practice. Narasimha's appearance embracing the middle and transitory nature is not a mere loophole but symbolizes something deeply embedded in the story, which is then reflected in the sacred geography and religious practices associated with Narasimha.

Sources of Study: Textual and Material History

This book represents an effort to bring all available sources together from textual and oral, as well as material evidence such as art-historical and archaeological sources to examine and shed light on the tradition of Narasimha. History hasn't taken kindly to oral sources, dismissing them as unreliable and hence not usable as authentic sources of history. However, for India, most of the important sources are frequently preserved in oral texts and stories. Considering orality as the preliterate mode of life representing less organized and less progressive thinking had been normalized in the twentieth century (Ong 1982: 37–49). Oral literature is considered to be overly expressive, loaded with epithets, redundant/repetitious, and not objective (Ong 180–230). Isn't it possible that the people who were able to keep prehistoric lifestyles intact for millennia might have been able to keep the lore from millennia ago intact? I, therefore, consider the oral tales collected from common folks and compiled within the genre of Sthalapuranas and preserved in the performance arts of Yakshaganam and Oggukatha to be equally authentic for understanding the religion and culture of Middle India as the classical texts.

Textual studies (based on Sanskrit texts) and anthropological studies (based on ethnography) remained exclusivist focusing on Aryan invasion theory refusing to bring together the numerous regional aspects, which symbolized gradual development, into broader analysis. Therefore, the field of Indian studies is dominated by theories of Sanskritization or Hinduization with the premise that Hinduism (Sanskrit) was imposed on the natives by invading Aryans. However, the Aryan invasion theory has been disproven (Vemsani 2014; Shinde et al. 2019) through genetic research and lack of evidence in archeological excavations. Hence, the presupposed theory of "invader vs. indigenous" is invalid. Scholars have previously proposed bringing together the textual studies and ethnographic studies in the hopes of bridging some of this gap in understanding the religious traditions (Van Buitenen 1966: 23–41; Singer 1961: 274). Singer has noted that "many a student of Indian culture on his first visit to India has been astonished and enchanted—as I was, to find so much of the epic and Puranic mythology and legends alive in contemporary oral traditions" in connection with Krishna, and wondered, "how are a legend and a cult so ancient, so varied, and widespread in their cultural expression, so profound in their significance, to be studied?" (Singer 1966: Foreword). This is true with regards to all major deities of Hinduism including Narasimha. Hence, the sources, practice, and my field trips to many of the places under study form the background of this study.

I discuss regional as well as classical texts of Narasimha in this work. The following Puranas, Upapuranas, and Sthalapuranas are used throughout this book:

I use Vedic sources since Rigveda (datable between 4500 BCE and 2300 BCE) and other later Vedic texts (2300 BCE–1300 BCE) provide cryptic references to the deity Narasimha. Almost all the classical texts beginning with the Mahabharata (400 BCE–200 CE) and Harivamsa (400 BCE–200 CE) and the Puranas (300 BCE–1000 CE) provide detailed accounts of the legend of Narasimha. The Sanskrit Narasimha Purana is a upapurana datable to 500 CE (R.C. Hazra). The Narasimha Purana (Jena 1987) contains six Kandas. The first is Shrishthi Kanda and contains Chapters 1–21. The second Kanda contains Vamsha, Manvantara, and Vamshanucharita containing Chapters 22–29. The third is the Bhugola Kanda containing Chapters 30–31. The fourth Kanda is the Haryavataradi Nirupana containing Chapters 32–56. The fifth Kanda is Varnasramadharmadi Nirupana of Chapters 57–62. The final section is Mantratirtha Mahima and Upasamhara. Chapters 36 to 54 contain the descriptions of avataras of Vishnu including Narasimha. The Narasimha Purana is translated into Kannada and published under the Jayachamarajendra Granthamala (Padmanabhacharya 1959). This Kannada translation follows the Sanskrit text closely.

It is difficult to date the Sthalapuranas, but I would like to date them to the 500 CE, about the time numerous temples began to be built in Middle India, even though these texts might have only existed in oral tradition and might been committed to writing much later. The texts of the Sthalapuranas are widespread and appear in poetical compilations beginning with the early second millennium CE. However, the Telugu Narasimha Purana, the most important and central story of Narasimha connected with his origin in Ahobilam, was composed in 1300 CE by Errana, which shows that the story might have been known and preserved in oral tradition at least 200 years prior to this literary composition. For example, even though the Mahābhāratamu is well known in the oral performance traditions (as noted in sculptures of the temples) of the Telugu region, it began to be committed to writing in Telugu in the eleventh century CE. Similarly, popular arts, such as Yakshaganam and Oggukatha, are known to have been practiced from the turn of the second millennium CE, even though literary compositions of Yakshaganas are only available from the fifteenth century CE (Somayaji 1955; Jogarao 1961; Emigh 1984: 21–39).

Historical sources including monumental and archaeological sources (inscriptions, seals, and coins) appear infrequently between 600 BCE to 300 CE. However, from 300 CE onwards the historical resources steadily increase, supplying substantial evidence for the widespread practice centered on the deity Narasimha.

Classical Story of Narasimha: Symbolism of the Middle

There are four elements which form the central theme of the story of Narasimha: (1) The animosity of the demon brothers, Hiranyaksha and Hiranyakashipu, toward the gods, (2) the death of Hiranyaksha and the vow of Hiranyakashipu to avenge the death of his brother, (3) the Ghastly Reign of Hiranyaksha, which threw the Earth off its usual course of movement, and (4) the incarnation of

Figure 2 Narasimha slaying Hiranyakashipu, lithograph from Calcutta (eighteenth century CE). Courtesy: Metropolitan Museum of Art, New York.

Vishnu as Narasimha to rescue the child devotee Prahlada and return the universe to its right course. However, some texts, especially the Shaiva Puranas, incorporate the events of the incarnation of Narasimha beyond this central event of vanquishing the demon. Popular performance traditions and local tales of Andhra Pradesh and Telangana extend the story of Narasimha to include his marriage and reign among the people (Figure 2).

Vishnu undertakes the unique incarnation of Narasimha to confront the evil brought about by the unique circumstances created by Hiranyakashipu due to the special boon he obtained from Brahma. The avataras of Vishnu, Varaha, and Narasimha appear in quick succession vanquishing the demon brothers Hiranyaksha and Hiranyakashipu. The next avatara, Vamana (Trivikrama), also uniquely relates to Narasimha. Comprehensive examinations of Vishnu's incarnations (Gonda 1970; Rao 1937; Trivedi 1972) and of Varaha incarnation in literature and art have been previously undertaken (Tripathi 1968; Soifer 1991; Becker 2010; Mitra 1963); hence I will focus my examination on Narasimha's story here. Due to the cryptic nature of the Vedas, the allusion to Narasimha and Vamana is brief, but their significance cannot be ruled out (Soifer 1991: 25;

Varma 1970: 323–34). Even though historical evidence shows that Narasimha is included among the avataras of Vishnu beginning with the earliest available evidence, some scholars have argued that the concept of Narasimha is not part of Vaishnavism, calling it by the variant term Vishnuism to demonstrate that the existence of the concept of the deity Vishnu exclusively, separate from the incarnations, especially Narasimha (Tripathi 1978: 44). Thus, they argued for the independent origin of Narasimha in the native traditions of India, prior to the arrival of Aryans and Vaishnavism. However, since the evidence connects Narasimha so closely to Vishnu beginning with the earliest evidence, including the Rigvedic references to the special features of Vishnu noted in the killing of Namuci, such assumptions remain false.

The story of Narasimha begins under the demanding circumstances after the death of Hiranyaksha upon the pledge of his younger brother Hiranyakashipu, who vowed not to spare any opportunity to take revenge on the gods for the death of his brother. The summary of the story of the incarnation of Narasimha below[8] is based on numerous Purana accounts of the story.

> Demon brothers Hiranyaksha and Hiranyakashipu harassed the gods incessantly. Hiranyaksha was killed by Vishnu. Thereafter, Hiranyakashipu vowed to take revenge on Vishnu for his brother's death. In order to materialize his plan of killing Vishnu, he sought to acquire immunity from death through the performance of difficult penances for the god Brahma. As it was against creation for anyone who had not drunk amrita to live forever, Brahma refused Hiranyaksha's desire to gain immortality. Hence, Hiranyakashipu chose a conditional death. He would not die of natural causes, and also he would only die under certain conditions. The conditions he chose were a time (which is neither a day nor a night), a place (neither inside nor outside), a non-weapon (neither a manufactured weapon nor a naturally existing weapon), a being (neither animal nor human or divine) born of nothing (vacuum) should kill with its bare hands, without spilling blood (any blood spilled on earth would give him rebirth), and his death or his killer should appear only on the invitation of Hiranyakasipu. It so happened that Hiranyakasipu's son was a born devotee of Krishna, who went about his day constantly chanting the divine names of Vishnu, which infuriated Hiranyakasipu. Hiranyakasipu used a number of techniques to change the mind of his son Prahlada to no avail. Hiranyakasipu then sentenced him to be killed through a number of methods. He ordered Prahlada to be thrown into a fire, drowned in water, and finally to be trampled on by elephants. Prahlada emerged alive from his dangerous death sentences and continued to praise Vishnu. An exhausted and infuriated Hiranyakasipu

asked Prahlada, where was his god Vishnu? Prahlada answered that Vishnu is sarvantaryami (inside everything and everybody). A further infuriated Hiranyakasipu hit a nearby pillar with his gada (mace) and demanded that Vishnu must emerge from it if what Prahlada said was true. Vishnu emerged from the pillar in the form of Narasimha and, as the time happened to be neither day nor night, grabbed hold of him and killed him by pulling his guts out and also licking the blood away so as not to spill any blood on the earth.

Method and Plan of Study

There is no holistic and comprehensive examination of the Narasimha tradition incorporating a variety of sources rather than a simplistic study of either texts or practice focusing on the extensive geographical region. Most of the previous works covered either classical texts or one or two of the sacred centers focusing on a limited geographical region (Sundaram 1969; Pidatala 1982; Eschmann 1978; Sontheimer1987). As a result, a number of disparate works are available, but no comprehensive examination of Narasimha has been carried out, so the current academic examination is missing crucial insights into the Narasimha tradition and the history of religion in the region of Middle India.

Interest in the study of Narasimha began in the late twentieth century. Even though one of the earliest studies was brief, it was a pioneering study of Narasimha that served to introduce the subject of Narasimha to academia (Biardeau 1975: 49–66). The next largest study is an analysis of avataras of Vishnu focusing on Narasimha in a joint analysis along with Vamana's incarnation of Vishnu (Soifer 1991) in the book *the Myths of Narasimha and Vamana*. The work is one of the most comprehensive examinations of the stories of Narasimha, even though the study combined this examination with the Vamana incarnation. Narasimha is not merely regarded as an avatara, but the ultimate god in numerous temple centers of Madhya Desha, the middle region of India. I will briefly examine the previous scholarship on the deity Narasimha in the following pages.

However, there are a number of works that focus on studying individual sacred centers associated with Narasimha (Subbulakshmi 1981: 35–52; Adinarayana 1993; 2006; Sundaram 1969; Sitapati 1982) and/or consider stories of Narasimha as part of a larger project (Soifer 1991; Guy 2016; Emigh 1984; Debicka-Borek 2016; Sontheimer 2004). Even though all of these early works focused on the Narasimha Telugu region, the center of the Narasimha tradition is not considered closely; some even avoid mentioning the Telugu region by its usual name Andhra or Telangana, instead opting for the less commonly known name, Deccan, while studying the Telugu performance traditions of Narasimha (Guy 2016). Eschmann studied the Narasimha tradition of Odisha in conjunction with Jagannatha and tribal religion (Eschmann 1978: 99–117). Although focusing on Jagannatha she utilized the symbolism of Narasimha noted in tribal religion as well as the Jagannatha tradition to advance the theory of the "Hinduization" of natives similar to the previous "Aryanization" theories. However, in her enthusiastic embrace of Aryanization theory, she failed to comprehend the deep symbolism and historicity embedded within the Narasimha tradition (see Chapter 8). Narasimha is equally represented in popular traditions as well as classical traditions, which is lost in her study as she did not focus on classical tales but focused on isolated references to the Narasimha tradition in practice from only a few temples haphazardly selected for examination in addition to the Jagannatha temple. Ethnographic studies (Sontheimer 1981; Eschmann 1978) exclusively focused on fieldwork while depending on the frameworks of textual studies, without coordinating with contemporary textual studies. As a result, Sontheimer borrowed the literary frameworks of Tamil literature, to apply it to that of the landscapes and practices of Maharashtra, two regions that are located far from each other and show distinct historical growth (Sontheimer 1978). The study would have been much more representative of the religion of Maharashtra if the historical literary sources of Maharashtra such as Hala's *Gatha Sattasai* or any of the later Vaishnava and Shaiva literary and poetical works composed in Marathi, were utilized to understand the religious and cultural landscape of Maharashtra. It is simply not clear why this author chose Tamil literary frameworks for a study focused on the Marathi region. Similarly, in her ethnographic study of Odishan folk religion Eschmann alluded to influence of Narasimha practices from Andhra Pradesh but she did not explore it further, ignoring Telugu sources in her study (Eschmann 1978: 108). If she had included Telugu sources in her study, her conclusion might have taken a different course from her purported theory of Hinduization (Aryanization or Sanskritization). In another stark example of the partisan nature of Narasimha studies, a recent study focusing on Telugu operatic practices of Narasimha Mela surveys most of the available sculptural and literary works, but completely ignores Telugu resources and research (Guy 2016: 17–22). On the other hand literary studies focusing either on Sanskrit or Telugu ignored the practices and ethnographic understanding of religion. Scholars focusing on Sanskrit classical texts showed an exclusivist focus, selecting Narasimha-related stories to study. They considered any type of diversion from the exclusive narratives preserved in Sanskrit texts, commonly noticed in regional practices, to be either an independent tradition which is later assimilated by classical Hinduism or a later introduction of syncretic tendency (Hacker; Soifer; Biardeau). Scholars focusing on Telugu literature and practice are at the receiving end of these classical literary works, frequently borrowing the Hinduization and Sanskritization frameworks and ignoring the latent evidence of Telugu work on hand (Sundaram; Madabhushini). Each of these scholars worked in an academic vacuum, not willing to consider evidence outside of their narrow area, thus leading to only a partial understanding of Narasimha. Therefore, my goal in this book is not to become entrenched in a single focus area but to focus on analyzing classical as well as oral literature along with monumental and contextual practice. I will examine the classical sources to bring out the most notable features associated with Narasimha. I will then proceed to examine oral literature and practice in relation to how these themes have permeated into all areas of religion associated with Narasimha in the wider area of Middle India. Therefore, I think my study in this book will be most helpful in bringing out the hitherto neglected aspects of religion in Middle India in addition to shedding light on the religious practices associated with Narasimha.

The *Fairs and Festivals* of Andhra Pradesh were collected in the Census of India 1961 (Volume II Andhra Pradesh VIIB) which listed more than 100 centers of Narasimha temples. An ethnographic and historical study carried out in the 1980s brought to light more than double that number of Narasimha temples in Andhra Pradesh (Madabushini 1989a; 1989b). These early surveys, one official governmental census, and other academic work are focused on documenting the extent of the centers of the Narasimha religion in Andhra Pradesh rather than the nature of religion. A number of studies analyze individual centers. Sacred centers of the deity Narasimha such as Ahobilam (Pidatala 1982) and Simhachalam (Sundaram 1969) attracted closer studies, which provide an exceptional understanding of localized traditions and practices of Narasimha, but fail to provide a comprehensive examination of either Narasimha or the overall regional practices of Middle India. Adinarayana studied the regional practices associated with Narasimha in the Kurnool district (Adinarayana 1993, 2006) including one of the most popular centers of the Narasimha tradition, the Ahobilam temple. One of the early works on Ahobilam, the central temple of Narasimha, conducts an examination of temples, inscriptions, and local stories (Sitapati 1982). A similar micro-study of a single temple of Narasimha located at Simhachalam was conducted in the early 1980s (Sundaram 1969). Emigh had explored the folk art traditions of Telangana state, specifically Oggukatha, which brought him to the story of Narasimha. Numerous close studies have been conducted on the

Ahobilam temple recently; however, the shadow of Aryanization still looms large over any studies of the religion of India (Debicka-Borek 2016). Although focused on Maharashtra, the regional traditions of Karnataka, and Andhra Pradesh also referred in the study of Sontheimer's ethnic studies (Sontheimer 1978, 1985, 1994). Madabhushini Narasimhacharya's ethnographic field surveys and the examination is comprehensive in bringing together the classical and regional tales of Narasimha through a study of temples of Narasimha in Telangana and Andhra Pradesh (1989a; 1989b), although it provides a basic survey rather than an in-depth analysis of the religion based on Narasimha.

Therefore, it is necessary to undertake a new study addressing the lacunae noticed in the previous works as well as bringing a deeper understanding of Hinduism as well as the popular nature of Hinduism. The goal of this book is not to undertake a basic survey of Narasimha temples or an exclusivist analysis of Narasimha stories either in classical or oral literature, but to advance the study of Narasimha further through an in-depth study through undertaking a thematic analysis of the symbolic nature Narasimha as well as symbolic religious concepts associated with Narasimha as these form part of the larger civilization within the Middle region of India. There is no comprehensive examination Narasimha incorporating the overarching nature of the deity spread across the specific geographical region studied in this book. This book will improve understanding of the overall religious landscape of the region.

A clear understanding of the transitional/middle nature of Narasimha is missing from previous scholarship on Narasimha. Narasimha's affiliation with Vishnu, Shiva, and Shakti was seen as enigmatic (Tripathi 1978), a synthesis of Shaiva and Vaishnava traditions (Soifer 1991; Sontheimer 2004), and his relation to the feminine aspect of divinity has been only partially studied to support Hinduization (Eschmann 1978). Regional legends composed in the Mahatmyas (Debicka-Borek 2019) and performance traditions (Emigh 1984) are studied in isolation rather than in comparison with classical sources, still utilizing the earlier frameworks of Hinduization or Sanskritization.

Despite a number of works focused on the religion of the area, there is not much work on Narasimha or comprehensive examination focusing on Middle India. Hence, the overall scholarship misses assessing the impact of Narasimha on the religious practices of Middle India. Narasimha is the deity incarnated in Middle India at Ahobilam, specifically to protect the folks of the region and release them from the tyrannical rule of the demon Hiranyakashipu. Hence, the region of Andhra Pradesh is the *leelasthali*, land of divine play, of the god Narasimha. His life and activities are etched on the land of Andhra Pradesh through temples and tales, which retrace the steps of Narasimha on this land millennia ago. Many temples and sacred centers in Andhra Pradesh and surrounding areas hold sacred memories of Narasimha's *leela*, similar to the Brajamandala, which holds the sacred spots of the *leela* of Krishna. However, microstudies focused on singular temples or texts have failed to bring focus to this unique religious background of the region centered on Narasimha. Hence, the current study is focused on examining the texts, sacred centers, and practices together to arrive at a comprehensive understanding of the theology and practice associated with Narasimha as well as religion in Middle India. This will also help bring out the unique cultural and social history of the region.

Significance of the Project

Classical texts depict the Hindu god Narasimha, in his cosmogonic role, not belonging to a clearly defined category of beings, which in practice is transformed as the "transitional middle," the most defining feature of Narasimha in the classical texts. The states of Telangana and Andhra Pradesh, geographically located in the middle land (Madhya Desha) between the northern region (Uttarapatha) and the southern region (Dakshinapatha), are also home to the most unique traditions and practices centered on Narasimha.

Narasimha, the man-lion incarnation of Vishnu, is a multifaceted deity within Hinduism, with strong connections to almost all traditional practices of Hinduism, centered on the major deities, Vishnu, Shiva, and Shakti, besides popular folk practices. Vaishnavism evokes Narasimha as the tamer of evil, while Shaivism remembers him Kala (Time) identifying him with Kala Bhairava, the deadly form of Shiva, as partly embracing death and danger that needs to be curtailed, hence the withdrawal of Narasimha is central to Shaiva texts. The lion face is also prevalent in folk practices in connection with female lion goddesses in Shaktism, and ganas of Shaivism. In a parallel development with ritual practices, it should be noted here that folk practices common across India utilize "kirtimukhas" or "kiriti mukhas," which also depict lion faces, frequently identified with Narasimha. It is also unique that these kiritimukhas also adorn mosques in Middle India, built in the syncretistic Hindu-Sufi tradition of practice. In addition, the lion's face is also associated with the demon Rahu and his family, who according to Hindu Puranas is responsible for the eclipses. Traditional theater festivals associated with Narasimha are also widespread across India. My research project in this book examines the stories of Narasimha from Vaishnava, Shaiva, and Shakta Puranas along with the folk, ritual, and theatrical practices to arrive at a comprehensive understanding of the religion of Middle India. This book examines the multiple aspects of the composite nature of the deity Narasimha as noted in his appearance, which is a composite of animal and human forms, which leaves him in the middle, neither belonging to the animal world nor the human world, although representing the unique form of the divine dictated by the swerving of the Earth from its proper course of movement, which overturned Time cycle, the kala, and Yuga. By being a composite of opposing elements simultaneously he unites opposing elements in other aspects as well, in religion that of being part of the Vaishnava, Shaiva, and Shakti; distinctions and oppositions vanish when it comes to Narasimha.

The current study examines the history of religion in the central region of India and the literary and oral traditions in Telugu and Sanskrit texts along with inscriptions of Narasimha connected with numerous sacred sites spread across central India. The goal is to understand the historical evolution of unique religious, socio-cultural, and historical contexts. This examination also contributes to the understanding of multiple historical Hindu traditions, through an analysis of the Vaishnava, Shaiva, and Shakta traditions as they interweave with the Narasimha tradition.

It is important that the historical traditions of central India be studied closely to gain a comprehensive understanding of Indian historical evolution. Although Middle India is treated as a distinct geographical region in the classical texts with the designation Madhya Desha, it is not treated as a distinct geographical region in modern scholarship. Hence, states of Middle India were previously combined either with northern states or with southern states leading to the obfuscation of unique features of the culture, religion, and history of the region. The eastern side of Middle India consisting of the two Telugu states Telangana and Andhra Pradesh received only marginal scholarly attention. Even those focusing on Narasimha seem to have ignored the region altogether. Hence, this project through its analyses of textual sources and oral tales of Andhra Pradesh and Telangana brings forward a fresh understanding of regional history.

My research has implicit as well as explicit goals. The explicit goal of this project is to examine the traditional understanding of Narasimha and the practice of Hinduism, while the implicit goal is to understand the unique historical, social, and cultural practices of Middle India. Therefore, my research has two primary goals. While the first goal is to examine Narasimha in history, thought, and culture, the second goal is to understand the history, thought, and culture of Telangana and Andhra Pradesh through close analysis of the historical texts, inscriptions, and arts in connection with Narasimha.

The following is detailed information on the chapters in this book.

Chapter 1

Introduction: Narasimha, the Lord of the Middle in Middle India

The background, scope, purpose, and introduction of the subject and methodology are discussed in the Introduction. Sequentially, Narasimha is the fifth avatara of the ten avataras of Vishnu, hence the middle avatara. In addition, the symbolism of the middle is depicted in the mythology of Narasimha, which presents him as a "neither here" "nor there" type personality, with regard to philosophy and cosmology, including his physical appearance. As a man-lion (Narasimha) he is depicted as a composite deity possessing the physical aspects of a lion as well as those of a man. Similarly, the time of his appearance, the place, and his life include numerous "middle" characteristics. Sacred geography also associates Narasimha with the middle region of India, with a large number of temples, and with regional traditions located in Maharashtra, Madhya Pradesh, Chhattisgarh, Odisha, Andhra Pradesh, and Karnataka. The first chapter focuses on introducing the subject matter of the book with regard to mythology, sacred geography, and regional practices such as festivals and theater traditions associated with Narasimha. The organization of the chapters and the methodology of the subject of study are also explained in Chapter 1.

Chapter 2

Classical Sources of Narasimha: Symbolism of the Middle

This chapter examines the Mahabharata and Purana stories of Narasimha along with Narasimha Purana. This chapter also presents a comprehensive examination of Narasimha stories and early academic studies, along with new perspectives on the study of Narasimha.

Chapter 3

Historical Narasimha from Prehistory to Present

This chapter examines the archaeological data, inscriptions, and sculptures to trace the historical practices associated with Narasimha and analyze the evolution of Vaishnavism in Middle India. This chapter also correlates the information from the inscriptions, sculptures, and other material sources to the textual information discussed.

Chapter 4

Narasimha in Middle India: From Rigveda to Oggukatha

This chapter also examines the concept of the middle as symbolically associated with Narasimha in mythology, art, and culture, and analyses how the concept of the middle is represented in his association with the sacred geography of India through representing the middle.

The earliest sculptural representation of Narasimha is documented in Andhra Pradesh and Telangana and is datable to the third century CE. This chapter also examines the sculptural representation of Narasimha in Middle India to understand the historical evolution of the Narasimha tradition in India, within the context of the historical development of Hinduism.

Chapter 5

Lakshmi in the Classical and Regional Tales of Narasimha: Gender and Family

Although not part of the classical texts of Narasimha, stories of Lakshmi and gender are uniquely represented in the regional stories of Narasimha. Each region provides a unique tale associated with the wife of Narasimha, popularly called Chenchitha in the states of Andhra Pradesh and Telangana. Some regional tales also include family perspectives which give rise to celebrations representing Narasimha as a son-in-law, especially noted in the Andhra Pradesh and Karnataka region. Examination of the feminine divine in association with Narasimha helps us to understand the social and familial perspectives of Narasimha.

Chapter 6

Narasimha in the Eastern Region: Odisha and Andhra Pradesh

This chapter examines the regional traditions associated with Narasimha in Andhra Pradesh and Odisha. Located on the eastern coast of India, Andhra Pradesh contains the most important temple of Narasimha, in Simhachalam, connecting it to the classical mythology of Narasimha. The regional legend of Simhachalam also depicts it as the place associated with Prahlada, the child devotee of Narasimha, upon whose prayers the incarnation of Narasimha occurred. A comparative study of the common themes in classical and regional mythology of Narasimha is undertaken in this chapter. This helps with understanding classical Hinduism and regional practices associated with Narasimha.

The regional practice of the state of Odisha associates Narasimha with goddesses and folk practices of the tribal groups, Sabaras and Konds. This chapter examines classical mythology as well as regional myths and practices in order to understand the social and religious history of Odisha. This chapter focuses on understanding the feminine divine in tribal and classical traditions as well as at the intersection of the Saiva (followers of Siva) and Vaishnava (followers of Vishnu) philosophical and theological traditions in connection with Narasimha.

Chapter 7

Narasimha in the Central Region: Madhya Pradesh, Chhattisgarh, and Telangana

This chapter examines the regional stories and practices associated with Narasimha in the states of Telangana, Madhya Pradesh, and Chhattisgarh. The regional stories of Narasimha in the state of Telangana connect Narasimha with classical mythology. Examining the history, regional practices, and temples of Narasimha, this chapter contributes to an understanding of the emergence of Narasimha as the most popular deity of this state, thus contributing to the evolution of the unique tradition of Telangana. Regional practices associate Narasimha with health and healing, especially at the central temple of Telangana, in Yadagirigutta. Swamy Narayana Tirtha, the author of Krishnaleela Tarangini, connects Narasimha to health and healing. Narayana Tirtha also composed a dance style, known as Andhra Natyam, to perform *Krishna Leela Tarangini*. Hence, artistic and devotional practices coalesce within the Narasimha devotional tradition. This chapter focuses on health, healing, and performance traditions associated with Narasimha. Similar practices are also noticed in the states of Chhattisgarh and Madhya Pradesh, which also form part of the discussion.

Chapter 8

Narasimha in the Western Region: Maharashtra and Karnataka

The most important temples of Karnataka associate Narasimha with Shiva, the symbol of Kala, time. As a deity beyond time, Narasimha is closely connected to

Shiva in classical mythology, which is also represented in the regional tradition of Karnataka. Narasimha is also connected with Mallanna/Mailer, a folk deity with connection to Shiva, in these regions. I will also examine the regional practices of the state of Maharashtra, which adjoins the state of Karnataka and demonstrates similar regional practices associated with Narasimha.

Chapter 9

Narasimha in Popular Culture, Performing Arts, and Devotional Practice

Narasimha is associated with the theater and performing arts of India, especially in southern India. Week-long theater festivals are organized across Middle India on the occasion of the Narasimhajayanti festival each year. The examination of theater and performance traditions associated with Narasimha also helps us to analyze the historical and social as well as cultural traditions of Middle India. Numerous artistic traditions in the popular art forms in Oggukatha, Harikatha, Yakshganam, and Jamukula Katha present the story of Narasimha. This chapter examines the folk and theater festivals associated with Narasimha, which present the concepts of evil and good.

Chapter 10

Conclusion: Narasimha in Totality

The conclusion draws together information analyzed in the previous nine chapters of the book to present a comprehensive summary of the subject of study. This chapter also provides the conclusions of the symbolic association of Narasimha with the middle, along with the representation of this concept in the sacred geography, mythology, ritual, and theatrical practice of Middle India.

2

Classical Sources of Narasimha
Symbolism of the Middle

Narasimha is represented with multiple features; however, symbolizing the state of the middle or transitions is the most distinct quality of the Hindu deity Narasimha which is also conspicuously represented in the classical stories and practice. The form of the deity and the stories, as well as the geographical associations of the Vaishnava deity Narasimha represent the symbolism of the middle and/or transition. Being part animal and part human and fully divine is the most complex concept of the divinity. Hence, his appearance is theorized as not fully being in a defined category of beings, but is noted as the concept of being a representation of "neither this nor that". However, representing the middle or being a combination of two opposing elements, that of the human and the ferocious animal represents the most profound early concept of divinity, which is reflected in the deity Narasimha in the Purana stories as well as the other arts and practices. The combination represents the multiple nature of Narasimha ferocious and yet yogic. The temples of Narasimha are also located in sites, hills and mountains that demonstrate aspects of this esoteric multiple nature of not belonging to a clearly defined category, yet serenely calm and yogic shaktipeethas.

Narasimha, Multifaceted Hindu Deity in Classical and Folk Tales of India

Narasimha is the most unique Hindu deity with extensive representation in almost all the prevalent Hindu traditions, that is, Vaishnava, Shaiva, and Shakta schools of thought and practice, with a very immense and all-encompassing popular practice. Any time Narasimha is associated with the central deities of the other Hindu traditions such as Shaivism and Shaktism, the central characteristics of Narasimha are overlayed onto the other gods rather than obliterating any characteristics Narasimha possesses. This chapter is dedicated to examining the central classical stories and other sources, which will be examined in detail below. The worship traditions of Narasimha are largely concentrated in the Vaishnava tradition in which he is depicted simultaneously as an avatara (incarnation), vyuha (emanation), and the other divine composite configurations of Vishnu such as Vishwarupa (universal multifaceted form), Vaikuntha (trimukha = three-faced or chaturmukha = four-faced), and chaturmukha (Gail 1983 197–207). Through his overarching and all-encompassing characteristics, Narasimha defies sectarian limitations as the deity is represented in close affinity with Shiva and Shakti, the goddesses. Therefore, it is important to examine the stories of Narasimha in detail to understand his all-encompassing nature, which is shaped by the unique features of Narasimha, defined by his most characteristic feature, the middle or transitional nature.

The earliest references to Narasimha are found in the Vedic sources (Rigveda I. 154.2; VIII.14.13). The story of Namuci (Rigveda VIII.14.13) only indicates Narasimha indirectly. Even though the Rigvedic references are cryptic they nonetheless include the most typical features of Narasimha. However direct reference comes from other Vedic texts, especially in the last section of the Taittiriya Aranyaka (1.7.1.6), in which the name Narasimha is used in conjunction with Vasudeva (Krishna). Here, the term Narasimha is used in the invocation of Vasudeva, which indicates that the identification of Narasimha with Vishnu as well as with vyuhas was well known during the composition of the last parts of the Vedas, the Aranyakas, and the Upanishads. It is also not out of context to note here that a notable class of Brahmins of the Godavari basin claim lineage from Tittiriaya, with a Tittiriya Samhita-based practice dating back 3,500 years here in Andhra Pradesh (Knipe 2015: 1–26). The Taittiriya Aranyaka although considered a late composition belongs to a period before the first millennium BCE as it belongs to the Krishna Yajurveda, the ninth and tenth sections of Tittiriya Aranyaka from the Taittiriya Upanishad. Hence, traditional worship and memory of Narasimha within the culture of Andhra Pradesh can be traced to the turn of the first millennium BCE if not earlier in Andhra Pradesh. The Epic and Purana sources of Narasimha are available from the middle of the first millennium BCE, gradually increasing toward the end of the first millennium BCE (the Harivamsa and the Mahabharata), and sculptural and pictorial representations of Narasimha are available from the middle of the first millennium BCE. (See Chapter 4 for an examination of archaeological and sculptural representations of Narasimha.)

However, this chapter examines the conceptual and theoretical elements associated with Narasimha in the classical texts as well as folk stories (for a full survey of folk tales and arts please see Chapter 9). This chapter does not provide a summary of the classical stories but strives to provide details that consistently connect him to central themes and concepts associated with Narasimha. Narasimha shows multi-valent nature through his affiliation and entry into multiple theological practices in association with numerous other deities within Hinduism such as Shiva, Bhairava, and the Matrikas. The multifaceted nature and unique symbolism also help us to gain insight into the evolution of Hinduism, in its historical evolution and geographical spread in Middle India.

Incorporating indigenous faith traditions as well as the mystical revelations of the Vedas, the Narasimha tradition represents the most popular blend of elements of prehistoric and early Vedic religion of India. The initial textual as well as the sculptural resources of Narasimha become available in the first millennium BCE India. However, the religious and theological elements might have long formed part of the cultural ethos and practice of India, becoming part of the established tradition by the first millennium BCE to have appeared in concrete form by then. The blend of the ferocious lion and the robust human representing the divine (Vishnu) is a fine representation of the indigenous Hindu practice of India based on native practices.

The most predominant themes associated with Narasimha in the classical texts are (1) the special nature of avatara (incarnation), (2) Pralaya, Kala/Kalanta, and yoga: Control of Time and conscious, (3) restoration and relationship with other deities and beings. These three aspects of Narasimha are frequently represented in practice and, hence, are important to examine here.

Special Nature of Avatara

Narasimha is the most commonly worshipped deity of Hinduism, as a folk and traditional deity in central India, especially Telangana. Narasimha appears to share his qualities, classical stories, and image with more than one deity in Hinduism, Shaivism, as well as folk deities, which demonstrates his middle or transitional nature, which is central to the deity Narasimha. It is this capability of his personality to fluidly represent more than one aspect that makes him affable to numerous social and religious groups, from traditional Hinduism to folk religion. Presently, in this chapter, I will discuss the classical stories associated with Balarama and the qualities that Narasimha shares with more than one deity of traditional Hinduism and how this shapes popular Hinduism in India, especially middle/central India.

The most important feature of Narasimha is that of not belonging to any definitively defined singular category but overstepping all boundaries and limitations. However, this special nature of Narasimha is developed to adequately respond to the conditions of Hiranyakashipu's special boon. This unique feature and the symbolism associated with it was simply misunderstood as it was designated superficially as a "loophole in the law" (Soifer). However, this is the most important element of the story, which is subsequently incorporated into almost all aspects associated with Narasimha. This special quality, dismissed superfluously as a "loophole in the law," embraces all aspects associated with the deity and is the most defining quality of the theology, stories, and practice associated with Narasimha. Hence, it is necessary to pay special attention to this aspect of the special nature of Narasimha. Therefore, in the following pages I undertake a comprehensive study of the stories of Narasimha taking note of his defining characteristics.

Narasimha as the name suggests is man-lion. The term lion is symbolically used to indicate strength and greatness in Indian classical literature irrespective of religious affiliation. Buddhism accords a special place for the lion with symbolism, but it does not evolve into divine status as seen in Hinduism. The Buddha was often called Sakyasimha, to denote that he is the lion among the Sakyas of the greatest of the Sakyas; its representation in Buddhism does not extend beyond placing the lion at the feet of Buddha in images (Coomaraswamy 1929). The man and lion connection of Narasimha extends far beyond such conceptual representations, as the depiction of Narasimha extends his name and indicates, lion, depicted in the form of man, which indicates a realistic depiction of the combined form of man with lion. This form is primarily lion with the torso of a man, while the head, hands, legs, and tail (almost all visible parts of the body) are those of a lion; this is the most usually depicted form of this deity (Vasishth 1977; Subbalaxmi 1981). The Vaishnava and Shaiva Puranas preserve different parts of the life story of the avatara (incarnation) of Narasimha. While the Vaishnava Puranas preserve the incarnation (origin) stories, the withdrawal (death) of Narasimha is preserved in the Shaiva Puranas. On the other hand, the goddesses (Shaktis/Matrikas) share the underworld residence and bloodthirsty nature of Narasimha. Therefore, the distinctive quality of Narasimha that does not make classifying the deity into a distinct traditional group easy is demonstrated through the stories: Not fully part of any single category but belonging to all categories simultaneously is one of the enigmatic qualities of Narasimha. Early studies confused the overarching nature of Narasimha as a cosmogonic deity limiting his role to Vaishnavism (Tripathi 1987). However, Narasimha is represented by transition or by the dangerous middle, which is also represented by his incorporation into Shaivism.

While Narasimha is described as an incarnation of Vishnu in the Vaishnava Puranas, he is also described as a deity akin to Shiva in the Shaiva Puranas. Narasimha is also adorned with a third eye on the forehead between the eyebrows and frequently depicted as wielding a trident similar to Shiva. In fact, the relationship of Narasimha with Vishnu and Shiva in the puranic stories is not one of rivalry but one that preserves the numerous factors that emphasize the neither-this-nor-that nature of the deity Narasimha. Narasimha's story is a clear example in which Vaishnava and Shaiva traditions share stories and deities, as noted in the Mohini and Shiva story (Mahabharata. Adiparva 17. 38–41) as well as the Harihara depiction of Vishnu and Shiva (Gopinatha Rao 1971 (reprint) Vol.II 334–5). Even though the Shaiva and Vaishnava sects involve various popular practices, they coalesce in Narasimha representing balancing as well as the destruction of creation of both these deities simultaneously as a representation of universal divinity involved with protecting creation.

My examination of Narasimha in this chapter shows that Narasimha is projected in the Hindu classical texts and practice as the central deity beyond the sectarian limitations of Vaishnava and Shaiva classifications. It is this capacity of Narasimha to surpass narrow limitations that is the central quality of Narasimha within theology, text, and practice. This is also frequently encountered in the sacred geography of the middle land. It is impossible to find a story or tradition associated with Narasimha devoid of the special quality of boundary-defying/middle.

Narasimha in the Vaishnava Tradition

Early scholarly studies of Narasimha were cryptic surveys of Narasimha examining the stories in classical texts. Narasimha stories first attracted the attention of scholars in the field of textual criticism who traced the textual history of the story and original core of the Narasimha story to understand the original concepts associated with Narasimha (Swain 1971: 1; Biardeau 1975: 1). Due to their focus on text history and textual criticism, these early studies analyzed basic themes of the story focusing on the classical story elements to understand the nature of the deity Narasimha. Early academic studies focused on understanding Narasimha in Bhakti theology since Bhakti was interpreted as a mode of Aryanization/Hinduization. This excessive focus on the basic elements misses the broader symbolism, multifaceted nature, and inclusive practice of Narasimha. Only two types of themes of Narasimha were noted in the Vaishnava stories which were frequently examined in these early studies at the expense of the most central aspects of Narasimha. These two themes are the incarnation stories and his divine-devotee relation with Prahlada. These themes continued to preoccupy the later scholarly studies, which focused on detailed analysis of Narasimha stories. These themes were closely studied to understand the cosmological and theological nature of Narasimha (Soifer 1991: 21–5). Most of these studies separated the incarnation of Narasimha from the story of Prahlada. It is said that the Prahlada story represents the evolution and adoption of Bhakti theology in Vaishnavism with Prahlada being represented as the foremost of the *Bhaktas* (Hacker 1959). These studies also considered Narasimha as an independent deity, conceived of as an embodiment of numinous potency (Otto 1942: 17). It is also proposed that Narasimha might have been an independent deity, who may have been assimilated into Vaishnavism (Hinduism) through the Bhakti theology centered on Prahlada (Hacker). However, early historical evidence of Narasimha disproves such assumptions (see Chapter 3). Vedic as well as early historic evidence datable to the middle of the first millennium BCE already includes the known elements of Hinduism. Hence, it is difficult to accept the premise of these early studies that Narasimha might have originated as an independent deity, due to a lack of evidence.

However, I think the lack of focus on broader themes and unique features of Narasimha led to only a partial understanding of Narasimha. Narasimha stories also record multiple aspects which show the popular and inclusive nature of practice which conforms with the personality of Narasimha as depicted in the stories of Narasimha. The stories of Prahlada and popular folk stories incorporating Narasimha in the tribal and classical culture of India simultaneously indicate the application of the middle/transitional nature of the deity in practice which is based on the textual directives of the unique symbolism of Narasimha. Popular modes of worship and beliefs associated with Narasimha in Odisha and Andhra Pradesh closely correspond to the tribal traditions (see Chapter 9; Eschmann 1978: 102–13) as well as textual traditions (Vemsani 2016a: 147–61).

The earliest Narasimha story is recorded in the Mahabharata (3.272.56–60), which is also briefly recounted later in another section of the Mahabharata

(12.326.72–84; 12.337.36). The original Mahabharata story of Narasimha is four verses long in the Vulgate texts, which was unfortunately reduced to one and a half verses in the critical edition. In the Bhagavata Purana (II.7.14), and Agni Purana (4.2–3) the Narasimha story is very cryptic and does not provide any information on the boon of Hiranyakasipu, which was the central theme of Narasimha stories in the other Puranas. Brahmanda Purana (2.5.3–29) and Vayu Purana (67.61–66) narrate this story beginning with Hiranyakasipu's penances and his boon from Brahma. A fully developed account along with the Prahlada legend is seen in Harivamsa (HV. 41), Brahma Purana (213.44–79), and Vishnudharmottara Purana (I.54). The Prahlada story is associated with the foundation of temples of Narasimha in India (Vemsani 2009: 35–52); an important aspect of Bhakti theology epitomizing the special relationship between the deity and the devotee forms a central aspect of the story, as Prahlada acquires the position of foremost Bhakta of Vishnu, eulogized through popular tales of Sthalapuranas in addition to the classical texts.

Hiranyakashipu's Boon and Universal Chaos

Hiranyakashipu was shocked and angered by the death of his brother at the hands of Vishnu in the Varaha avatara (Bhagavatapurana VII.2). He vowed to avenge the death of his brother by taking control of the trilokas (three worlds) and directing his anger at Vishnu for killing his brother, Hiranyaksha (Shivapurana II.5.43.5a). Bhagavata Purana's story of Narasimha depicts the enmity of Hiranyakashipu toward Vishnu. Hiranyakashipu said, "My best friend and beloved brother has been slaughtered by my puny adversaries, with whom Hari, though professing impartiality, has sided attributing his action to their devout worship unto him" (Bhagavata Purana VII.2.6). To fulfill his desire to avenge the death of his brother Hiranyaksha, he decided to obtain the grace of Brahma. Therefore, Hiranyakashipu performed 10,000-year-long severe penances (Brahmanda Purana 2.5.3–29; Vayu Purana 67.61–66) while the Harivamsa lists a slightly longer penance at 11,500 and Brahma Purana lists 11,000 years, which is similar to the length of his penance in the Vishnudharmottara Purana. Eventually, at the end of his long penances, Brahma appeared to him and granted him his desired boon. Hiranayakashipu obtained a calculated wish that would place the created world as well the world of gods under his control. According to the Vayu Purana (67.62), Hiranyakashipu requested "immortality and inviolability from all beings. Having conquered the gods with yoga, to become the god of all. Danavas, Asuras, and gods must be equal, and I must possess the great sovereignty of Maruti. Give me this wish." Although the first two wishes noted here, immortality, and conquest and sovereignty over the gods, are clear, his last wish, sovereignty over Maruti, is not clear. It is also interesting that the demon Hiranyakashipu wished to conquer the god through yoga. This name is used as a patronymic to refer to a number of gods including Bhima and Hanuman, who were notable heroes connected to the god Vayu as his children. As a boon recorded in the Vayu Purana this may indicate an esoteric meaning unique to the Vayu Purana even though previous works have not deciphered any special meaning (Soifer 78). The boon of Hiranyakashipu is more overt in the Brahmanda Purana. While demanding invincibility, immortality, and conquest over gods through yoga similar to the Vayu Purana, he emphasized that "Danavas and demons, gods together with celestial singers, all these must be my subjects, close at hand, and serving me. Inviolable by wet or dry, by night or day" (Brahmanda Purana 2.5.16–17). Thus, the Brahmanda Purana version brings forward the ulterior motive of the demon, that of universal sovereignty, including the gods as his servants. He did not merely demand immortality and inviolability but included the conditions of "neither wet nor dry" and "not by night or day," the most crucial aspect of the story of Narasimha that required a specific avatara. The Harivamsa and Brahmapurana add other beings also to the list saying Hiranayakashipu, "may not be killed by gods, demons, Gandharvas, Yakshas, Nagas, Rakshasas, men or Pisacas, nor cursed by rishis; to be killed neither by weapons, swords, rocks or tree, by neither wet nor dry (Harivamsa)/high or low (Brahmapurana)." Brahmapuarana, Harivamsa, and Vayupurana also note that he must be killed by one stroke of the hand. Harivamsa notes that "not die in heaven nor in the ether region, not in the air nor on earth, neither during the day nor at night. I may only succumb under the force of one who, in the middle of my officers, soldiers, and animals which serve for vehicles, triumphs over me by the power of his arms" (Harivamsa 226.15–16).

The Shiva Purana story notes an elaborate list as part of Hiranyakashipu's boon:

> never may I have the fear of death from weapons, missiles, thunderbolts, dry trees, mountains, water, fire, or onslaught of enemies—gods, daityas (demons), sages, Siddhas, or in fact from any living being created by you. Why should I expiate on it? Let there be no death for me in heaven, on earth, in the daytime, at the light, from above or below, O lord of Subjects.
>
> (Shiva Purana II. 5.43.16–17)

The next phase of the story in the Brahmanda Purana describes the conquest of the world by Hiranyakashipu through his special powers acquired due to Brahma's boon he thus obtained. He replaced all the natural phenomena of the worlds: "In heaven, he became the sun, moon, and wind. . . . He became the herdsman, the shepherd, and the cultivator, he became the knower of all the worlds, giving interpretations of the mantras; Leader, protector, preserver, giver of the sacrifice, and the sacrifice" (Brahmandapurana 2.5.20b–22a). This makes it clear that the demon replaced Vishnu as the "leader, protector, and preserver" of the world, a role predominantly attributed to Vishnu. In addition, the Brahmandapurana also says that Hiranyakashipu also usurped Vishnu in his central quality of spreading throughout the world in many forms. Brahmana Purana described that "having pervaded (vyapya) the world . . . everything standing and moving, he lived in many forms" (2.5.19b–20a). Shiva Purana describes how, endowed with the special boon, Hiranyakashipu "disturbed all righteous activities and defeated all the gods in battle" (Shivapurana II.5.43.20b). This overzealous actions of the demon Hiranayakasipu in the upturning of the world is also noticeable in other Purana stories of Narasimha. The Vishnu Purana says that "He had usurped the sovereignty of Indra and exercised of himself the functions of the sun, of air, of the lord of waters, of fire, and the moon. He was the god of riches, the judge of the dead; and he appropriated to himself, without reserve, all that was offered in sacrifice to the gods" (Vishnupurana I.17.2–3). This describes the complete overturning of the world order in which Hiranyakashipu monopolized all the activities associated with the divine and banished them from their roles and abodes (Figure 3).

Even though Narasimha (the man-lion) is presented as an incarnation of Vishnu in the developed theology of Vaishnavism, the lion theme appears more frequently in Shaiva classical texts in association with Shiva than in the Vaishnava Puranas. The appearance of Narasimha is the only lion-related theme in Vaishnava classical texts. For purposes of ease of examination, this chapter is divided into five thematic sections. In the first section, I will survey the stories of Narasimha from the classical Vaishnava texts to examine the central features associated with this deity and his position in Vaishnava tradition, and in the second section, I will examine the Shaiva and Shakta sources to analyze the deeper symbolism embedded in the Narasimha stories representing the relationship he shares with Shiva and Shaktis. The third section will examine the popular practices associating Narasimha with the Shiva as well as Vaishnava traditions. The final section is the conclusion summarizing the depiction of Narasimha in Vaishnava and Shaiva texts and popular practices. My examination

Figure 3 Narasimha slaying Hiranyakashipu with gods in attendance, lithograph from Calcutta (eighteenth century CE). Courtesy: Brooklyn Museum of Art.

of Narasimha in this chapter shows that Narasimha is accepted as a central deity beyond the sectarian limitations of Vaishnava and Shaiva classifications. It is this capacity of Narasimha to surpass narrow limitations that appeals to large sections of devotees which could be understood as one of the main reasons for Narasimha's immense popularity as the most commonly worshipped folk deity.

Vaishnavism incorporates numerous concepts of the appearance of the divine within creation such as prabhava, vibhava, avatara, rupa/vishwarupa/swarupa, Vaikunkta rupa, vyuha, etc. (Vemsani 2016c: 19–20). However, two concepts of the appearance of divinity predominate in the stories of Narasimha in connection with creation. The primary emanations of Vishnu prior to the emergence of creation are termed vyuhas, while the incarnations within creation with regards to correcting the imbalance of the created universe are termed avataras (Shreiner 1997: 1–27). Although it is not pertinent to discuss in detail the differences and nuances between the varieties of forms of appearance of Vishnu in relation to creation, it is pertinent to note here that the subtle differences between the concepts of avatara and vyuha demand careful consideration for understanding the true meaning of these terms and their usage is not simply interchangeable.

Hence, Narasimha, although predominantly presented as an avatara (incarnation) of Vishnu, is also represented as a vyuha (emanation), since Narasimha functioned fluidly within creation in order to straighten the course of the overturned Earth, which was moved off course of its usual path by the actions of the demon Hiranyakashipu. The concept of Time and correction in the course of the Earth is discussed later in this chapter. The concept of Time and the cosmogonic understanding of time and a correlation with the rotation of the Earth form part of the stories of Narasimha. However, presently, the discussion continues by noting the association of Narasimha simultaneously as and an avatara as well as a vyuha of Vishnu is an affirmation of the esoteric traits associated with Narasimha.

Since Narasimha is depicted in the context of avatara and vyuha in classical texts and art it is pertinent to discuss these two aspects here in connection with Narasimha. Being represented as avatara and vyuha simultaneously also underlines the capacity of Narasimha to exist within and beyond creation at the same time. This again supports the symbolism of the middle and/or transitions associated with Narasimha.

Another important task this story accomplishes in addition to firmly underlining the entrenched Narasimha avatara in the milieu of Bhakti theology of Vaishnavism is that it supports the connection of Narasimha with Shiva and the Matrikas, the mother goddesses. In the Vaishnava texts Narasimha is seen to have withdrawn his form soon after killing the demon Hiranyakashipu. However, this was not the case in the Shaiva texts and folk stories. I will examine Shaiva texts and the local tales of Narasimha temples in Andhra Pradesh briefly in the following pages, which further demonstrate his synergy through his depiction as a blend of Shaiva, Shakta, and folk beliefs (see Chapter 9).

Avatara and Vyuha Correlation of Narasimha

Narasimha is presented in the ethos of Vaishnava theology through his identification as the fourth/fifth avatara of Vishnu. Narasimha follows immediately after the Varaha incarnation, assuming which the god Vishnu killed Hiranyaksha, brother of Hiranyakashipu, while Narasimha killed the demon Hiranyakashipu. These two incarnations appear in sequence close together killing demon brothers in quick succession. There is also a close affinity between these two incarnations as they are represented in the classical literary and artistic forms. Narasimha and Varaha are also represented together in a combined form as Varaha-Narasimha as the central deity in the temple of Narasimha in Simhachalam (Vemsani 2009: 35–52).

However, the Vaishnava theology presents the assimilation of Narasimha in symbolic as well as realistic representations. Narasimha is symbolically represented as the second vyuha Samkarshana while in his real form Narasimha is presented as the avatara of Vishnu. The first four avataras of Vishnu are theriomorphic and Puranas depict an effort to identify these first four avataras, Mastya (fish), Varaha (boar), Kurma (tortoise), and Narasimha (man-lion), symbolically with the caturvyuhas, Vasudeva, Samkarsana, Pradyumna, and Aniruddha. Padyumna is identified as Mastya, Aniruddha as Varaha, Samkarsana as Narasimha, and Vasudeva as Kurma. The first four avataras are therefore depicted as symbolic representations of the *caturvyuhas*. I will discuss below how the avatara, vyuha correlation of Narasimha and Samkarshana is achieved through the identification of Narasimha with Sankarshana/Balarama indirectly.

The avatara stories of these first four vyuhas are said to have been derived from similar stories in Vedic literature (Jaiswal 1973: 140–51). Although depicted as an avatara of Vishnu, Narasimha's story is noted to contain elements similar to those of Namuci-Indra stories (Soifer 1991) of the Rigveda. This affiliation with Namuci is represented in the Narasimha temple at Mangalagiri in Andhra Pradesh.

Narasimha as Vyuha Samkarshana/Balarama

Narasimha is identified with the second vyuha, Samkarshana. Samkarshana also known as Balarama, is symbolically depicted with plow frequently topped with lion head, which earns the title of Simha- Langala (the Lion Plow holder) for Balarama (Vemsani 2006). Balarama also represents Kala (Time). As Kala, both Balarama and Narasimha are in turn identified with Kalabhairava, a form of Shiva. The lion is also associated with Balarama as he is also symbolically represented by the emblem of combined lion and elephant.

The Vaikuntha form of Vishnu depicts Samkarsana with a lion head on the right side and Aniruddha with a boar on the left side, which establishes the identity of Narasimha and Samkarshana, the second vyuha. The boar is the representation of Varaha avatara of Vishnu, while the lion's head is considered a representation of Narasimha. In this case, Aniruddha is identified with Varaha, and Samkarshana is identified with Narasimha. Since the vyuha Samkarsana is identified with Balarama, Balarama is repeatedly depicted in close association with Narasimha. The first four incarnations are identified with the four vyuhas identified with Krishna's associated family members. The four vyuhas are identified with Vasudeva (Krishna), Samkarshana (Balarama), Pradyumna, and Aniruddha. The caturvyuha image from Bhita depicts a seated cat or small lion on the south side, the side associated with Samkarana/Balarama in the caturvyuha depictions (Srinivasan). Balarama is also described as Simhalanguli, and his weapon the plow is topped by a symbolic lion head sculpture (N.P. Joshi 1978). The representation of Narasimha as Langala Narasimha indicates special affiliation of Narasimha and Balarama/Samkarshana, who is symbolically represented by langala, the plow.

The association of Samkarshana/Balarama with Narasimha might have been a well-established phenomenon for it to be recorded in the Jain texts also. The Jain texts also preserve this identification by recollecting a different type of story. The Jain Puranas explicitly call Balarama Narasimha (Harivamsapurana 69) describing the final event of his life. Harivamsapurana of Punnata Jinasena describes that Balarama undertook austere penances in preparation for his leaving the world. While he was undertaking his penances in the middle of this forest a number of lions surrounded him as he sat in his yogasana. Harivamsapurana says that since he was surrounded by lions at the time of his final ascent to heaven, Baladeva was known as Narasimha. The Jain Puranas also mention that his mother, Rohini, saw the vision of a lion entering her mouth before his birth (Harivamsapurana 33). It is clear that the Narasimha avatara and vyuha correlation is well preserved in the classical texts and sculptural representations datable to the middle of the first millennium BCE. Therefore, Narasimha's position in Hinduism is well known from the early phases of the beginnings of Hinduism.

In the following pages I will examine Narasimha as represented in relation to Shiva and Shaktis. Narasimha is also associated with Kala (Time)/Kalanta, and yoga. Narasimha is well known as the master of yoga similar to Shiva, and he is commonly worshipped in his form as Yoga Narasimha. As noted in Vayupurana (67.62) Hiranayakashipu wished to conquer gods through yoga and become master of all through yoga. This indicates the awareness of Hiranyakashipu that the gods are noted as masters of yoga in addition to highlighting the awareness of the demon regarding the mastery of the god Vishnu over yoga.

Pralaya Kala/Kalanta, and Yoga: Narasimha in the Shaiva Puranas

The appearance of Shiva in affiliation with Vishnu is not unusual. The close affinity of Shiva and Vishnu is clearly documented in the classical texts and the Purana stories. One of the most popular stories is the courtship of Mohini, a form of Vishnu, and Shiva. This episode is known as the Mohini-Sundara Murthy episode widely depicted in texts and temple sculptures. The story begins with the demon Bhasmasura (Lingapurana Ch. 93). The Bhasmasura story is multidirectional and connects to Vishnu and Shiva in multiple ways. Bhasmasura performed severe penances for Shiva to obtain a special boon. Shiva appeared in front of him and blessed him with Bhasmasura's desired boon that "anybody touched by the palm of his hand on the head must die" immediately. However, Bhasmasura wanted to check the efficacy of the boon immediately and wanted to touch Shiva's head with his palm. Alarmed Shiva began retreating pursued by the demon Andhra now bolstered by the boon. At this juncture Vishnu assumed the form of a beautiful female, known as Mohini, to distract the demon Bhasmasura. As Mohini, Vishnu was able to distract the demon, and cleverly tricked the demon into placing his palm upon his own head, which killed him instantly. However, another issue ensued as the demon died as Shiva began pursuing Mohini. This story introduces another aspect of the gender fluid and gender-swapping role of Vishnu. Another story following this episode indicates that the child born of the special relationship of Shiva and Mohini is Ayyappa, another of the most popular deities in southern India (Younger 2002: 18–25). Hari (Vishnu/Mohini) and Hara (Shiva) are also widely depicted together in classical literature and art (Agrawala 1970: 348–51). However, the relationship between Narasimha and Shiva acquires symbolic meaning as both Narasimha and Shiva represent Kala (Time) predominantly associated with Shiva. Shiva is also called the Mahakala or Kala. Narasimha becomes Kala as he ends the Yuga, while setting the Earth on its right cycle ending the reverse cycle imposed by Hiranyakashipu (see below: Overarching Concept of Time/Kala; Pralaya, Kala/Kalanta, and Yoga).

Narasimha is identified as a form of yoga (Yogamurthy). Yoga (mindful state) is capable of moving beyond the limitations of physical existence and thus expands beyond the bounds of Time (Kala) and Matter. Narasimha through the cosmogonic role of overturning the passage of Yugas remains the ultimate god of yoga and Time/Kala, frequently noticed in practice. Kala/yoga is one of the aspects which connects Narasimha with Shiva extending beyond the perceived categorical differences (Figure 4).

My examination of Shaiva classical stories is twofold: In this chapter, I will first analyze the lion theme in the Shaiva classical stories; second, I will discuss the death of Narasimha as depicted in the Shaiva stories, which was not clearly described in the Vaishnava Puranas.

The central theme of the basic story of Narasimha is that Vishnu incarnated in the form of a man-lion, to kill the demon Hiranyakashipu. As noted, in the pages above, the Narasimha story appears twice, once as a brief four-line story in the Mahabharata, which does not supply much detail, and other classical Puranas provide information only about the incarnation, and scanty details on the withdrawal of his form. Although the last part of Narasimha's story is recollected in a more detailed form in the other Puranas, details of the withdrawal of the

Figure 4 Yoga Narasimha (wood carving) from Kulathupuzha, Kerala, India, fifteenth century CE. Courtesy: Napier Museum of Art.

Narasimha incarnation remain unclear, only to be found in the Shaiva Puranas. However, some questions remain as to what happened after Narasimha killed the demon Hiranyakasipu. While the Vaishnava Puranas are silent on these questions, the Shaiva Puranas and Sthalapuranas provide additional information that shows that Narasimha was regarded as an important deity in Shaivism as well and closely connected to Shiva. Animal forms are more commonly noted in the Shaiva tradition; the son of Shiva, the most commonly worshipped deity Ganesha, possesses an elephant face. I will discuss below the prevalence of Lion forms in Shaiva texts.

The Lion in the Shaiva Puranas

As noted above, the lion form occurs more frequently in Shaiva classical stories than in Vaishnava classical stories. It is interesting to see that Shiva creates mythical lion forms for destruction. Shiva creates Kirtimukha from his third eye to control Rahu when Rahu creates a disturbance in the wedding ceremony of Shiva and Parvati (Padmapurana IV, Uttarakhanda, Cha. 104–22; Skandapurana

II, Vaishnavakhnada 4, Karttikamasa Mahatmya Ch. 17.21). To deal with Rahu, Shiva created the Kirtimukha, who has a lion face with flaming eyes and protruding tongue and is also described as another Narasimha (*Nrusimha iva ca aparah*). The Kirtimukha attacks Rahu and is stopped by Shiva only when he is about to swallow Rahu (Gail 1990: 27–36). On another occasion, Daksha performed a sacrifice and did not invite Shiva and humiliated Parvati when she attended the sacrifice without invitation; unable to bear the humiliation, she sacrificed herself. Infuriated by the news of his wife's death, Shiva created Virabhadra, a lion, to destroy Daksa's sacrifice (Skandapurana, Critical Edition, Ed. Hans Bakker, Brahmapurana, Ch. 39). In the Narasimha story, Narasimha emerges from the sthambha (pillar) in the court hall of Hiranyakasipu (Linga Purana I, 95–6). The sthambha is identified simultaneously with the linga, the aniconic representation of Shiva (Janaki 1988: 6), and Narasimha. Narasimha is represented as sthambha in the temples at Dharmapuri in Telangana and other temples in Andhra Pradesh and Karnataka. The creation of lion forms by Shiva, which is similar to Narasimha, and finally the emergence of Narasimha from the sthambha which is identified as the aniconic representation of Shiva, in his form Sthanu, emphasize the overlapping identity of the deities Shiva and Narasimha. The relation of Shiva and Narasimha indicates that Narasimha shares more with Shiva than it appears at the first reading. This is the only Vaishnava avatara to be associated so closely with Shiva, the central deity of Shaivism. I think these overlapping characteristics indicate the unique shared identity of Narasimha and Shiva, which might be due to their association with Kala/Time.

The Overarching Concept of Time/Kala

The overarching concept of Time/Kala unites the gods Shiva, and Narasimha symbolically. However, the story elements help us to glean the meaning of this relationship. The concept of Time has two different dimensions within the Hindu cosmological understanding. Linear Time and periods of Time such as Yugas are part of the cosmology of Time cycles of the Earth and creation, which change with each cycle. The divine Time in comparison to human Time is measured in the Kalpa (a day of Brahma), with the units measured with a blink of the eye of Brahma (Vishnu Purana I.3). The cycles of Earthly time are coordinated with the divine Time like clockwork. The stories of Narasimha include information to indicate that the balance of the three worlds is shifted off course of its characteristic revolution due to the activities of Hiranyakashipu.

As the multiple worlds of the universe are interconnected their revolution and cyclical Time are interdependent. The Time cycles of the Earth are connected with the super world of the gods and the underworld of the demons. As the demons overturn this order, bringing the world of demons to the top and the world of gods to the bottom to the underworld, the Earth, even though it is in the middle, begins to reverse the course of its revolution, and hence the Time cycles begin to proceed in the reverse course. Hence, the progression of Yugas is marked by regression, which is dangerous for the gods as well as the humans. Vishnudharmottara Purana (I.54), Harivamsa (41), and Brahma Purana (213.44–79) include Pralayic (end of the universe) imagery as the demon Hiranyakaipu shifts the order of the world with the new powers he gained due to the special boon Brahma had given him. Vishnudharmottara Purana (I.54.40) compared Narasimha to the Pralaya with light and fire emanating from him. "Having flaming breath which, going in and out, sounded like the cloud at kalpanta (the end of a kalpa)" (Vishnudharmottara Purana I. 54.42a). Narasimha is further compared to Pralaya and Shiva, as "having the appearance of the submarine fire (vadavanala varcasam) to consume the great ocean of Daitya troops." Shiva is compared to vadavanala and Pralaya at the end of Time. It is in this aspect of Kalanta/Kalpanta that Narasimha and Shiva are related and function as one and the same. As Narasimha assumed the terrible form that was beyond the universe, it was the role of Shiva that he assumed, but not to support the end of creation, but to reverse its end to bring it back to the normal course of progression. Vishnu, assuming the form of Narasimha, which was compared to that of vadavanala (badavanala), was successful in accomplishing his task of vanquishing the demon Hiranyakashipu as well as setting the three worlds (trilokas) on their proper course. However, as he went outside of the course of the universe in his efforts to accomplish these tasks, Shiva was needed to bring an end to this avatara Narasimha to restore Vishnu to his world. To this end, Shiva created Kala Bhairava to absorb Narasimha, so that the further danger of Kalanta was averted and Vishnu was returned to his world. Kala Bhairava symbolically represents the end of Kala for the Narasimha incarnation, so that Vishnu could return to his eternal abode to his original form. I will discuss these aspects in detail in the following pages.

Shiva is known to create forms similar to Narasimha as noted above, and he is also known for his creation and control of Matrikas. Interestingly this aspect of Shiva is also shared by Narasimha, which indicates that the Puranas are in fact trying to present the two deities as very similar in nature and their affiliations. Further, the narration of the death of Narasimha demonstrates that Narasimha is depicted as one with Shiva, supporting the synthetic origin of the theology of this deity. In the following pages, I will examine the stories of Narasimha's death.

Death of Narasimha and Shaivism

After killing Hiranyakasipu, Narasimha goes on a rampage due to his predominant nature Kalanta. In the Lingpurana story, it is said that god requested Shiva to appease Narasimha. For this purpose, Shiva creates Virabhadra, but he is not successful. Then Shiva goes to the underworld by himself and, there assuming the form of a Sarabha, he kills Narasimha and assimilates the prana (life) into himself (Linga Purana 95–6). In the Shiva Purana, Shiva absorbs Narasimha into himself (Shiva Purana 10–12). These stories reveal a clear desire to identify Shiva and Narasimha.

Narasimha is identified with Shiva more than once in the above stories unlike any of the Vaishnava avataras. The Linga Purana describes Narasimha and Shiva as one (Linga Purana I. 96.112). The Saura purana (29.49.52) describes Bhairava and Narasimha as one. In the Vaishnava stories of the origin of Narasimha avatara, he emerges from the sthambha (pillar) in Hiranyakasipus's palace and has three eyes. His weapons when he goes to Hiranyakasipus's palace are a club and trident (Linga Purana I. 95–6); in another description, he is said to have taken the Vajra (thunderbolt) (Harivamsa 226–33) and trident. The trident is traditionally the weapon of Shiva (J.N. Banerjea 1942: 65–8). The description of Narasimha as having a third eye similar to Shiva, and taking the weapon of Shiva (trident) demonstrates the close connection of Shiva and Narasimha and the synthetic views in the development of Narasimha. In the following pages, I will consider how this representation of Narasimha as Shiva in the Puranas has its parallels in the practice and worship.

According to *Kalikapurana* when Sharabha killed Narasimha, the god split into two forms: From the human (nara) part of Narasimha, avatara gave rise to Nara, while Narayana was produced from the Simha (lion) part of the avatara. Sharabha is also represented with a lion face in numerous sculptural representations.

While the above stories indicate the origin of Narasimha from Shiva or similar to Shiva, the following stories indicate extending this connection of Shiva and Narasimha further by depicting the relationship of Narasimha with the goddesses, who are also frequently depicted as close associates of Shiva.

Narasimha: The Creator and Controller of the Matrikas

The story of the demons Bhasmasura and Andhaka reveals the close connection between Shiva, Narasimha, and the goddesses. The Bhasmasura and Andhaka stories appear related even though they are described in different sections of the Puranas. Andhaka (Kurma Purana 179), the son of Hiranyaksha, develops an enchantment for Parvati (Shiva's wife). Andhaka creates 100 other Andhakas to fight Shiva's army. In the Kurma Purana, to help Shiva, Narasimha creates the Matrikas to fight the 100 Andhakas created by Andhaka. The Matrikas, having killed the Andhakas, go on a rampage and Shiva asks Narasimha to pacify them. Narasimha goes to the underworld where they are controlled and their powers are transferred to Bhairava (Kurma Purana 179.36). The control of Matrikas created by Narasimha and their transfer by him to Bhairava indicate that Narasimha is related to these gods as a mediatory deity who has similar powers and strengths as they do. This legend is longer in the Mastya Purana, which provides more details and attributes more importance to Narasimha as a median deity between Shiva and Bhairava. In the Mastyapurana story Shiva creates Matrikas to drink the blood of the Andhakas, but after having done that, they go on a rampage. At Shiva's request, to appease them, Narasimha creates another set of Matrikas who successfully appease Shiva's Matrikas (Mastya Purana 179.36). The creation of Matrikas by Narasimha to aid Shiva or to control Matikas created by Shiva demonstrates the similarity of Narasimha and Shiva in connection to Matrikas. Both Shiva and Narasimha can create and control the Matrikas. In this case, Narasimha is almost like another Shiva. Furthermore, in creating the Matrikas or appeasing the Matrikas, Narasimha is associated with another tradition of Hinduism, the Matrikas, who are seen as a part of Shaiva traditions. Indeed, the female counterpart of Narasimha, the goddess Narasimhi, is worshipped as one of the Saptamatrikas (Meister 1986: 233–62). The Devimahatmya mentions Narasimhi as a Matrika among the nine Matrikas (Meister 234). The first inscription of Narasimha is also dedicated to his female counterpart Narasimhi in Odisha, dated to 423 CE (Meister 1996: 291–301). Mother goddesses represent complex personalities with graceful/pleasing nature as well as fiery/terrifying with flexible status in Hinduism. Narasimha's association with Shiva and the Matrika traditions, show indigenous origins of Narasimha similar to the goddesses. Narasimha's close affiliation with a number of gods and goddesses shows the multifaceted as well as the middle or transitional nature of Narasimha. This flexible nature and transitional nature is noted amidst traditions associated with other local goddesses and popular traditions as noticed in Andhra Pradesh and Odisha.

Worship of Narasimha as Shiva in the Puranas and Practice

Numerous examples of worship of Narasimha as Shiva are described in the classical texts, which support the identity of Narasimha as Shiva, even though Narasimha is an incarnation of Vishnu. This again supports the nature of Narasimha as a deity not limited by narrow identities or boundaries. The Skanda Purana and Vishnudharmottara Purana mention that Narasimha is worshipped as Shiva. Vasista advised King Suratha to worship Shiva in the Bhirava form with the Narasimha mantra at Hatakeswara kshetra. He did so and obtained his lost kingdom by exterminating all his enemies (Skanda Purana VI. Nagara Khanda. Ch. 151.45–61). In the Vishnudharmottarpurana account, a devotee of the Pancaratra tradition, Visvaksena, was threatened by death, and he worships Narasimha in linga form, and from the linga emerges Narasimha and saves Vishvaksena (Vishnudharmottara III. Ch. 354–5). The images of Narasimha, Shiva, and Bhairava are seen as one in the above examples.

While in the Skandapurana Shiva is worshipped with the Narasimha mantra in the form of Virabhadra, in Vishnudharmottarapurana Narasimha is worshipped in the linga form from which he emerged to save his worshipper. Here Shiva is Narasimha and Narasimha is Shiva. Shiva is appeased by chanting the names of Narasimha and Narasimha appears from linga. This shows that the worship of Narasimha and Shiva as one was practiced.

Pralaya, Kala/Kalanta and Yoga

The Bhagavapurana (3.29.33) expounds on the relationship between Time and Space. This verse explains that Kala is the shelter of everything in the universe; Kala enters into everything and destroys the beings. This verse also describes Kala as Vishnu while also depicting Kala as a master of substances which subjugates others (Chattopadhyaya 1992: 86–7). Kala also denotes Samkarshana and Rudra. Kala (Time) follows different measure of time in different realms (spaces) of the Universe (see Chapter 4). Three measures of Time are noticed in the Puranas in connection with Narasimha: planetary time interconnected Cosmogonic time of Yugas, divine time, and the yogic time in which the enlightened mind surpasses time. When the space changes, the time extends or shortens, as seen in the planetary time: The length of a day on the

Earth differs from the length of day on the other planets. Similarly, the length of time is described as longer or shorter between different divine worlds. This aspect is clearly noted in the story of the marriage of Samkarshana (Balarama). The father of Revati decided to consult Brahma regarding the marriage of his daughter. However, when they reached the Brahmaloka music was playing; hence they waited. After a while when consulted Brahma smiled and said that, "a moment in Brahmaloka equals a long time on the Earth." He then informed Revata to marry his daughter to Samkarshana born in the next Yuga. This specifically indicates Balarama's capacity to remain beyond that realm of Kala. The vyuha Samkarshana is also identified with Narasimha, which also indicates the common characteristic of their capability to remain beyond the ravages of Time. Narasimha and Samkarshana are not subject to Kala, but masters of Kala.

Narasimha is referred to as Kala in the narration of vanquishing the demon Hiranyakashipu. Images of Kalanta (end of the world) were also noted in the course of the narrative. The incarnation of Narasimha also takes place toward the end of the Krita Yuga (Mastya Purana 161.2; Padma Purana V.42.2; Harivamsa 226.2; 41; Brahma Purana 213.44); appearing at the transitional phase he oversees the transition of Kritayuga to Tretayuga. The symbolism of the transitional middle is unmistakable in this depiction of Narasimha. Narasimha is referred to as Yuganta/Pralaya (Bhagavatapurana VII.2-10). Previous scholarly examinations of Narasimha noted the immense symbolism of cosmogonic transitions between two Yugas (Soifer 101; Biardeau 177). The appearance of Narasimha is referred to as Kala (Harivamsa 226; Shivapurana II.5.43). Narasimha has also been described with Kalanta (end of time) imagery of Pralaya. Narasimha acquires the form of Kala bringing about the Yuganta (Kalanta) of the Tretayuga, the first age, to a proper end to begin the next age. Therefore, it is absolutely important that the course of Time is not interrupted or abruptly changed. The story of Hiranyakashipu indicates that by overtaking the world Hiranyakashipu reversed the course of the universe, while also overturning the order of the worlds, bringing the world of gods down. Restoring the course of the universe as well as restoring the proper course of Kala is the primary goal of the Narasimha avatara. However, this aspect of the avatara confused scholars who have analyzed the story of Narasimha previously (Biardeau 1976: 111-263). However, the avataric nature and the yugadharma are also explained in connection with the avataras (Hiltebeitel 1972; Soifer 148-50). Narasimha avatara brings forward the deeper concerns of cosmology and universal harmony embedded in the concept of yugadharma. Soifer remarks in concluding her analysis of classical stories of Narasimha that "the unique nature of the avatara lies in its ability to join cosmological structures, particularly the kalpic and yugic understanding of both pralaya (destruction and recreation) and dharma. But the avatara does not stop at this already significant unions, it goes on to integrate into this context the central religious structure itself, soteriology" (Soifer 150). The kalpic, Yogic, and Pralayic nature of Narasimha brings together disparate elements. Therefore, even though seemingly disjointed and containing several elements of popular culture, the story of Narasimha succeeds in bringing together disparate elements of Indian culture and religion.

Interestingly, for the god who is identified as Kala/Kalanta, the end of universe/Time, his end is to be brought by another god, who is overwhelmingly identified as Kala Bhairava, another form of Shiva. Intriguingly, this is exactly what is represented as the last episode of the avatara of Narasimha in the classical texts. Shiva's destructive forms Bhairava (Kalabhairava) or Sharabha appear to bring about the end of Narasimha avatara on the Earth.

Restoration and Relationship with Other Deities and Beings

In the following pages, I will consider the local tales associated with some of the temples, which further demonstrate the syncretistic origin and worship of Narasimha.

Worship of Narasimha in a Form Similar to Linga in Andhra Pradesh

Although the syncretistic nature of Narasimha is only partly depicted in the Puranas and not stated clearly, it is seen clearly in the practice of the Narasimha tradition in Andhra Pradesh. In the Simhachalam temple (Sriramachandracharya 1991: 26) Narasimha is worshipped in a symbolic form covered by a several thick layers sandal paste. This paste is taken out only once a year to reveal the original form (nija rupa) of Narasimha. In his symbolic form wrapped in layers of sandal, he appears similar to a linga (Sundaram 1969: 122–3). Narasimha here is represented with three eyes like Shiva.

A legend about Ahobilam temple (Ramesan 1962: 28) states that the Kakatiya king Prataparudra planned to install an image of a golden Shivalinga in that temple. But he saw a vision in his dream in which, from the cast of the Shiva, linga Narasimha emerged. Prataparudra was perturbed by this. However, Narasimha appeared in his dream and told him that it was futile to make distinctions between Shiva and Narasimha. So even though Narasimha appeared from sthambha this story indicates the centrality of Narasimha at Ahobilam as distinct from Shiva, even though sharing divinity. As discussed here in the previous pages Narasimha's origin from sthambha has already established the aniconic representation of Narasimha in the form of sthambha similar to Shiva in his form as Sthanu.

The repeated association of Shiva with lion forms, as seen in the creation of Kirtimukha and Virabhadra, suggests that the lion form was with the forces of destruction and Shaivism. Surprisingly the lion motif never appeared in a systematic form in Vaisnavism except in the form of Narasimha.

Even though all the Vaishnava texts stress the association of Narasimha as an avatara of Vishnu, the above narrative and worship practices demonstrate that Narasimha evolved as a syncretic deity in practice while the Vaishnava and Shaiva texts laid claims to incorporating his stories equally. This only indicates the nature of transitions represented by Narasimha, which defines his boundary defying nature.

Restoration, Bhakti, and Symbolism

Vishnu Purana and Bhagavatapurana provide more information on the restoration and return of the world to positive order as well as Bhakti (devotion). As Vishnu is an all-pervader (vyapya) and conservator of the world order it is important for the avatara Narasimha to vanquish the demon, Hiranayakashipu, but it is also equally important to restore and establish the positive order of society. The cosmogonic role of Vishnu entails the maintenance of the harmonious order of the world.

The Symbolism of the Middle

The form of Narasimha and the stories, as well as the geographical associations of Narasimha represent the symbolism of the middle of the transition. Narasimha is the personified/deified concept of "neither this nor that," but something representing both aspects equally, a type of transitional center. This is closely reflected in the Purana stories of the deity Narasimha as well as in practice and popular representations. The geographical locations of temples are also noted in sites that demonstrate aspects of the middle/transition as well as the esoteric multiple nature of Narasimha of not belonging to any static position.

This symbolism of Narasimha also pervades numerous aspects of Narasimha tradition including practice.

The appearance of Narasimha from the pillar in the palace of Hiranyakashipu had been interpreted variously as symbolizing the ritual of a sacrifice (Bieardaeu 40–3; Soifer 97; Hacker 590–4; Eschmann 102). However, this is not plausible in the light of the event as it is described in the Narasimha stories in the Mahabharata and other puranas. Even though the pillar was compared to the stake in these early scholarly readings, its deep symbolism embedded in this event is misconstrued due to hasty comparisons. Early readings of the stake had been hastily applied to this event even though the similarity is lacking other than the term sthambha (pillar) also mistakenly identified with another Sanskrit word, skambha, which is previously used in the Vedas to denote stake (Gonda 1970: 81–4). Even though both of these words are used without discretion, the terms differ greatly in context. While sthambha simply denotes a pillar, skambha denotes a ritual stake. However, this does not apply to the emergence of Narasimha from the pillar in the palace. A stake is a ritually constructed free-standing pillar, but not a structural pillar as noted in this event and a stake is not destroyed or cut in a ritual of sacrifice. Besides, Sanskrit terms denote multiple meanings and should be properly contextualized to understand the precise meaning. More important here is the emergence of Narasimha from the structural pillar of the palace, while sacrifice holds no symbolic connection to the deeper meaning of the story. I think the exact meaning of sthambha bears deeper symbolism in connection to Narasimha in this event rather than a prop for sacrifice. Understanding it as a stake based on unrelated evidence has led to missing the true symbolism of pillar as representative of Narasimha, as "neither high" "nor low," but a state of the transitional middle, not belonging to either the ceiling or the floor of the palace. The internal evidence of the story must be considered closely in order to learn the embedded contextual meaning of the event prior to employing any unrelated external evidence, such as this case. Hence, the description of the Narasimha story shows the pillar in a palace cannot be assumed to be a stake based on the internal evidence of the story.

According to the Bhagavata Purana and Vishnu Purana versions, the person who was under duress, who was also the victim of the wrath of Hiranyakashipu, was his son, Prahlada. Due to the Bhakti of Prahlada Narasimha emerged from the pillar to save Prahlada from the wrath of his own father Hirnyakashipu. As Hiranyakashipu burst the pillar in anger with his Gada (mace), Narasimha emerged from the pillar as depicted in the Bhagavata Purana (VII.5), while in the Vishnupurana Vishnu makes his appearance in yellow robes (Vishnupurana I.20. 1,3) and the event of killing Hiranyakashipu is described briefly in the Vishnu Purana. In this process, Hiranayakashipu is vanquished, and the one who was intended to be decapitated, the child Prahlada, was protected. So, the symbolism of the event as a sacrifice is misplaced even though a concession could be made to understand it as one since the subjects are reversed. The one intended to be decapitated is replaced by the one who was performing the task of decapitation, who was then killed by Narasimha. Therefore, the fact of the emergence of Narasimha from the pillar marks a reversal as well as the transitional middle, symbolism associated with Narasimha closely in all the depictions of him in the Puranas. The pillar signifies one of the qualifiers of the boon of Hiranyakashipu which said neither "high nor low" which makes the pillar neither part of the ceiling, which is high, nor part of the floor, which is low, and it is also the middle here by not being high or low.

After Prahlada was thus saved, he requested Narasimha to pardon his father Hiranyakashipu and grant him "liberation from existence" thus exemplifying one of the important aspects of Bhakti, salvation. Here again, the early scholarly interpretation focused on the aspect of sacrifice. Even though Bhakti, the special bond that Narasimha shared with Prahlada, is central to this event, it was interpreted that "as a sacrificial victim in the Bhagavatapurana story, Hiranyakashipu is assured liberation" (Soifer 97), while adding that "it is besides, the sacrificial nature of this violent act accomplished for the good of the worlds which gives the victim a chance of salvation" (Bieardeau 43). Comparing this event to a sacrifice and presenting Hiranyakashipu as a sacrificial victim, these early works misconstrued the symbolism of Narasimha and the central event of the story and its connection to Bhakti. This is one of the ways Hindu studies misconstrued the symbolism and internal evidence of a particular classical story. Some have even gone further to pronounce that the avatara, Narasimha, on which the entire story is based as not being central to the story. Others have misconstrued the event of his appearance to vanquish Hiranyakashipu as not important noting that "But the avatara has become superfluous here" (Hacker 594). One has to disagree with these previous interpretations of the killing of a demon, Hiranyakashipu, as sacrifice or of Narasimha granting liberation to the demon after his death as negating the purpose of avatara. The central event as well as the conclusion of the event are in fact a demonstration of the profound nature of the avatara as central to the incarnations of Vishnu, but it was overruled in earlier scholarly interpretations using external evidence, rather than internal textual evidence associated with Narasimha. In the Narasimha stories depicted in Bhagavatapurana, Vishnupurana, Skandapurana, and Lingapurana stories, Bhakti is central to the story of Narasimha as the stories venerate Narasimha as an important avatara of Vishnu. In the Skanda Purana (II.10–12) and Lingapurana (I.95–6), Prahlada was called on to approach the raging Narasimha to appease him as all others were too scared and not sure on how to appease him. However, Prahlada's Bhakti was seen as the best way to approach Narasimha.

In the Bhagavata Purana upon the restoration of the world back to its harmony each group of beings, gods and humans, thanked Narasimha. Indra thanked him for the restoration and return of the sacrificial portions, the sages for their penances, the Pitrs for their oblations, the nagas for their gem crowns, and so on. This shows the centrality of the avatara within Hindu cosmology, and Bhakti is an ancillary development of this primary role of the avatara.

Although the Vaishnava and Shaiva sectarian debates are recorded in some regional texts, these polemical debates are limited in influence and did not affect the popular practice of the region. The central region as the *leelasthali* of Narasimha accords primacy to Narasimha and equal status to Shiva and Vishnu. These Shaiva and Vaishnava traditions are fused in Narasimha within the historical Hindu tradition and practice, in a symbolic representation of the transitional nature of Narasimha, which defies boundaries. Studies on Shaivism and Vaishnavism indicate that the practice, philosophy, and sacred centers worked in concert regardless of minor differences. Overarching themes of philosophy, yoga, and belief in the universal soul led to concerted efforts to link these numerous pluralistic practices under a uniform direction, indicating the indigenous origins. Embracing contradictory features in his representation and practice Narasimha appears as the greatest example of sectarian unity noticed in practice as well as textual sources. Shaivism in Karnataka and Andhra Pradesh is pluralistic, but its philosophical tradition coalesces with other Hindu sectarian traditions in practice (Fisher 2018: 9–23). This fusion is notable in how the pilgrimage circuits are organized encircling the Vaishnava and Shaiva sacred centers in Andhra Pradesh and Telangana. One of the most important pilgrim circuits of Andhra Pradesh includes the most popular Vaishnava and Shaiva temples. The Narasimha temple at Ahobilam forms the central part of the pilgrimage circle along with the Shiva temple at Sri Sailam and Venkateshwara temple at Tirupati (Debicka-Borek 2019: 79–81). The overarching unity of the deities spread out in the vast landscape of mountains and rivers is imagined through identifying the mountains stretching from Tirupati to Sri Sailam as the world-carrying divine serpent Shesha, on whose hoods rests the Earth, and on whose coils rests the meditative Vishnu. In the second millennium when traveling by foot, commonly, this is one of the most well-known sacred pilgrimages. Ahobilam is in the middle, as the other two important sacred centers, Srisailam and Tirupati, are located on each side. The distance between Ahobilam and Srisailam (about 150 miles) could be covered in three days, and the distance between Ahobilam and Tirupati (about 150 miles) could be covered in another three days; hence a pilgrimage of two weeks would allow the devotees to complete the pilgrimage circuit and return home. This could be completed in a day's journey currently; hence a weekend of travel covers this circuit as modern travel and tourist services are available. This pilgrimage circuit is still currently in use in southern India (Eck 2012: 251–2, 317). The evolution of the Narasimha tradition in Middle India, therefore, shows unity mediated by Narasimha rather than sectarian rivalry as noticed elsewhere in India. The Ahobilam temple of Narasimha also epitomizes the simultaneous relationship of Narasimha with Shiva and Vishnu symbolically superimposed on the landscape as the temple is located in the middle of the mountain ranges equidistant from the most popular Vishnu temple and Shiva temple of the region. It is not coincidental that three of the most popular temples of Andhra Pradesh dedicated to different gods are located in a unified pilgrimage circuit. They might have developed due to the shared nature of Narasimha with Shiva and Vishnu within the religious landscape of the middle region of India.

Conclusion

This chapter examined the classical texts of the Mahabharata and the Harivamsa and other Mahapuranas to understand the predominant concepts associated with the deity Narasimha. Even though the Narasimha story has been examined extensively in previous scholarly works, their analysis has failed to bring the true symbolism of Narasimha to the forefront since they misconstrued the central features of the story. Several mistaken interpretations and identities imposed on Narasimha based on isolated references from external sources hampered the holistic understanding of Narasimha based on the internal evidence of the Narasimha stories. In particular the symbolism representing the state of the middle/transition has been interpreted variously in the previous scholarship. In particular understanding the appearance of Narasimha from the pillar and the place of Prahlada has caused tremendous confusion. It was considered a symbolic sacrifice (Bieardeau 1976: 111–263; Soifer 199: 97), while others considered it the poet's lack of knowledge (Hacker 1959: 594) or due to derivation from folk traditions (Eschmann 1978: 102–3).

The first theme of universal chaos demonstrates the success of the extreme penances that the demon Hiranyakashipu performed lasting up to 11,000–12,000 years to reap the karmic benefits by obtaining the special boon of qualified immunity from the god Brahma. However, as soon as Hiranyakashipu obtained the special boon he reversed the order of the universe, removing gods from their stations. This also pushed the human world, the Earth, into chaos as the reversal of the upper world of gods and the lower world of demons resulted in a unique error for the middle world, the Earth, to take a reverse course in Time. The second theme of the Narasimha story, *viz.*, is the special nature of the avatara Narasimha necessitated by the special boon of Hiranyakashipu. Hence, the special feature of transitions, not belonging to either-this-or-that, becomes the dominant quality of the persona, activities, and theology associated with Narasimha. The third theme of yoga in the stories of Narasimha is generally associated with Vishnu in his rest as Anantasayanamurty, but not usually associated with his incarnations. Vishnu's rest is referred to as yoganidra. However, here in the incarnation of Narasimha yoga is his predominant quality. Yoga and Tantric practices form part of the religious practice associated with Narasimha. The fourth theme of Pralaya, Kala, and Kalanta, in the stories of Narasimha, is associated with the Ugrarupa, the terrifying form of Vishnu, Narasimha. These qualities are predominantly associated with Shiva. Hence, Shiva's close affinity with Narasimha is symbolized through his activities, which closely resemble Shiva. As an incarnation of Vishnu, Narasimha predominantly represents qualities of transitions and Time (Kalanta/end of Time). This has been central to avatara Narasimha which is crucial to accomplish the task of vanquishing the demons as well as returning the three worlds (trilokas) to their original balance. As Narasimha accomplishes his desired tasks adapting terrible form he also transforms himself into a form that is akin to Shiva, which requires Shiva, in the end, to help him withdraw from his transitional as well as this transgressive terrifying man-lion form. Hence, as an incarnation of Vishnu, Narasimha does not comfortably fit into known categorizations and hence he was considered a vyuha and avatara, equating him with other forms of Vishnu such as Samkarshana-Balarama. Not only is Narasimha a complex incarnation within Vaishnavism, but a multi-faceted deity of Hinduism as his incorporation into Shaivism is also paved by his not-so-conventional characteristics which present him in Pralayic form incorporating the Kalanta (end of time) aspects of Shiva. This is the reason he is also unified with Shiva through Kala Bhairava a form of Shiva. Narasimha is also unified with Shiva through his relationship with the goddesses, the Matrikas. While Shiva created the Matrikas, Narasimha holds the power to calm and contain them. Finally, as Narasimha accomplished the task of returning the world to its proper order, Narasimha had also evolved close relations with demons through Prahlada, and with the other important gods Shiva and the goddesses, as well as the humans. This fifth and final task is the most important aspect of as the multi-valent deity of Hinduism. Overall, this chapter showed the multi-valent and multi-functional nature of Narasimha through an examination of Hindu texts. It is this quality of Narasimha to connect with each and everyone emphatically, which made him accessible deity with the most inclusive practices propelling him as the favorite deity to the diverse communities of devotees in Middle India.

3

Historical Narasimha from Prehistory to Present

Literary evidence along with historical and monumental evidence helps establish the historicity of the Narasimha tradition. Hence, this chapter is devoted to examining the archaeological data, inscriptions, and sculptures to trace the historical practices of Narasimha and analyze the evolution of Hinduism in Middle India. This chapter also correlates the information from the inscriptions, sculptures, and other material sources, which provides additional resources to the textual information discussed in Chapter 2 in the previous pages of this book to fathom the historical development of the Narasimha tradition. This chapter focuses on the monumental and historical evidence from the region under study, Middle India. Although early material evidence of Narasimha is noted from across India, which is roughly contemporaneous with the textual evidence, the preponderance of material evidence in Middle India supports the advent of the region of Middle India as the *leelasthali* of Narasimha. None of the evidence available indicates the imposition of the tradition from northwestern India due to invasions and occupations.

Historical information about Narasimha can be divided into two categories. The first category of data identifies Narasimha through name, depiction, and so on, while the second category of information is not directly identified but can be deduced from symbolic similarities and coincidences of occurrences. Aniconic (symbolic) representations of Narasimha as a seated or standing lion can be identified since the prehistoric era and, even though it is difficult to know for sure if the symbolism of lions, the story of Narasimha, and later iconic representations are connected or not with these early aniconic representations, their appearance itself is symbolic of the profound regard for lion within the culture of the region. However, it is not unusual to find the historic roots of Hinduism in excavations at Paleolithic and Mesolithic sites in India. Common themes of religion might have persisted and evolved among the living populations of indigenous communities of India notable since the Mesolithic era, noted in India from about 10,000 BCE.

It has been theorized that Narasimha might have been absorbed from popular or prehistoric practice into classical Hinduism although whether these two aspects of Hinduism have ever remained distinct enough to support this dual perception of practice is questionable (Jaiswal 1973: 140–51; Murty 1997: 179–88). However, the lion remains a major aspect of prehistoric symbols and totems of current tribal groups (vanavasi) of Middle India, which connects Mesolithic life with modern vanavasi cultural life of this region. Even though continuity is noticed between prehistoric practices and modern vanavasi societies, which are also shared commonly among Hindus of all stripes, a forced dichotomy is imposed within Hindu practices. Continuity noticed within the practices and historical religion associated with Narasimha is ignored as a way to promote this theory of Aryan occupation and imposition. However, the examination of evidence in this book proves the futility of imposing such a dichotomy through establishing the overarching affiliation and continuity within the practice of religion between prehistoric and modern religious practice. As historical evidence is discussed in this chapter, I will also consider prehistoric lion representations which might have been primal religious symbols. This chapter is dedicated to surveying relevant information on Narasimha, but this is by no means exhaustive, as the central focus here is to trace the historical development of the Narasimha tradition, and not to chronicle all the available evidence.

Hinduism is the foremost indigenous faith of India developed over the millennia. Hence, numerous elements form part of the practice, which make it part of the traditional practice of all the indigenous population groups of Indian society, be it forest-dwellers or non-forest-dweller Hindus. This becomes even more obvious in the practices associated with Narasimha. Non-tribal and tribal populations have different lifestyles and practices rather than different religions. It is apparent in the practices associated with Narasimha that the religious practices once may have overlapped and diverged gradually. Tribal and non-tribal groups have had more shared culture and practice historically within Narasimha tradition and practice. In fact, lion symbolism is preserved in the tribal religion and practice, while the others merely preserve the practices associated with Narasimha.

It has been theorized that the worship of Narasimha might have been a tribal tradition assimilated into Hinduism. It is difficult to assume that tribal and non-tribal Hinduism were always distinct since the indigenous populations might have shared their religious and social practices based on indigenous practice and faith.

Whether tribal or non-tribal, all Indian population groups show shared genetic heritage according to recent genetic research that has established that large sections of current populations of India have autochthonous origins connected to the subcontinent derived from the first Founders about 80,000 years ago (Vemsani 2014). As the original inhabitants of the subcontinent's population groups and their lifestyles evolved and developed over a long period their beliefs and practices might have also gradually evolved from the symbolic original core noted in the prehistoric roots. Although efforts have been made to coordinate prehistoric human groups with the modern social groups of India, they haven't been successful beyond establishing the autochthonous origin of all current human groups of India, either caste or tribe. An individual's belonging to a social group does not determine the nature of his religion or his devotional practice.[1] However, no consistent efforts have been launched to coordinate the historical data with the textual data of India in connection with Narasimha. The human groups must have preserved their inner consciousness of early symbols in some form in the texts as well as through depictions in the caves and rock shelters. However, although this early depiction might not show the direct adaption or evolution of the Narasimha tradition from previous totemic representations or other early lion paintings, it definitely shows the enduring legacy and longstanding practice of revering practices associated with the lion, but also establishes the lack of social distinctions among the followers of the deity. The contribution of any of this early imagery is only symbolic and does not mean direct constructive contribution, but only indirect contribution.

Concept of Time and Hindu Time Cycles

Classical Puranas note three types of time: The divine time cycle, the cosmogonic time cycle, and historical time. The divine time cycle is measured in connection with Brahma, the smallest measure of which is the blink of the eye of Brahma, which is used to build large measures of time such as Brahma's day and Brahma's year. The life of Brahma is equal to one cycle of creation.

Cosmogonic cycles are also measured in Brahma's time cycles, which is interconnected with the human world as a measure of Time, by the equation of one day of Brahma is equal to that of the one human Yuga.

According to the Vishnu Purana,

> that Time is a form of Vishńu: hear now how it is applied to measure the duration of Brahmá, and all other sentient beings, as well as of those which are unconscious, as the mountains, oceans, and the like. "Oh best of sages, fifteen twinklings of the eye make a Kashtha; thirty Káshthás, one Kalá; and thirty Kalás, one Muhúrtta. Thirty Muhúrttas constitute a day and night of mortals: thirty such days make a month, divided into two half-months: six months form an Ayana (the period of the sun's progress north or south of the ecliptic): and two Ayanas compose a year. The southern Ayana is a night, and the northern a day of the gods. Twelve thousand divine years, each composed of (three hundred and sixty) such days, constitute the period of the four Yugas, or ages.
>
> (Vishnu Purana Book III.2.3)

According to this comparative measure, a year for humans is a day for the gods. The Vishnu Purana provides further information on the length of the Yugas in comparison with the year of Brahma.

> Twelve thousand divine years, each composed of (three hundred and sixty) such days, constitute the period of the four Yugas, or ages. They are thus distributed: the Krita age has four thousand divine years; the Tretá three thousand; the Dwápara two thousand; and the Kali age one thousand: so those acquainted with antiquity have declared. The period that precedes a Yuga is called a Sandhyá, and it is of as many hundred years as there are thousands in the Yuga: and the period that follows a Yuga, termed the Sandhyánsa, is of similar duration. The interval between the Sandhyá and the Sandhyánsa is the Yuga, denominated Krita, Tretá, &c. The Krita, Tretá, Dwápara, and Kali, constitute a great age, or aggregate of four ages: a thousand such aggregates are a day of Brahmá, and fourteen Manus reign within that term.
>
> (Vishnu Purana Book III.2.3)

The Indian cosmogonic system divides the universal time into four eras: the Krita, Treta, Dwapara, and Kali Yuga, which are again part of a Kalpa, one cycle of Time. The Krita Yuga is also called the Satya Yuga, the golden age of human life ruled by truth. The Treta Yuga is marked by divisions and enmity between the demonic and divine forces and human suffering. The Dwapara age is marked by deteriorating truth and quality of life. The Kali Yuga is the current age marked by declining morality. The length of these ages and the period of time in the historical era do not match the time scale as we know it currently. The current history of India notes three Paleolithic periods of which the Upper Paleolithic period beginning 80,000 years ago (YA) is notable as this period denotes the replacement of hominids by hominins in India, which is also noted in the genetic heritage of India. The genetic heritage of India traces male genetic heritage to clade C datable 73,000 YA, while the female genetic heritage is traced to M clade datable to 74,000 YA (Vemsani 2014: 594–620). Even though it is difficult to coordinate these time cycles with the current periodization of history, the description of the qualities of the ages depicts unmistakable similarities between the first ages, the Krita Yuga and prehistory. The story of Narasimha takes place toward the end of the Krita Yuga during the transition to the next age, the Treta Yuga.

The Satya Yuga/Krita Yuga denotes the first and best age in cosmogonic cycles in which humans lived happily and there was no greed or theft. Similarly, the prehistoric golden age represents a period free of greed and theft as the concept of personal property or social stratification is not noticed. Thus, the stories of Narasimha resemble some prehistoric early configuration of lifestyles seen through symbolic association. Incidentally, Narasimha traditions contain numerous prehistoric symbols such as the association with caves and hills, and affiliation with social groups that practice hunter-gatherer lifestyles, similar to the Paleolithic hunter-gatherers. These features appear even more prominently in the case of accounts of Narasimha in regional accounts, the Sthalapuranas and the Mahatmyas, which may represent an early vague recollection of the former stage of Paleolithic life during which humans roamed the Earth sustained by the available natural resources, which mostly resembles the hunter-gatherer stage of life, now preserved among very few of the vanavasi populations of India.

According to the popular tales, Narasimha also connects with the hunter-gatherer lifestyle and roaming in the forests. Narasimha's marriage to Chenchulakshmi, a daughter of the Chenchu tribe, which still practices a hunter-gatherer lifestyle, is also indicative of Narasimha's symbolic association with the hunter-gatherer lifestyle.

The symbolism of the historic events of the Toba volcanic eruption about 74,000 years ago (Basu, Biswas, and Acharyya 1987: 66–72), fire, and destruction are also noted in the end-of-world symbolism preserved in Narasimha's tale. Incidentally numerous prehistoric era habitation sites excavated in Middle India preserve Toba volcanic ash deposits, which indicates that the prehistoric population might have experienced this cataclysmic event. According to the classical texts, the world is pushed into Pralaya with the arrival of Narasimha who defeated Hiranyakashipu and set the world on the straight path. The symbolism of transitions and the fiery end to the world, as well as the population recovery from calamity described in the Narasimha story, bears close semblance to the Toba volcano eruption and population recovery of hominins as the hominids gradually disappeared from the world as hominins recovered from this natural calamity. However, nothing can be established for certain as these popular stories and classical stories of Narasimha only preserve symbolic associations.

In this chapter, I will begin my examination of historical data noting the depiction of Narasimha as standing and sitting lions from prehistoric cave sites followed by examination of early historical evidence. Even though numerous Hindu practices bear resemblances to prehistoric cave paintings and pottery depictions, historians have hesitated to closely analyze the similarities. I would not suggest that Upper Paleolithic culture gave rise to religion, but it is possible to think that early indigenous conscious played a role in shaping the early religion of India, which might denote the symbolic connections of divinity depicted as lion discussed here.

The Upper Paleolithic period is a transitional period, which faced the natural calamity of the Toba volcano eruption. There were numerous distinct lifestyles in the Lower Paleolithic and Middle Paleolithic periods, while after the Toba volcanic eruption the number and variety of cultural settlements decreased. This is also the period of population replacement noted in the interaction of earlier hominids (*Homo erectus/Homo sapiens*) and new arrivals the hominins (*Homo sapiens sapiens*) (Vemsani 2014).

The historical events of the Upper Paleolithic period closely resemble the narrative elements of the Narasimha story. The symbolic idea of the utter destruction of creation or the imagery of *Kalanta*, in which the world was destroyed and then revived, bears close similarities to the imagery of destruction and revival about 74,000 years ago due to the Toba volcano eruption. Excavations conducted in Kurnool district not too far from the sacred center of Narasimha at Ahobilam, located less than 50 miles from there, have preserved Toba volcanic evidence as well as continued habitation from the Paleolithic era (Petraglia 2007).

In addition, the social groups associated with Narasimha are also known for their predominant Paleolithic lifestyles. Chenchus are known for their hunting and gathering skills and their familiarity with forest produce. Forest produce is still one of the mainstays of the Chenchu tribe. The similarities in the descriptions of Pralaya and end of Time events such as vadavanala and the re-emergence and recovery of historical evidence could be hardly missed. Narasimha's relationship and commonality with tribal groups following the Paleolithic hunter-gather lifestyle are also another important aspect of note here (see Chapters 4 and 9 for more information on popular traditions). Lions live in small family groups in deep forests where water and game are fairly abundant. The easy availability of resources was also one of the special qualities for establishing human settlements during the Paleolithic period. Presence of lion indicates availability of resources and might have been regarded as a symbol of strength and abundance during the remote prehistoric era. Such reverential attitudes gradually lead to historical religious symbols and motifs. Hence, it is not unusual that the lion was worshipped as a totem among many early tribal groups as a symbol of abundance, which might have been considered as savior in this remote period of the Paleolithic age during which humans came close to extinction only to find revival in deep forests into which the Toba volcanic ash could not infiltrate to effect their extinction. Therefore, I am inclined to consider Paleolithic era representations of standing or sitting lions as proto-Narasimha symbols of the early religion of the prehistoric golden age.

Although the Yugas and prehistoric timelines need to be further examined, it would be helpful to examine the resemblances of descriptions of the characteristics of the Yugas and note their similarities with the prehistoric period. For a historical examination, this close examination reveals similarities between the Yugas of the Indian calendrical system and the early phases of the prehistoric evolution of human beings at least for the cosmological golden age and prehistoric golden age. The Narasimha story mentions the last part of the Krita Yuga and its interregnum as the chaotic period leading up to the beginning of the Treta Yuga. These events closely represent the Paleolithic period, especially the Upper Paleolithic period (Figure 5).

Prehistoric Precedents

Historical data on Narasimha is available in archaeological, inscriptional, and sculptural sources. One important aspect of sources related to Narasimha is the availability of lion/lion-faced depictions from as far back as the beginning of civilization, from the Upper Paleolithic period datable to about 40,000 years ago (YA). These early cave paintings have been interpreted variously by archaeologists, cultural anthropologists, and early historians, sometimes ruling out eliminating the possibility of understanding the profound symbolic meaning embedded in these depiction, by calling these sketches as childish scribbles of some prehistoric human without attributing any deeper meaning to them. However, it appears that due to the selective nature and repeated appearance of certain motifs and the continuation of these symbols in religious practice in a symbolic manner, it is plausible that these early cave paintings may have served a similar type of spiritual and pedagogical purpose as the modern sculptural depictions/pata chitras or

Figure 5 Appearance of Narasimha, wooden image (Andhra Pradesh seventeenth to eighteenth century CE). Courtesy: Metropolitan Museum of Art, New York.

inscriptions carved on temples, whose main goal was to preserve and disseminate the deeper thought for later generations. The fact that these engravings and sketches were preserved, but not erased or drawn over for millennia by many generations of folks living in or visiting these Paleolithic caves and rock shelters is reason enough to think that these paintings might have held some solemn message/meaning from the past, even though long lost currently, due to the passage of time. These early depictions hold the key to understanding the roots of early human civilization, especially religion. Similarly, the cave paintings are most prolific from the Upper Paleolithic period. They may hold the key to understanding indigenous religion through interpretations of pictures, which are encyclopedic in nature in preserving a large number of primal motifs and lifestyle information in cryptic symbolic depictions. What is necessary is close examination and careful analysis to reach the core of the symbolism. In fact, it is impossible to separate the tribal and non-tribal themes of practice within the Narasimha tradition, since oral and textual practices are incorporated within the temple stories (Sthalapuranas) and practices simultaneously. Therefore, studying Narasimha traditions might also provide clues to the development of religious practice in India including several strands of indigenous practice since the prehistoric era.

Prehistoric paintings noted at Bhimbedka rock shelters and other early caves contain numerous animal drawings including lions, tigers, rhinos, elephants, and peacocks (Misra 1979: 29–33; Neumayer 1993). However, the early emphasis on examining the art and lifestyles of prehistoric paintings, through their emphasis on human figures and their activities rather than the symbolic nature of animal figures, missed the deeper meaning embedded in these depictions. It is certainly possible that they may indicate religious symbolism since some of these symbolic depictions of animal motifs such as lions, elephants, boars, and peacocks continue to appear in the Hindu religion.

Lion images and symbolic representations of lions are noted across the world. However, it is not out of place to discuss one of the rare images of prehistoric standing lion sculpture to understand the prevalence of prehistoric lion symbolism to understand the profound nature of prehistoric nature symbolism. The admiration of humans to see lion as majestic animal verging on being identified with humans has taken many forms across the world. An interesting sculpture is noted in Europe dated to the Paleolithic era: An ivory image of a lion called Lowenmensch, which coincidentally translates as Narasimha, for its symbolism of anthropomorphic bipedalism. The figure was discovered in fragments recently in the Hohlenstein-Stadel cave in southern Germany. It could easily be one of the oldest images of Narasimha as it is dated between 32,000 and 40,000 years ago. The image measures 29.6 centimeters (11.7 inches) in height and 5.6 centimeters in width and 5.9 centimeters in thickness. This image is currently on display in the Museum of Ulm. Although some pieces of the sculpture were discovered in 1938, the head and other parts were discovered between 1997 and 1998, and the sculpture was reassembled. The image was carved out of woolly mammoth ivory using a stone tool (flint flake tool) kit. It can be noted that great care had been shown in carving the image as indicated by the facial features and grooved upper right arm, which indicate its use as a ritual image.[2] This indicates ceremonial rather than decorative use of the sculpture. It appears similar to the early Narasimha image depicted on the Kondamotu panel, and in its standing posture it bears similarity with the Nrusimhanatha image at Padampur. This is not to suggest that these figures are connected, but only to indicate that prehistoric lion symbolism is widespread.

The posture of Lowenmensch is very similar to Kevala Narasimha, which is a lion-formed anthropomorphic depiction of the deity Narasimha in standing or sitting posture. Although no weapons were found at the site, the posture of the image indicates that the image must have held some long weapon such as a trident or a spear. Ivory image carving was one of the long-known sculptural practices of India.

I will examine the early historical sources (sculptures, coins, and archaeological data) to understand the early evidence and themes associated with Narasimha. The literary records of Narasimha (the Mahabharata and the Puranas) and historical sources are contemporaneous, beginning in 600 BCE. The information might have been much older than the historical and archaeological records, and it might have survived in the popular memory and practice before being recorded in permanent sources as it remains as lasting evidence for the veneration of Narasimha. Such widespread occurrence of images of Narasimha across India in archaeological excavations belonging to early historical levels dating from at least 400 BCE to 300 CE demonstrates the early widespread worship of Narasimha across India.

Early Historical Tracts of Narasimha from 600 BCE to 600 CE

Historical evidence following the prehistoric era begins with the foundations of kingdoms and empires on the fertile river basins of India. The Janapadas and Mahajanapadas noted in Buddhist, Jain, and Hindu classical literature spread across India were also identified through historical excavations and the abundance of seals and other clay objects at these notable centers in the first millennium BCE. It is important to note that early evidence of Narasimha begins from this early period, continuing and multiplying over the centuries. I will note the early evidence from these early settlements (600–100 BCE) during the first millennium BCE and continuing into the ancient period of India (100–900 CE). From the turn of the second millennium, inscriptions as well as historical sources concerning the religion centered on Narasimha multiply. Hence, for this later period, I will limit my consideration of historical evidence to the notable historical temples of Narasimha.

However, it seems that numerous early centers of Narasimha may have been destroyed since most of the early seals and sculptures datable to the sixth century BCE to the third century CE have been discovered in isolated excavations in ruins (Thaplyal 1972). Although it is not clear when these temples might have been originally built or destroyed, the invasions of the second millennium followed by numerous others are recorded as very destructive in this region in oral tales. The Sri Simhadri Narasimha Satakamu recollects one such temple-destroying attack of the Islamic armies (Gogulapati 1983), while another destructive attack on

Ahobilam temple is recollected in the historical accounts of Aurangzeb's son and the Nizam of Hyderabad (Eaton 1995: 59–71; Ticku, Srivastava, and Iyer 2019).

Early historic representations of Narasimha from 600 BCE to 600 CE are discussed here. Although there are only a few resources that have survived from this period, these resources certainly indicate widespread and well-known practices centered on Narasimha. Most of the resources have been either excavated or survived in the caves, which shows that there might have been active centers of Narasimha during this early historic period, which might have been destroyed or lost.

An early seal from Basrah (ancient Vaisali) in the state of Bihar, excavated by Spooner, superintendent of the Eastern Circle of the Archaeological Survey of India during 1910–15, shows the ancient Narasimha in his most popular form, seated on a high seat (Nagarch 1985). This seal depicts Narasimha seated in Lalitasana on a high pitha. This might be one of the oldest depictions of Narasimha which could be historically dated. The site of Vaisali has been dated to at least 600 BCE if not earlier. Vaishali is the capital of the Vrijji confederacy dated between 600 and 400 BCE. Hence, the monuments, punch-marked coins, and other discoveries found in lower levels of excavation were dated to this period based on their prevalence in these early historical layers during excavation.

Sculptures of a seated Narasimha datable between 1 and 300 CE, found in ruins among the excavations at Motadaka and Kondamotu, revealed unique early sculptures of Narasimha. A green limestone image of a seated four-armed Narasimha was excavated from a ruined brick structure in Motadaka, Guntur district (Sarma 2000: 301–2), datable to the early centuries of the current era. The dating of these sculptures from Kondamotu and Mothadaka varies between 100 BCE and 300 CE (Khan 1964; Srinivasan 1979: 39–51; Vasantha 1991; Jaiswal 1973: 140–51). The sculpture of Narasimha from Motadaka depicts Narasimha (Kevala Narasimha) seated at ease (sukhasina) termed as lalitasana on a high chair (pitha).

The sculpture from Kondamotu depicts a seated Narasimha at the center with Pancaviras flanking his sides (Khan; Nigam 2000–1: 114; Banarjea 1942: 65–8). Narasimha is depicted with a conch (shankha) and wheel (chakra); the Pancaviras are depicted with their respective weapons. The identity of the Pancaviras remained a mystery until their identification based on the Vayupuarana (97.1–2) reference was correlated to explain it (Banerjea 1942). The sculpture seems to represent Narasimha as Vishnu from whom the vyuhas emanate.

The vyuha and avatara symbolism is fused in this early representation. The Pancaviras represented are Samkarshana (Balarama), Vasudeva (Krishna),

Pradyumna, Aniruddha, and Samba. While the vyuhas Samkarana, Vasudeva, Pradyumna, and Aniruddha are identified as the four vyuhas, Samba shares the identity with Samkarshana partly as the destroyer of creation, as described in the Mausalaparva of the Mahabharata in which he is depicted as bringing the annihilation of the Yadavas. The vyuha and avatara correlation of Narasimha is unmistakable as the depiction of Samkarshana as lion/cat is again encountered in the sculptural depiction of the vyuhas (Srinivasan 1979: 39–55). The depiction of Narasimha as a cat is a reminder of the Bidala Narasimha noted in the Padampur Nrusimhanatha temple in Odisha (see Chapter 6).

The most intact image of caturvyuhas was discovered in the Saptasamudri well in Mathura. Even though extracted in pieces it was put together to make a complete vyuha image, which is preserved in the Mathura museum (Gupta 2013: 86–7). Few other vyuha images are noted later. Although this image does not contain Narasimha, it helped explain the configuration of deities of another vyuha image containing the Cat, on the back, generally noted as the southern side associated with the second vyuha Samkarshana, identified with Balarama. The second vyuha Balarama is uniquely connected with Narasimha. Symbolic representation of Balarama involves Simha (lion). Balarama's weapon is Simha-langala, the lion plow, and his symbol is the combined lion-elephant form; both involve lions (Agrawala 1976: 281).

Numerous ruling dynasties of the middle region of India adopted Narasimha as the central deity. The Vakatakas adopted Narasimha, depicting him on their royal insignia and flag. The Vakatakas also built one of the earliest temples of Narasimha on Ramtek (Bakker 1993: 46–74; Jamkhedkar 1987a: 335–41; 1987b: 217–23). Even though reverence of Narasimha as the central deity of the Vakatakas is attributed historically to Queen Prabhavati, daughter of the Guptas, wife of the king of the Vakataka empire spread in the mid-west region of India, it could be attributed to regional influence. Ruling dynasties of the middle region of India regardless of their personal preferences adapted Narasimha as central deity alongside other popular gods and goddesses. The Maharashtra region is dotted with temples and depictions of Narasimha under the support of Prabhavati Gupta.

Personal names of kings as well as of common folk representing Narasimha profusely appeared from the third century. Gupta emperor Narasimha Gupta I (414–55), also known as Baladitya, was a Gupta emperor ruling northwestern India including parts of Kashmir and southern Afghanistan. Emperor Narasimha Gupta issued gold coins with the title Nara inscribed on the coins, and numerous special sculptures of Narasimha seated cross-legged and leaning on a symbolic pillar with his upper arms touching the top of the pillar are attributed to his period. These sculptures are found in Kashmir and Afghanistan. While one of these sculptures is housed in the Sri Pratap Singh Museum in Srinagar, another is in the process of being obtained by the Metropolitan Museum of Art, New York (see Figure 9). Another is listed on the Sotheby's website. There might have been many more sculptures of this variety, but only a few survived, currently held in the museums due to the destruction of temples between Afghanistan and Kashmir between the tenth and twelfth centuries CE.

The Gupta era temple complex at Eran contains temples for the nine avataras of Vishnu. The Narasimha temple was destroyed completely even though a broken Narasimha image was found lying there. Another image of Nrivaraha (Narasimha-Varaha) found there is housed at the Sagar University. Exploration conducted here by Cunningham (1847; 1874–5) revealed occupational layers from the Chalcolithic era, while the early historic phase (700 BCE–100 BCE) is noted in a large coin hoard discovered here, which contained about 3,268 coins of various dates and materials. Further explorations and excavations were conducted here under the auspices of Sagar University between 1960 and 1965 (Bajpai 1971: 21–6). The Gupta temple complex is datable from the early Gupta period to the later phase, until it was destroyed in the late first millennium CE. Eran is also located at 78 degrees east longitude and 24 degrees north latitude within the central zone associated with Narasimha. Numerous temples of Narasimha are located along the line of 78 degrees east longitude including the Ahobilam and Simhachalam temples in Andhra Pradesh.

Historical Period 600–1600 CE: Representations of Narasimha

Numerous Chalukya dynasties ruling the Karnataka, Telangana, and Andhra Pradesh region between the sixth and ninth centuries CE also sponsored Narasimha temples in Andhra Pradesh.

The gods Varaha and Narasimha are sequential incarnations vanquishing the demon brothers, Hiranyaksha and Hiranyakashipu. Numerous temples were constructed for the gods Narasimha and Varaha avataras of Vishnu, since these two deities were simultaneously adapted together by numerous dynasties ruling the geographical areas of the Madhya Desha.

Early evidence of depictions of Narasimha datable to 600 CE is noted at the Badami caves in Karnataka (see Chapter 8). Important depictions of Narasimha are noted from the Ellora caves in Maharashtra. Eastern Chalukya

(Vengi Chalukya) ruler Jayasimha I (647–73) issued coins with a punch-marked image of a standing lion. The name Simha is also indicative of his devotion to Narasimha.

Pallava ruler Narasimha Varma II also known as Mahamalla (Mamalla) was the founder of the Mamallapuram (Mahabalipuram) shore temple complex. The Pancharathas, Shore temple, and massive canvas of sculptural carvings on a large rock surface represent the vision of Narasimha Varma II (690–725 CE). One of the interesting depictions on the rock surface is a cat in the yoga posture. It is difficult to know if it is related to sacred story of Bidala Narasimha noted in Odisha, in the narrative of Padampu templer the story indicates that Narasimha appears as a cat in perpetual yoga posture there, immersed in his watch to vanquish the demon Mushikasura. However, given the depiction of the cat on the caturvyuha image as well as the cat standing in impressive yoga posture in the Mahabalipuram sculpture, we may consider it to indicate a connection with Bidala Narasimha. Therefore, it is possible to propose the identity of this cat as representative of vyuha Narasimha (Bidala Narasimha) worshipped in Padampur in the state of Odisha (see Chapter 6).

Some of the earlier images of Narasimha are depicted in the caves in India indicating his close affinity with caves, mountains, and forested regions: Important examples are noticed in the Udayagiri caves (300 CE) and the Ellora caves (700 CE). The standing Narasimha image classified as Kevala Narasimha in the Udayagiri caves bears a resemblance to the Ulm Museum image of Narasimha, with the exception that the Udayagiri image is depicted with four arms. However, the Ellora cave 15 Narasimha image from the Dasavatara cave depicts Narasimha with eight arms, emerging out of a pillar, while a happy and prayerful devotee Prahlada looks on. There might have been another image of the demon on that sculptural panel, which might have been destroyed or removed, leaving only the feet of the third image on the opposite corner of the niche. The standing Narasimha image from the Aihole Durga temple (600 CE) also bears similarity to the Ulm Museum image in posture (Ulm Museum publication 2013). The Badami Narasimha image is carved in the veranda of cave III in the Badami (Vatapi) caves. This image also depicts Ugra Narasimha killing the demon Hiranyakasipu.

Another interesting early sculptural representation may connect Narasimha to the flaming pillar represented in Indian temple and ritual sites. Although identified with Buddha and Siva, the flame-pillar (Agni-Sthambha) may in fact represent Narasimha. This represents the central event within the legend of the incarnation of Narasimha. Narasimha burst out of the pillar which broke with an immense sound and sparks emanating out of it as the angry demon-king Hiranyashipu hit the pillar with his mace. Therefore, any pillar depicted with flames or splitting with fire should be considered as representative of Narasimha's incarnation. However, a breaking pillar with noise and sparks is associated with Narasimha. Depictions of Narasimha with the pillar are also not unusual and found at Narasimha temples in Ahobilam and Dharmapuri.

The Kakatiya emperor Prataparudra (1289–1323) was a known devotee of the god Shiva. However, it is said that he desired to construct a large temple of Shiva installing a golden image of Shivalinga. However, the emperor had a dream vision in which Narasimha emerged from the golden Shivalanga, prompting the emperor to regard Shiva and Narasimha as one and not two. Emperor Prataparudra visited the Narasimha temple at Ahobilam donating the golden image of Narasimha studded with various large precious stones such as rubies and emeralds, and he also contributed to the revival of Narasimha temples in southern India. The mercenary armies of the Nizam of Hyderabad attacked and looted the golden image of Narasimha in 1579 (Eaton 1995: 70; Ticku, Srivastava, and Iyer 2019).

Although the Chalukyas and Vijayanagara adapted Varaha as their royal emblem, they supported the construction of large Narasimha temples, and the Yoga Narasimha sculpture at Hampi, the Vijayanagar capital, is the largest sculpture of Narasimha (Michell 1998). The Vijayanagara emperor Narasimha Devaraya (Devaraya I) regarded Narasimha as his ishtadaivam, personal favorite deity, participating in temple rituals of Narasimha, while also reviving, repairing, and rehabilitating numerous temples of Narasimha across Andhra Pradesh and Karnataka. Saluva Narasimha Devaraya ruled the largest empire of southern India in the fifteenth century extending from Karnataka to Odisha. He is also known for his skills with letters and arts as well as sponsoring poets and saints of fifteenth-century central India. His magnum opus Ramabhyudayam is a well-known literary work in Sanskrit. His minister is named Narasanayaka also shows the importance and prevalence of the worship of Narasimha during this period. His son and successor Narasimha Raya II also known as Narasimha II/ Immadi Narasimha Raya (1491–1505) also took an active role in Vasantotsavam as well as sponsoring rituals and constructions of Narasimha temples across Andhra Pradesh and Karnataka including the largest temples of Narasimha located at Ahobilam and Simhachalam. He was assassinated by Tuluva Vira Narasimha Raya, who usurped the throne and began the rule of the Tuluva dynasty. However, the prevalence of the name Narasimha among the rulers of Vijayanagara between 1430 and 1530 is notable and lays the foundation for the keen interest of the Vijayanagara empire in worshipping the deity Narasimha. The Sanskrit composition, *Vasantika Parinayam*, and celebration of the wedding of the god Narasimha and the vanavasi woman, Vasantika (Chenchulakshmi), is also dated to the fifteenth century, which was a continuation of the traditional lore in Andhra Pradesh that connects forest folk with the temple. This story is also symbolic in culmination of prehistoric symbols with the deity Narasimha, which are predominantly preserved within the life style of vanavasis. The association of Narasimha with the Chenchu woman indicates this primeval connection as well as his association with the forests and hills as lion, which form part of the Narasimha symbolically represented as his central characteristic, the middle or transition. Most tribal societies preserved early Hindu religious symbolism, while the Sanskrit texts and traditional practice represent the deep symbolism embedded within these practices as they evolved over time. The Vijayanagara emperor Narasimha proclaimed his loyalty to the god Narasimha and sponsored the construction of as well as repairs to temples at Ahobilam. He is also known to have connected with the Vasantotsavam (Debika-Borek 2019: 69–106).

Important evidence of the historical Narasimha and his transitional association with Shiva and Vishnu is also noted from inscriptions as well as traditional practices in Odisha. The god Narasimha is commonly associated with Jagannatha (Purushottama) in Odisha, while he is also commonly associated with Shiva and Shakti in common practice. One of the early inscriptions to invoke Narasimha and Jagannatha together is the Sirpur inscription datable to the eighth century CE (Stietencron 1978: 1–30; Rajaguru 1971: 101–2; Eschmann 1978: 113). In this inscription invocation of Jagannatha is followed by a lengthy praise passage dedicated to Narasimha, identifying Purushotthama as Narasimha (Om Namaha Purushotthamaya Nrisimha . . .). A similar invocation of the gods is noted in the combined name of the deities Purushasimha, which represents Purushotthama and Narasimha joined together. An inscription from Khajuraho (953 CE) refers to Narasimha as Purushasimha, noting "He who incarnates in the form of boar and Purushasimha" (Rajaguru 103; Eschmann 114). Although Purusha is another term for Nara, this name is predominantly associated with Jagannatha in his name as Purushotthama. The centrality of Narasimha in the Jagannatha temple of Puri is noted. However, an early inscription of Anantavarma Chodaganga noting the construction of the monumental temple of Jagannatha (1132) is located on the door jamb of the Narasimha temple, which indicates that the temple of Narasimha was constructed prior to beginning the construction of the central temple of Jagannatha (Eschmann 114–15; Joshi 1961: 47). Similar to the tradition of worshipping Narasimha prior to the beginning of the Navakalevara ritual as well, the daily puja shows that Narasimha forms an intricate part of Jagannatha temple and is not seen as distinct from Jagannatha, but one with Jagannatha, a representation of Krishna Vaasudeva, considered the purna avatara of Vishnu, hence Vishnu himself who is not different from Narasimha. Another Chodaganga inscription with similar descriptions is also noted at Puri issued by Anangabhima III, the great-grandson of Chodaganga, which includes a praise passage (prasasti) of the emperor presenting him as incarnated Narahari, another name for Narasimha (Epigraphia Indica XXIX: 126; Vasu 1898). This shows the centrality of Narasimha in this region (Odisha and northern coastal Andhra Pradesh) during the twelfth to the fifteenth centuries. The Chodagangas also elevated Purushotthama-Narasimha to the position of their reign lord, worshipping him as the lord of the state. They also continued to worship Shiva calling themselves Parama Shaiva while also continuing to call themselves Parama Vaishnava, while worshipping Narasimha and Jagannatha simultaneously. This again shows the continuity of themes noted in connection with Narasimha in classical texts (see Chapter 2), that of close affiliation with the gods Vishnu and Shiva, thus equally represented as a form and worshipped regardless of whichever tradition the historical practice might represent.

Sculptural Representations of Narasimha

Art history preserves the earliest representations of Narasimha; hence the earliest history comes from disparate images of Narasimha excavated at sites from the four corners of India. Historical data also shows the immense popularity of Narasimha across India in the early centuries of the current era.

Initially, Narasimha's images were sparsely examined leading to a partial or frequently misplaced understanding of Narasimha. Early study of Hindu iconography only lists three types of Narasimha images, Girija, Yoga, and Yanaka (Gopinatha Rao 1971: Vol. I. 49–154). However, the Sthalapurana of Simhachalam enumerates that Narasimha was worshipped in thirty-two different forms (Sriramachandracharya 1991; Ramesan 1962: 136–41).

However, the nine forms of Narasimha are commonly encountered across the subcontinent. The most common forms of representation seen in the sculptural representation of Narasimha are Kevala Narasimha, Yoga Narasimha, and Lakshmi-Narasimha. These are also discussed in early scholarly works (Gopinatha Rao 1971). However, I think new categories of images of Narasimha need to be added to do justice to the variety of images of Narasimha available currently, especially central images in numerous temples across Middle India. In addition to the images of Narasimha, including Kevala Narasimha, Lakshmi-Narasimha, and Yoga Narasimha, the following images are commonly represented.

Samharamurthy (Slaying Hiranyakasipu): This is the image of Narasimha killing the demon Hiranyakashipu. The demon is lying flat on the thighs of a seated Narasimha, while Narasimha is slitting open his bowels. This is a fearsome representation of Narasimha, rarely worshipped in the central sanctum (garbhagudi) of Narasimha temples, although it is not unusual to find this representation on the outer walls of the temples.

Anugrahamurthy (Blessing Prahlada): Also known as Prahladanugrahamurthy, this is the most widely represented image of Narasimha. According to the Vishnu Purana and Bhagavata Purana narratives, Narasimha appeared due to the pleas of Prahlada, and hence Prahlada is depicted as the foremost Bhakta (devotee) of Narasimha.

Girirupa (Hill Form/Natural Form): This form is also called Girija (hill born) in previous scholarship (Gopinatha Rao 1971; Eschmann 1978), but it is a misnomer. Girija is not reflective of the nature of the deity, since Narasimha is not born from the hill, but assumed the form of a hill in numerous local tales. Numerous hills across Andhra Pradesh and Telangana are identified as Narasimha. The hill surface is symbolically adorned with tripundra, eyes, and mouth for convenience of worship (see Chapters 6 and 7).

Yanaka (Riding Garuda) or **Gandabherunda Narasimha**: This form of Narasimha is also represented in temples for central worship. Narasimha is depicted as riding Garuda (eagle), or Gandabherunda (double-faced eagle).

Sthauna (standing): This image is commonly depicted in temples on the outside walls and sometimes in the sanctum also.

Varaha-Narasimha (Boar-Lion form of Narasimha): This is a representation of two avarataras of Vishnu, Varaha and Narasimha. It is one of the rare forms represented for worship. Simhachalam is one of the famous temples representing this image for worship (see Chapters 6 and 8). However, it is not uncommon to see these two avatars represented alongside each other as in the Badami caves, Udayagiri caves, and so on.

Bidala Narasimha (Narasimha in Cat Form): The cat-formed Narasimha represents a rare depiction of Narasimha seen in the Padampur temple in the state of Odisha. However, the representation of Vishnu as a cat does not seem to be unusual as seen in the caturvyuha image. The yogic cat depiction at Mahabalipuram might also represent Vishnu in Narasimha avatara.

Sthambha Narasimha (Narasimha in Pillar Form): This is one of the rare forms represented in the sanctum, but not unusual. A simple pillar is identified as the representation of Narasimha (see Chapters 7 and 8).

Jwala Narasimha (Fiery Narasimha): This is a symbolic representation of Narasimha seen at the Narasimha temple in Yadagiri, Ahobilam, and numerous other temples.

Vishwarupa and Vaikuntha forms of Vishnu: In addition to these exclusive Narasimha images, he also forms part of combined representations along with other deities, including Vishnu Vishwarupa. The Vaikuntha form of Vishnu has three faces, that is Vishnu flanked with the images of the heads of Varaha and Narasimha forming a three-headed composite form of Vishnu (Gail 1983: 297–307).

It is difficult to understand historical religion especially for the first millennium BCE. Between 600 BCE and 300 BCE many new philosophical and yoga traditions including Buddhism, Jainism, and Ajivika traditions took root in India. However, even though these new practices attracted a massive following in urban centers (nagaras/pattanas) their influence beyond the urban core was limited. Their reach beyond the forest regions was even more limited. Therefore, early historical evidence of Narasimha is frequently noticed preserved in forest regions as well as the rural areas. From the turn of the first millennium CE sculptures and temples of Narasimha predominate, especially in the Middle India, indicating the prevalence of Narasimha traditions.

The eastern coast of India (Odisha) was ruled by the Pitribhakta or Matharas dynasty from their capital Simhapura/Singapura (near Srikakulam/Chikakole), the name of which also indicates the practices associated with Narasimha (EI Vol. 28 pp. 175–9). Early temples of Vishnu in Odisha, the Lakshmana temple mentions Narasimha even though the central temple is dedicated to Vishnu/Purushottama (Stietoncron 1978: 12). In Odishian culture, the association of Narasimha as Vishnu/Purushottama or Jagannatha is also noticed in the recitation of a Narasimha mantra and special temples dedicated to Narasimha at Jagannatha temple in Puri.

Even though the Saiva traditions including the Pasupatas gained an immense following in Karnataka and Andhra Pradesh from 800 CE, Narasimha remained central as he shared a close affinity with Shiva and the goddesses.

Even within the Vishnu temples of the east coast of India (Odisha, Andhra Pradesh, and Tamil Nadu), Narasimha is projected as the central deity. The Purushottama/Jagannatha temples of Odisha identified Purushottama as Narasimha at Lakshmana temple at Sirpur (EI Vol II pp. 184–20), and Jagannatha temple at Puri (EI Vol 3 p. 226). This trend of representing Purushottama as Narasimha is representative of the trend of the centrality of the Narasimha aspect of Vishnu in Odisha (Stietoncron 12). The central role of Narasimha in the ritual and temple of Jagannatha at Puri remains a symbol of this supreme role of Narasimha in Odishian tradition. The Narasimha temple of Simhachalam is also datable to this period supported by the Eastern Ganga and Gajapati rulers.

Many natural formations not part of the general landscape are frequently associated with Narasimha.

Early Modern and Modern History 1600–1950

The Narasimha temples faced difficulties from this period onwards since the Vijayanagara empire was defeated and three Sultanates were established in the Deccan region, who began sponsoring Islamic culture and saw no reason to support the previous temples. These Sultans also ordered some temples to be destroyed, which were recorded in local literature and court records. For example, the Golkonda Sultans sent their armies to destroy the Ahobilam temple and loot the treasures housed in that temple. Elaborate data was recorded of jewels and golden images taken from this temple. Gogulapati Kurmanatha Kavi recorded the attack of the Golkonda Sultan's army on the Simhachalam temple in his Narasimha Shatakam.[3] Many temples fell into disuse during this period, rediscovered and renovated in the later part of the nineteenth century and early twentieth century. The Narasimha temple at Dharmapuri was attacked an rebuilt, but contains an Islamic monument incorporated forcefully into the temple compound. Other temples were destroyed beyond recognition only to be rediscovered and rebuilt in the early twentieth century. For example, according to my family legend, the Narasimha temple in Khammam was discovered in the early twentieth century. Part of the territories of Golkonda Sultanate, now forming part of the current state of Andhra Pradesh, was transferred to the East India Company (EIC) upon conclusion of the Military Co-Operation Treaty between the Sultan and the EIC. The EIC began administering the temples; this also resulted in corruption in Company administration in the south and in the looting of numerous temple jewels from southern India. However, the situation of temples in southern India did not improve as the temples came under state administration following independence in 1947, continuing the corrupt administrative system of the colonial state.

Conclusion

This chapter examined the historical data on the prevalence of worship of Narasimha in utilizing oral sources, as well as textual, archeological and monumental data. Prehistoric depictions of the lion may indicate the symbiotic relationships of hunter-gather societies with wild animals and wilderness in general. However, the memory of life recorded in the Narasimha story bears an uncanny resemblance to prehistoric events, which happened about 74,000 years ago. The Toba volcano eruption destroyed the human population and life in general across the world leaving only a small population. The imagery of Pralaya, the fiery nature of Narasimha, and a new beginning from a reversal may recollect this historical memory in a symbolic form. The close relationship of Narasimha and hunter-gatherer societies is widely recorded in India. This chapter also examined the historical evidence in seals, coins, and sculptures. Historic evidence for the worship of Narasimha is dated from the turn of the first millennium CE. Central regions of Middle India (see Chapter 7) predominantly preserve evidence of early temples and depictions of Narasimha. Examination of historical data showed the consistent increase in the Narasimha tradition and growing popularity of his worship through the building of a great many temples of large proportions in this region. It is also notable that ruling dynasties of the middle region of India adapted Narasimha as the regal deity by imprinting his image on their insignia. A survey of historical evidence in this chapter showed that the story of Narasimha may have preserved the memory of the prehistoric golden age and the large calamity that changed the world. In the Hindu cosmogony, this is recorded as the end of a golden era, the Krita Yuga, and the beginning of the next age, the Treta Yuga.

The story of Narasimha is important for its historical importance: First, for preserving the memory of early prehistoric societies in the lion form, and second, for the impact of the stories and the Narasimha tradition on the historical evolution of the middle region of India. The middle region of India preserved unique features of Narasimha along with innovative practices and local stories (Sthalapuranas), which show the special place Narasimha holds in this region.

4

Narasimha in Middle India

From Rigveda to Oggukatha

Geography as well as cosmogony forms an important part of Narasimha stories. The symbolism of Madhya or Madhyastha (middle/transition) is also central to the geographical and cosmogonic motifs associated with Narasimha (see Chapter 2). Although not clearly explored in the previous scholarship this word is reflected in the geographical provenance of Hinduism in Middle India as it relates to Narasimha symbolically. The middle region (Madhya Desha) in general and the Telugu states, in particular, are considered the Mandala (sacred space) of Narasimha, due to the prevalence of sacred centers associated with Narasimha as well as the identification of this land as the *leelasthali* (land of divine play) of Narasimha. The earliest sculptural representation of Narasimha in Middle India is documented in Andhra Pradesh and Telangana, datable to the first to the third century CE. Therefore, this chapter examines the classical Sanskrit texts, ethnography, geography, and regional culture to understand the geographical affinity of Narasimha, symbolized by the middle. Narasimha represents the transitional middle in his incarnation and theology, as well as defying the sectarian boundaries in his connection with Shiva and the Matrikas (goddesses) in practice.

This chapter also examines the concept of the middle as symbolically associated with Narasimha in classical literature, art, and culture. This chapter analyzes in the following pages how the concept of the middle is represented in Narasimha's association with the sacred geography of India through representing the middle.

For the purposes of religion, the subcontinent of India had been considered as a unit, and the middle region historically referred to as Madhya Desha is taken up for analysis in this chapter. The region of Madhya Desha had been interpreted variously in the previous research identifying it with the Ganga and Yamuna Doab region, considering India's expanse from west to east. Early scholarship considered merely northern India as the civilizational zone of Aryans proposing the theory of invasions for the spread of Hinduism beyond the Vindhyan ranges. This theory doesn't remain valid now as the Aryan invasion theory has been disproven due to lack of sufficient evidence as well as striking similarities of religion and culture datable to the early Neolithic and Chalcolithic periods traced throughout India (Vemsani 2014 Shinde 2019).

However, in this current work, the land of India is considered from north to south, considering the peninsular region as Middle India. This is the region associated with Narasimha, as the transitional and middle qualities of the Narasimha story are closely superimposed on the geography and practices. Middle India under examination in this chapter does not indicate any empire or state; the region within the geographical entity of the Indian subcontinent is imagined as a geographical unit in connection with the Narasimha tradition. Although at certain points in time this region was unified as an empire under the well-known dynasties of Middle India such as the Shatavahanas, the Vakatakas, and the Rashtrakutas, and so on, the region remained fragmented throughout major periods of its history.

The religious fabric of India has remained intact even though the middle region has been divided into numerous smaller kingdoms for most of its historical era. Interactions between religious networks located in different kingdoms continued even though the region was divided into multiple independent kingdoms as their pilgrimages and travel continued uninterrupted between temples in different political states.

However, what is interesting is that being part of a different kingdom for a long time has also given rise to distinct cultural traditions. Culturally each part of the Madhya Desha has given rise to distinct regional practices associated with Narasimha, yet preserving the overarching symbolism of Narasimha. Thus, examining Hinduism in Middle India focusing on regional oral traditions associated with Narasimha helps conceptualize the sacred geography of this region as well as the multiple aspects of Hinduism as an inclusive pluralistic inclusive practice.

The current region under study is spread between the latitudes of 24 degrees north and above 12 degrees north roughly spanning the middle of India. This includes the central region of Narasimha spread across the states of Andhra Pradesh, Telangana, Maharashtra, Chhattisgarh, Odisha, Madhya Pradesh, and Karnataka. This region under study also includes small parts of other states including, but not limited to, northern Tamil Nadu. The largest number of Narasimha temples are located in the core areas, the states of Telangana and Andhra Pradesh, which are connected with numerous events of the life of Narasimha marking his earthly sojourn.

Shtalapuranas of Andhra Pradesh connect Narasimha incarnation and events of the life of Narasimha to specific places in Andhra Pradesh, thus forming the *leelasthali* of Narasimha within the landscape of Andhra Pradesh. Nava-Narasimha temples, the central temple complex of Narasimha, which are connected with the appearance of Narasimha, Ahobilam is located at 16 degrees north latitude and 78 degrees north longitude. The most important Shaiva temple of this region is located at Sri Sailam, which is also located between 16 degrees north latitude and 78 degrees east longitude. Yadagirigutta is located at the confluence of 17 degrees north latitude and 78 degrees east longitude roughly at the midpoint of this region. The Gupta era Dasavatara temple at Eran containing a Narasimha temple is also located at 78 degrees east longitude at 23 degrees north latitude. Numerous Narasimha temples are located at 78 degrees east longitude and 79 degrees east longitude. Similarly, 78 degrees east longitude and 79 degrees east longitude are marked with numerous Shiva temples including eight temples of Jyotirlingas. However, in the Andhra Pradesh and Telangana region, the Shiva temples located at 78 degrees east longitude at Sri Sailam and Kaleswaram are also connected to important Narasimha temples located close to these cities. Another significant temple of Narasimha in this region is located in Simhachalam between 17 degrees north latitude and 83 degrees east longitude roughly forming the eastern most temple of Narasimha, while Narasimha at the Dasavatara cave in Cave 15 of Ellora located at 20 degrees north latitude and 75 degrees east longitude represents the most western most early representation of Narasimha. The Narasimha temples on the 78 longitude, including Ahobilam, Yadagirigutta, and Eran, are located in the center while an important temple of Narasimha on the East Coast is located at Simhachalam on the 83 longitude, while the important early temples of Narasimha on the Western Coast are located at Ellora. Hence, the most important temples of Narasimha are spread in a region shaped like a trapeze roughly spanning the Middle section of India, that forms a distinct cultural and geographical zone, separate from the northern and southern regions.

Narasimha stories condensed symbolic memory over millennia along with social and cultural practices as they preserve symbols that are associated with the divinity in Vaishnavism. Hence, the typical characteristics of Narasimha reflect the crystallization of indigenous cultural practices of Indians over the millennia. Transitions and not belonging to a set category are some of the central characteristics of Narasimha. This central characteristic of Narasimha is also reflected in the traditional practices associated with Narasimha in the areas of arts, geography, and popular practice. The concept of the transitional middle is represented in sacred geography as well as in reflecting his affiliation to the land.

The Earth is sacred and considered to form part of the divine sphere. The Bhumisutra of the Atharvaveda[1] specifically mentions it in the verse invoking the special qualities associated with the Earth. It is noted that (Atharvaveda VII. BhumiSuktakam Verse 5) "The earth upon which of old the first men unfolded themselves, upon which the gods overcame the Asuras, shall procure for us (all) kinds of cattle, horses, and fowls, good fortune, and glory!" This demonstrates that it was the place of origin of the humans as well as the sphere of action (*leela*) for the gods in their war against the demons, while also providing sustenance and glory for humans. Atharvaveda further notes that (Book VII. Verse 6), "The earth that supports all, furnishes wealth, the foundation, the golden-breasted resting-place of all living creatures, she that supports Agni Vaisvânara (the fire), and mates with Indra, the bull, shall furnish us with property!" It also adds that the gods protect the Earth relentlessly (Verse 7), "The broad earth, which the sleepless gods ever attentively guard, shall milk for us precious honey, and, moreover, besprinkle us with glory!"

However, each part of the geographical region is connected with a unique deity due to affinity in shared common features. The deity is represented within the land and other natural features of the region owing to the shared unique symbolic features between the land and the deity. Although the deity's unity with the universe is clear, it finds expression in different forms based on the symbolic expression of the Earth.

Hence, the middle part of India is closely connected to the middle avatara of Vishnu, Narasimha, whose incarnation conceptualizes the middle/transition within the symbolic nature of incarnations. The universal energy/the principle energy might take a form that is reflective of the conditions on the Earth, providing the necessary conditions as well as the purpose of the incarnation.

This chapter contains three sections: the first section examines the main aspects of the divine nature of Vishnu and his affinity with the Earth, personified divinity, and the goddess Bhumi (Prithvi) as well as the universe and creation as part of the divine self. Creation arose from the body of god and creation is also within the body of the god.

The next section examines the geographical features of the middle region of India and their descriptions in early literature. This section also considers some important temples and their special features in association with the geographical region noting the symbolism of the middle within the temples and the deity.

The next section considers the practices associated with the ruling dynasties as well as the common folk of the region focusing on practice.

Geography and spirituality come together through the representation of the divine body of god in the sacred spots marked with temples. For example, the Dvadasa Jyotirlingas (Twelve Jyotirlingas) crisscross the divine land of India. Similarly, the Chatuhshashti (Chausat) Shakti Pithas (64 seats of goddesses) are also spread across India. Sacred centers of Krishna are localized in Mathura Mandala and Vraja Mandala, even though Krishna temples are spread across India. Therefore deities are associated with distinct geography. However, this does not preclude the construction of the temples of the deities anywhere. Even though Narasimha is closely linked with the land of Middle India, Narasimha temple can be constructed anywhere in the world, even though this specific region is considered as the specific spiritual land of Narasimha. Narasimha Mandala noted in the middle region of India only shows this special geographical connection of the deity to a specific region as the land of divine play (*leela*). The following pages discuss the deity Narasimha, the lord of the middle, and the Middle Land (Madhya Desha), as well as the communities that share a close affinity with him.

The Divine Nature of Vishnu and Affinity with the Earth

Creation arose from the divine energy represented variously as the gods Shiva and Vishnu. However, the view that the universe forms part of the divine whole of the god pervades the classical texts of India. This is even more clearly expressed in the conceptualization of Vishnu. Vishnu is closely connected with the Earth, with creation forming part of himself.

Creation arose from Vishnu and creation is also within Vishnu, which is also presented explicitly as part of the narration of the avataras of Varaha, Vamana, and Krishna, while it is symbolically indicated within the stories of all incarnations of Vishnu. Vishnu Purana recollects the all-embracing nature of Vishnu in connection with creation including Brahma as follows:

> He is Brahma, the supreme lord, eternal, unborn, and imperishable, and undecaying; of one essence; ever pure as free from defects (2.12). He (Vishnu), that Brahma, was all things; comprehending in his own nature the expressed (vyakta) form and unexpressed (avyakta) form (2.13). He then exists in the

forms of Purusha and Kala. Purusha (soul) is the first form, of the supreme; next proceeded two other forms, the expressed (vyakta) and unexpressed (avyakta); and Kala (time) was the most important (paramam) (2.14). These four—Pradhana (primary matter), Purusha (soul), Vyakta (expressed/indiscrete form), and Kala (time)—the wise consider being the pure and supreme form of Vishnu (2.15). These four forms, in their due proportions, are the causes of the production of the phenomena of creation, preservation, and destruction (2.16). Vishnu being thus expressed (vyakta) and unexpressed (avyakta) as well as substance (pradhana), soul (Purusha), and time (Kala), sports like a playful boy, as you shall learn by listening to his play (leela) (2.17).[2]

The Vishnu Purana (2.17) summarizes his connection with creation adding that Vishnu "sports like a playful boy, as shall learn by listening to his play (Leela)." This indicates the concept of avatara, and the god Vishnu. He is beyond creation as a playful boy and within creation. Hindu cosmology gives a special place to Vishnu within and beyond creation. Vishnu is in two forms as expressed (created universe) and unexpressed (the divine) within cosmology (Vishnupurana 2.14). Vishnu is also represented by the four important aspects of Pradhana (primary matter), Purusha (the soul), Vyakta (matter/space/creation), and Kala (Time) which constitute the pure and supreme form of Vishnu (Vishnupurana 2.15) as well as creation. These four aspects of Vishnu in their due proportions are the causes of the production of the phenomena of creation, preservation, and destruction (2.16). These are the aspects represented in the accounts of the incarnation of Narasimha. This chapter focuses specifically on understanding the three aspects of Pradhana (primary matter), Purusha (the soul), and Vyakta (creation/matter/space). The presence of the soul (Purusha) within matter (land and creation) and space (vyakta: Created world) is expressed symbolically within the symbolic connection of Narasimha (Purusha) with matter (land) and the expansive space (vyakta/land/creation). The earthly nature of Vishnu is noticed in the Vyakta and Avyakta aspects of Vishnu. I will examine the close affiliation of Vishnu with the Earth as created world as well the Earth as the goddess Bhudevi, his wife.

Vishnu is spread (vis) within the creation as vyakta (seen/known/revealed) and avyakta (unseen/unknown). The presence of Vishnu within the universe as well as the presence of the universe within Vishnu is depicted in the Puranas examined in the following pages. Vishnu's close affinity with the Earth and creation is reflected in the incarnations, especially the Narasimha incarnation.

Creation within the Body of God

Vishnu is depicted at the root of the beginning of creation as well as creation itself. The Vamana incarnation depicts this spread of Vishnu beyond creation connecting the three worlds in a clearly physical spread of Vamana as he spreads himself to reach beyond the created world reaching the heavens and the underworld in a physical form (Rigveda Book 1.22.16–18; Glucklich 2008: 4–5; Soifer 1991: 113–40; Kuiper).[3] While Vishnu represents the universe, regional expressions embrace the avatara of Vishnu closely resembling the symbolic features in nature, geography, and society. Vamana also represents transition and the middle, similar to the Narasimha avatara. The Varaha avatara similarly depicts vanquishing Hiranyaksha and rescuing the goddess of the Earth, Bhulakshmi, from the grasp of the demon Hiranyaksha.

The expression Vishwarupa (universal form) is noted in the Mahabharata[4] when Krishna provided divyachakshu (divine eye) so that Arjuna could catch a glimpse of the Vishwarupa of Vishnu. As Arjuna visualizes the universal form of Vishnu he is overwhelmed as he described the form of Vishnu, which contains the whole universe, along with the Earth, within the divine body (Bhagavadgita 11.5–15). This description of the Mahabharata gives expression to the concept of Vishnu described in the Vishnu Purana as expressed and unexpressed aspects. It is not merely the human and divine worlds that are contained within the body of the god, but also everything known in the universe including the solar system.

Krishna's mother Yashoda sees the brahmanda (universe) in the mouth of Krishna in another incident narrated about the childhood of Krishna (Harivamsa 33).[5] Yashoda is not the only person to view the universe within the mouth of her child, the god Krishna. Another person to view the universe within the mouth of Krishna was the sage Markandeya, who also saw the universe within the body of god as described in the Mahabharata (3.183–90), and Mastyapurana (ch. 167), etc. The sage Markandeya came across a child floating on a banyan leaf in the ocean. Curious, he entered the mouth of the child. As Markandeya entered the mouth of the child saw the universe and realized the boy was Vishnu and came out immediately.

Narasimha accomplishes the cosmogonic role of Vishnu by being within and beyond creation simultaneously. Narasimha entered creation as he appeared in the palace of Hiranyakashipu and killed him, and he was beyond creation, while he corrected the overturned world order by returning it to its proper course of movement.

These stories establish the unity of Vishnu and the universe including creation within his body. However, it is only in the classical stories of Narasimha that the transitional and border-defying qualities of Narasimha come to the fore. As Narasimha, he is associated with geographical features that stand out from the surroundings. Many temples of Narasimha are founded on mountains and forest regions associated with his incarnation. Narasimha is also the most commonly noted deity in the central states of India, Maharashtra, Madhya Pradesh Chhattisgarh, Odisha, Andhra Pradesh, Telangana, and Karnataka, Middle India.

The Earth as Mother and God as Carrier/ Protector of the Mother

Atharvaveda-Bhumi Suktam in the Atharva Veda exposes the relationship of Vishnu and the Earth as well as humans (see "The Divine Nature of Vishnu and Affinity with the Earth"). The references to Vishnu also contain the desire for protection and protection afforded by Vishnu. As Varaha Vishnu rescues the Earth from the demon Hiranyaksha by lifting her and carrying her on his tusks, or shoulders. As Vishnu Trivikrama he traverses the Earth and the universe. These two avataras are specifically noted in the Bhumisuktam of the Atharvaveda, which indicates the early origin of the concept of this unique affiliation of Vishnu with the goddess Earth. Atharvaveda mentions that (Book VII. Bhumisuktam Verse 10) "upon which Vishnu has stepped out" indicating the three steps Vamana took covering the universe. As Vamana Trivikrama traverses the Earth horizontally and vertically he expands to embrace the Earth.

The Earth is described as the goddess connected to Vishnu. The Varaha avatara demonstrates the relationship between the Earth and Varaha, also referred to in the Atharvaveda (Book VII. Verse 48), "The earth holds the fool and holds the wise, endures that good and bad dwell (upon her); *she keeps company with the boar (Varaha)*, gives herself up to the wild hog." This verse shows the relationship between Varaha and Bhulakshmi, who is frequently depicted as the wife of Varaha.

Another layer of this relationship is brought forth through the Narasimha avatara. From this period onwards, Lakshmi or Bhulakshmi, as the representation of the wealth[6] of the Earth, is represented as the wife along with each incarnation of Vishnu. The Bhulakshmi might also be represented as the second wife of Vishnu. Overall, the wife of Vishnu is Lakshmi, a representation of the wealth, who can also appear in multiple forms, in her incarnations.

The goddess Bhulakshmi in fact takes a human incarnation to become the wife of Vishnu in each of his incarnations. Even though there are two versions of the story of the marriage of Narasimha and Chenchitha, it also brings forward this relationship with Bhulakshmi/Bhudevi. The first wife is Lakshmi and the second wife is an incarnation of Bhudevi. She is represented as a second wife in many regional stories. The Earth is described as nourishment and in other words, the giver of life itself, while Vishnu is depicted as her companion and protector.

Appearance and Weapons of Narasimha Representing the Middle

Narasimha appears as an incarnation in the middle preceded by animal form incarnations and succeeded by human form incarnations. Narasimha's appearance from a pillar that was broken by Hiranyakashipu in anger symbolizes the middle nature of Narasimha. Narasimha is part human and part lion form. As noted in the boon of Hiranayakashipu which stipulates numerous conditions, Vishnu assumed an unusual form.

The boon of Hiranyakashipu in Vishnu Dharmottara Purana (I.54) notes that

> Neither gods, demons, nor Gandharvas, nor Yakshas, snakes, or Rakshasas, neither men nor Pisachas shall kill me, O Excellent God. Nor may angry rishis, endowed with tapas, curse me. Grandfather of the world, that is the boon I choose. Not by weapons nor by missiles, nor by stones or trees, neither by wet nor by dry; in no way at all may death be mine. I am the sun, the moon, the wind, the fire, the air, the stars, and the ten regions. I am wrath and passion, Varuna, Indra, Yama, Kubera, the supervisor, a Yaksha, and the chief Kimpurusha.

A similar but shorter boon of Hiranyakashipu is recorded in Brahmanda Purana (II.5.3–29) which adds the time clause by stipulating that the demon should not be killed by day or night: "Immortality and inviolability from all beings. Having conquered the gods with yoga, to become the god of all and make the sovereignty full of strength and vigor. Danavas and demons, gods together with celestial singers, all these must be my subjects, close at hand, serving me, inviolable by wet or dry, by day or by night."

Three aspects are clear from the boon: (1) Inviolability by all beings, (2) sovereignty over all beings, and (3) inviolability by weapons, by wet or dry, and by day or night. As a protector of the Earth noted here, Vishnu incarnated in the world as Narasimha taking advantage of the conditions of the boon of Hiranyakashipu. When Vishnu appeared as Narasimha in the palace of Hiranyakashipu, all of these conditions stipulated by Hiranyakashipu as part of his boon were met. So a new being, which is not known within the divine or human world is to be created to vanquish Hiranayakashipu, since his boon provides him impunity from all beings. Therefore, his form was a new being unknown in the universe. Hiranyakashipu obtained sovereignty over all beings including the divine and reversed the world order placing the underworld at the top and bringing the divine world (svarga) to the bottom. This reversed the course of the world, placing the universe in the transitional dangerous phase. Hence, it was necessary for Vishnu to assume the form of a composite being, as well as to not use any weapons to meet the third condition. The only weapons Narasimha used were his nails, although the Puranas mention that he carried a trident with him, which is symbolic in nature indicating his close affinity with Shiva in his incarnation as Narasimha.

Narasimha's Affiliation with the Land and Life

There are two major levels of spiritual concepts represented in the temples and practice. The first is the two concepts of land as the body of god and symbolism of the middle, which are represented through the temples and sacred sites spread throughout the middle region. Secondly, there are the broader concepts expressed in the classical literature as the Earth, sacred as a goddess, Bhudevi, Vishnu as the protector, is expressed through sacred energy, the fusion where these divine elements come together identified as Shaktipitha; these spiritual concepts are represented symbolically in practice.

Hence, I will examine here in this section the geographical features of the middle region of India and their descriptions in early literature. This section also considers some important temples of Narasimha and their special features in the geographical region. The middle region of India is bordered on each side by the mountain ranges called the Western Ghats and the Eastern Ghats, and in the region between these ranges are the fertile river basins of numerous rivers. Almost all the large rivers of this region originate in the Western Ghats and flow toward the Eastern Ghats. The Mahanadi, Krishna, Godavari, and Tungabhadra are the major rivers with numerous tributaries. Major Narasimha temples are located frequently in the Godavari and Krishna river basins, two of the major rivers in the Telugu region, a core part of the sacred space associated with Narasimha in Middle India. Incidentally, the largest image of Narasimha is located on the banks of the Tungabhadra river at Hampi (UNESCO heritage center) in one of the central temples of Narasimha (see Figure 6).

Figure 6 Yoga Narasimha, the largest known image of Narasimha at Hampi (fifteenth century CE) UNESCO Heritage Complex. Photo by Cathleen Cummings; courtesy of John C. and Susan L. Huntington Photographic Archive of Buddhist and Asian Art.

Sacred Geography and the Middle Region of India

The land beyond the Vindhya ranges spreading up to the Kaveri river is geographically located in the middle region of India. This region contains a mountainous region with the Vindhya and Satpura ranges toward the northern side and the Eastern and Western Ghats on the eastern and western sides. Hence, the region contains dense jungles, which are also widely inhabited by numerous vanavasis. Most of the vanavasis are also closely associated with Narasimha in their religious practice.

The Eastern Ghats, Mahendra Giri Ranges

The Eastern Ghats are hilly ranges running parallel to the east coast of India, also called Coromandal Coast. The northern portion of Eastern Ghats ends in Dadakaranya as it spreads through the states of Odisha and Andhra Pradesh on the east coast. Unlike the Western Ghats, the Eastern Ghats are not continuous, but disjointed ranges, hence acquiring numerous local epithets where a significant rise of the mountains is noticed in the landscape of the east coast.

Historians also consider that the Mahendra hill denotes the northern part of the Eastern Ghats near Ganjam, which is also called Mahendragiri. It is also noted that the Mahendragiri is between the Ganga Sagara and Sapta Godavari (Law 1968: 15). The mountainous zone of the Eastern Ghats is seen between the Mahanadi and Godavari rivers. Copious numbers of temples are located on these mountain ranges. The tallest mountain of the Eastern Ghats is called Mahendragiri, located in the state of Odisha. The southern section of this range is Nallamala hill, which runs parallel to the Coromandel Coast. The southern part of this range called the Palkonda range runs from Palnad basin in Guntur district to Tirupati hill in the south. The length of the Nallamala ranges is 430 kilometers, and the height ranges between 900 and 1,000 meters, with a width of about 30 kilometers. Numerous temples including the important Narasimha temples (Simhachalam and Ahobilam) are located on these ranges in the states of Andhra Pradesh and Odisha.

Sri Sailam-Ahobilam-Venkatadri

One of the most auspicious ranges in the Eastern Ghats is the Sri Parvata known as Sri Sailam (Sri's Mountain) which is mentioned in Markandeya Purana (LVII.15), Kurma Purana (30.45–8), and Agni Purana (109). The Padma Purana notes that on the summit of this auspicious and beautiful mountain resides the god Mallikharjuna, who is identified as one of the twelve Jyotirlingas of India, the holy center of Shaivism. This mountain is also important for Narasimha as Ahobilam is also located in the middle of this mountain range. On the western side equidistant from Sri Sailam is Tirumala (Tirupati)/Venkatadri noted in the Skandapurana (Chapter I). The Tirumala hills host the temple of Vishnu, known as Venkateshwara. Ahobilam is located in the middle, equidistant from these two sacred sites, Sri Sailam and Venkatadri on this mountain, which is the most important temple of Narasimha symbolizing the appearance of Narasimha (see Chapter 6). This mountain range is considered the most sacred regionally and compared with the divine serpent Shesha upon which Vishnu rests in his Yoganidra. The three temples form the most important sacred temple complex of southern India. The seven hills of Venkatadri represent the seven hills of the divine serpent Shesha, on which the presiding deity, the Venkateshwara, stands, and the middle of the serpent's body is several folds occupied by the nine temples of Narasimha, and the tail end is the temple of Shiva as Mallikharjuna on Sri Sailam (Law 1968: 19).

Udayagiri hills

The Udayagiri hills are located near Vidisha in the state of Madhya Pradesh between the Betwa and Besh rivers, one of the important historic sites of India. The Udayagiri inscription of Chandra Gupta II (401 CE) is noted here. The cave temples here preserve early imagery of Narasimha carved in high relief on the cave walls (see Chapter 7).

The Western Ghats, the Sahyadri Mountain Ranges

The Western Ghats are western mountain ranges also known as Sahyadri in the classical literature of India. The length of the ranges is about 1,600 kilometers with an average elevation of about 1,000–1,200 meters above sea level. The northern part of this mountain range, almost 650 kilometers in length, was formed by horizontal sheets of volcanic rock formation. Numerous mountains and caves are noticed in these high-rising hill ranges in the Western Ghats. Early Narasimha temples are located in these hill ranges and caves. The Badami caves are also located in these hill ranges.

The Western Ghats are referred to as the Sahyadri mountains in the ancient inscriptions and classical literature, the Puranas and Epics (South Indian Inscriptions Vol. I. pp. 168–9). The Sahyadris form a continuous range beginning at Kundaibari Pass in the Dhulia district of Maharashtra and ending at Cape Comorin, the southern tip of the subcontinent of India (Law 1968: 17–18). The Sahyadris contain numerous caves and passes and are known by numerous local epithets in each location. Important temples of Narasimha are located in these ranges and river valleys near these mountains (see Chapter 8).

Therefore, the region under study, between 16 degrees north latitude and 22 degrees north latitude, consists of the sacred hills of the Eastern Ghats and the Western Ghats as well as the sacred rivers, Mahanadi, Godavari, Krishna, and Tungabhadra. The temples of Narasimha are located on the hills and the banks of the rivers in this region. The eastern longitude of 78 degrees is adorned with numerous important temples of Narasimha including the Ahobilam temple.

The landmarks are identified as a profound manifestation of the god Narasimha as they also represent the special features associated with Narasimha, the middle, and sacred characteristics of Saktisthana. Thus, Middle India uniquely represents the sacred land as well as the body of the god, a central concept discussed in "The Divine Nature of Vishnu and Affinity with the Earth" in the previous pages. I will consider the special relationship of the deity Narasimha with certain groups of people of the land in the middle region expressed in the local stories.

Narasimha's Affiliation with Common People

The classical accounts of the avataras relate Narasimha in a special relationship with the common folk of the region in which the *leela*, the divine play, of the deity is located. The deity, even though he appears in a miraculous divine incarnation, becomes one with the simple folk of the region. This is noticed in conjunction with almost all the incarnations, although it is more obviously noted in the case of Bhagavan Krishna, since the *leelas* of Krishna are elaborately recorded and studied closely (Ingalls 1966: Foreword). Krishna lived among the simple folk of Vraja as one of them; even though his grace blessed them as part of his maya, it was an undercurrent, and not manifest to the extent that it disturbed their relations. Vraja is known as Brajamandala regarded as the most important sacred centers of India discussing the leelas of Krishna in detail in the Garga Samhita (Vemsani 2016: 99–100). Similarly, the *leelas* of Narasimha are depicted as taking place in the Ahobilam hills of Kurnool district, now located in the state of Andhra Pradesh. Hence, the Ahobilam region hosts nine temples memorializing the divine play (*leela*) of the appearance of Narasimha as well as his close connection with simple folks of the region, living among them and belonging to them (Chenchus) as one of them. Hence, the sacred center of Ahobilam and the numerous temples in the Telugu states of Andhra Pradesh and Telangana (Simhachalam, Yadagiri, Mangalagiri) remember unique events from the life of Narasimha and form the *leelasthali* (land of divine play) of Narasimha. However, since the different parts of the legend of Narasimha are depicted in different genres of texts and present Narasimha in different contexts, academics studying the deity Narasimha refuse to accept all these tales as representing part of a single unified account of the deity Narasimha. Indigenous origin of the concepts of divinity associated with Narasimha and Vishnu help understand the historical religion of India.

Initially, scholars showed reluctance to see the deity in the classical texts as one with the deity represented as Narasimha in local traditions, instead proposing two Narasimhas, the classical avatara and the folk Narasimha. They consider this second folk Narasimha as part of the process of assimilation of the indigenous folk, through marriage (see Chapters 5, 7, and 8). A similar tendency is noted in the early scholarship on Krishna which proposed three Krishnas (Hopkins 1914: 727–38; Bhandarkar 1965), even though they all seem to coalesce into one within the practice. These types of efforts were proven fruitless in the case of Krishna, and the efforts to separate classical Narasimha from folk Narasimha are equally futile for understanding the religion and culture of Middle India. It is much more useful to consider the accounts from both genres together to arrive at a comprehensive understanding of the deity, which would also be helpful to understand the religion of Middle India. I will discuss the basic information related to the vanavasis of the region whose account is intimately connected with Narasimha through oral literature as well as history.

The Sthalapuranas (the regional sacred lore of temples) preserve numerous elements, which depict the unity of the nature of Narasimha with the natural geographical features of the region as well the common folk of the region. The Sthalapuranas are preserved in oral traditions committed to writing in the past 500 years. Therefore, in this section, I will consider general information on the common folk of the region; their participation and oral stories are considered in Chapters 6 to 9 in this book.

The temples and the multiple forms of sculptural representations of Narasimha uniquely incorporate the special features and divine events (*leelas*) noted in the Sthalapuranas (see Chapter 3). The storytelling and performance traditions of Narasimha (melas) are not mere performance traditions but incorporate ritual and spiritual tradition entrenched among the masses. Performance traditions such as Yakshaganam, Oggukatha, and Harikatha ganam incorporate the Sthalapuranas in oral performance. The concepts of transition, movement, and the non-binding nature of Narasimha are related in the stories of Prahlada Charitam, Chenchu Natakam, and Hiranya Natakam performed through various genres in Oggukatha, Yakshganam, and Bhagavatamela (Narasimhamela) held at numerous temples on the occasion of Narasimha Jayanti (Emigh 1984: 21–39; Guy 2016: 17–22). The stories of bygone eras are brought to life during the melas. Due to these oral tales presented in performance traditions, even though they are performed at the temple, scholars considered these stories as evidence to support their hypothesis that Narasimha might have been a folk or tribal deity before his assimilation into Hinduism (Escmann 1978: 97–114; Kulke Jaiswal 1973: 140–51). This theory fails miserably in the presence of immense evidence for the worship of Narasimha along with his classical representation beginning with the Rigveda. Are they speaking of tribal culture prior to absorption of the deity Narasimha into the Vedic religion? The classical stories and oral stories of Narasimha may be equally old and represent a different aspect of indigenous culture. Both traditions and practice must be considered together to arrive at the immensity of the practice associated with Narasimha. I will consider the basic information of the common people of the region with whom the deity Narasimha lived as one according to the oral tales and performance traditions. How are oral traditions less valuable as tools to understand culture?

The most commonly used theory to analyze indigenous Indian religions is that the tribes are autochthonous while the others are invaders according to the Aryan migration theory, which was disproven due to recent genetic research (Vemsani 2014; Shinde 2019). The fact that the tribes follow a similar religion and worship the same deities noted in the Vedas is ignored. The tribes and castes are not different racially or genetically and possess similar genetic heritage in male and female genetic lines. The tribes, Chenchus, who are associated with Narasimha in the Telugu states possess the oldest genetic heritage (Vemsani 2014; Shinde 2019). Ethnographic archaeology in Andhra Pradesh and Telangana states has also revealed the parallel development of different lifestyles (Murty 2003: 73–85). Ethnography has revealed that Mesolithic cultures and Neolithic cultures existed side by side through sharing and symbiotic relationships. At the same time some population groups might have continued practicing the original lifestyle of Paleolithic hunter-gatherers, which is what most of the tribes, including Chenchus, Savaras, Koyas, and Khonds, discussed in this chapter practice.

Ethnographic studies observed that tribes constitute clans, which live in close-knit family groups that practice a similar lifestyle. It is not unusual for clans to separate and form new tribes when they disagree with a significant decision of the tribe. It seems to me that that might have been the common practice in societies historically. While the original tribe might have stayed loyal to the original lifestyle and lived in the forests, others might have adapted different lifestyles and moved in different directions. Indian society shows historical evolution since the foundation of early human societies in the Upper Paleolithic period.[7] However, staying within closer proximity in the same geographical regions they might have continued to maintain symbiotic relationships exchanging products and services. That seems to be the relationship that Chenchus maintained with their neighbors, the plains people, until the eighteenth century. It is also notable from Kakatiya and Vijayanagara records. The tribes are skilled hunters, and also gatherers of forest produce such as honey and special herbal plant products. They were valued for their products and services by the Kakatiya and Vijayanagara rulers.

Since the forest-dwellers (vanavasis) and plains-dwellers share genetic heritage and cultural heritage it seems only natural that they also shared their religious practice. In fact, research has shown that Chenchus and Koyas preserve numerous practices of early Hinduism now rarely associated with current practice. In my previous research on Balarama, I noticed that elements that are represented symbolically in the depiction of a deity are seen in practice among the vanavasis of Andhra Pradesh (Vemsani 2006). While the plow is represented symbolically in the images of Balarama, he is directly connected with religious practice in association with the agriculture of Koyas. An ethnographic survey in the late twentieth century revealed that while sowing the Koyas utter the name of Balarama (Satyanarayana 1991), which strengthens the association of Balarama with agriculture and bountiful harvests, which is clearer than it is in the Balarama stories in the Puranas.

The examination of regional stories and classical texts and religious practices with relation to Narasimha reveals similar trends. Narasimha is the deity closely connected to the life and heritage of Middle India. Even though different groups adapted and changed their lifestyles, the practices associated with Narasimha continued to flourish among the different population groups of this region.

Personality and Association with Social Groups of Middle India

Narasimha's part lion and part human form and his association with transitional nature are also represented in the stories and temples associated with Narasimha. Narasimha temples are located in geographically transitional in-between locations such as hills and forests. Narasimha is also associated with tribes including Sabaras, Chenchus, and Koyas. Narasimha's personality and nature are intentionally transitional due to the special boon Hiranyakashipu received from the god Brahma. The tribes show close affiliation with Narasimha. Sacred centers of Narasimha are frequently located in the favorite locations of vanavasi communities of Middle India. The religion of vanavasi social groups is referred to as little tradition even though the differences with the mainstream practice of Hinduism are limited (Sinha 1958: 504–18). Separating the practicing traditions of religion into folk or little traditions indicates a type of colonial authority, which dictated some practices as great traditions and others as folk or little traditions based on measures that were not part of Indian civilization. Even though Hinduism is the most commonly practiced religion, many clans and families maintain their own family deity, kuladeva or kuladevi. Hence, separating certain practices as little or folk traditions, other practices as village traditions, and still others as great traditions is problematic and shows a lack of sensitivity to the native cultures of India. Considering book-based religion and practice as primary and juxtaposing other religious practices as folk or little traditions wreaks of western concern for book religion rather than religious practice as understood in India. Colonial administration promoted a narrative based on Aryan invaders bringing language (Sanskrit) and religion (Hinduism) into India, which is far from the truth. This is not the place to consider this question in detail; however, it is adequate to note here that the religious traditions including Hinduism are indigenous to India and mutually coexisted as well as being co-practiced for millennia. The close affinity of religious practices of vanavasi communities of Middle India noticed within the practice of Narasimha traditions does not support the theory of dichotomy within the religious practice as one religious tradition overtaking the other. The Narasimha tradition is too entrenched within popular practice and memory that it is too strange to imagine it to be brought from elsewhere.

Gonds are the most numerous of the vanavasi communities in Middle India. The large area of the central plateau of India is occupied by the Gond community, which is divided into Agariya, Ojhas, Pardhans, Parjas, Koyas, Bhatras, Marias, and Murias. The religion of Gonds is passed on through oral tradition. Gond lore records that thirty-two disciples of Pari Kupar Lingo founded the "Koya Punem" thousands of years ago which guides the religious life of Gonds. Pari Kupar Lingo is denoted as Padda Devudu (Mahadev).[8] Pari Kupa Lingo appears similar in depiction to the Linga depiction of Shiva. Koyas are spread across Telangana and Andhra Pradesh, and their religious practice is centered on Hindu deities, which also connects them to the Mahabharata. Numerous Narasimha temples and Rama temples were built and maintained under the service of Koyas. One of the important temples of Narasimha in the state of Telangana on the hill at Koyilkuntla was built and maintained by the Koyas of the region until it was destroyed in the thirteenth century repeatedly in the Muslim raids of the Delhi Sultanate followed by other, successive Islamic states in Delhi and Hyderabad.

Chenchus live in the Nallamala hills of the Eastern Ghats noted as their habitation since the Paleolithic period (Heimendorf 1982: 2). Although some practice agriculture, their main mode of life is based on a hunter-gatherer lifestyle similar to the prehistoric Paleolithic modes of life. Chenchu religion includes worship of numerous village goddesses in addition to Narasimha and Shiva. The village goddess Maisamma is worshipped as Garla-Maisamma by the Chenchus as she is offered garelu (fried black-gram dumplings), a popular fast food of Telugus. The Chenchu lore records their origin from the Shiva temple at Sri Sailam, and Narasimha is their son-in-law as he married their daughter. So Chenchus are well connected with the religion of the land.[9]

Khonds

Khonds live in the Eastern Ghats region of Odisha and Andhra Pradesh. Even though known as inhabitants of the hilly region, they also practice horticulture and agriculture. Practice of Hinduism here is interconnected with the traditional Khond style of practices and cultural aspects. Narasimha temples and especially the Padampur Nrusinhanatha temple are connected with the Khonds of Odisha.

Although Narasimha is the central deity of the Telugu region, the simple folk of the region, the Chenchus, Koyas, and Khonds, preserve oral tales of intimate association with Narasimha. It is ultimately the people of the region, the followers of Narasimha, that bring together the land and the god, by their practice, pilgrimage, and rituals.

Conclusion

This chapter examined three aspects brought into focus by the tradition of Narasimha. The first section examined the association of Narasimha as an incarnation of Vishnu with the Earth, the goddess Bhudevi/Bhulakshmi. The second section examined the geographical features of Middle India, while the third section examined the common folks of the region, who preserved the oral traditions and protected the sacred centers of Narasimha. This chapter also examined the features of the middle/transitions associated with Narasimha as these features play a significant role within the religious tradition of Middle India. The land and the god Narasimha are brought together in oral accounts, religious practice, and finally, life itself as his simple life among the community is memorialized through the celebration of the wedding of Chenchitha and Narasimha.

5

Lakshmi in the Classical and Regional Tales of Narasimha

Gender and Family

Although not part of the classical texts of Narasimha, stories of Lakshmi and the feminine divine are uniquely represented in the regional stories of Narasimha. Examination of the long preserved oral tradition connected with Chenchulakshmi overturns the previously held approach to religion in India, by placing oral tradition at the center of understanding the religious tradition of Middle India. This region preserves a unique family perspective associated with the wife of Narasimha. In the states of Andhra Pradesh and Telangana she is popularly called Chenchitha or Chenchulakshmi. Some regional tales include family perspectives in association with Chenchulakshmi, which give rise to celebrations representing Narasimha as a devious son-in-law, especially noted in the southern Andhra Pradesh and Karnataka region. Examination of the feminine divine in association with Narasimha helps us to understand the socio-cultural perspectives of Narasimha. It also helps us to understand the prevalence of the Narasimha tradition in Middle India considered as the *leelasthali* of Narasimha due to his connection with the land and life of people of this region, especially Andhra Pradesh and Telangana. Narasimha is a multifaceted divinity with extensive ties to other goddess and gods of Hinduism. There are two types of relations noted with the feminine divine in the classical accounts of Narasimha. One is his relationship with Lakshmi, and the second is his relationship with the Shaivite goddesses, which forms part of the larger involvement of Narasimha with Shiva (see Chapter 2). As the examination of Narasimha's close affinity to Shaivite deities has been already undertaken in the previous chapter, I will limit my examination to understand the feminine divine within the incarnation and marriage accounts of Narasimha.

After killing Hiranyakasipu Narasimha begins to roam in the forests around Ahobilam, still raging with anger. The gods and others were unable to pacify him and persuade him to come out of his raging form of Narasimha and return to his original form.

The second part of Narasimha's life begins here with the arrival of Lakshmi as Chenchulakshmi. However, there are two strands to this story of the marriage of Narasimha and Chenchulakshmi or Chenchitha as she is popularly called in central India. The regional story of Narasimha has two parts. The first part depicts the story of the incarnation of Narasimha and vanquishing Hiranyakashipu to establish dharma. The second part is the story of Narasimha's marriage and life on Earth. This is an independent story representative of the symbolism associated with Narasimha.

It is important to examine the classical accounts of Lakshmi before the stories of Chenchulakshmi are examined in this chapter. This chapter is divided into two sections. The first section examines the origin stories of Lakshmi to understand her forms and her connection to the Earth and her incarnations on the Earth. The second section examines the stories of Chenchulakshmi and her marriage to Narasimha. Even though the stories of Lakshmi and Chenchulakshmi appear distinct, there are points of agreement, which help us to understand the cultural practices associated with Narasimha in the Telugu region.

Lakshmi (Sri or Srilakshmi) is the feminine counterpart of Vishnu, even though the Bhudevi is also considered the wife of Vishnu. Lakshmi did not incarnate along with the Varaha incarnation, but Bhudevi is depicted as the female counterpart, frequently referred to as Bhulakshmi, a composite of the goddess Lakshmi and the goddess Bhumi. It is with the Narasimha incarnation that the female counterpart of Vishnu begins to appear in a full-fledged account. The female counterpart of Narasimha appearing as Chenchulakshmi is lively and independent as is commonly noticed in the warrior culture of the Chenchus. Regional stories popularly narrated in the Telugu states of Andhra Pradesh and Telangana represent Chenchulakshmi as the incarnation of Lakshmi or occasionally as an incarnation of a Gandharva maiden. Both versions of the story are well known. I will begin my examination with Lakshmi as the counterpart of Vishnu and proceed to the stories of Chenchulakshmi. Examination of the stories of Lakshmi helps us to understand the special role of the feminine divine within Vaishnava tradition, as the wife of Vishnu. The examination of Chenchulakshmi's story brings forward the vivacious culture of the Telugu region and the warrior culture of Chenchus. Two versions of Chenchulakshmi's story are known, which connect her to Lakshmi uniquely.

Figure 7 Lakshmi Narasimha, seventeenth century CE (Narasimha seated with Lakshmi) from Nepal. Courtesy: Brooklyn Museum of Art.

Vishnu is depicted as the guardian of creation, while Lakshmi is the provider of wealth and prosperity. Hence, Lakshmi accomplishes an equally important role within the maintenance of the universe, the prosperity of beings, as noted in the popular stories of Narasimha (Figure 7).

Narasimha becomes part of the regional culture through Lakshmi as she incarnates as the beautiful daughter of the king of Chenchus. According to the classical stories and popular tales, Lakshmi born as Chenchulakshmi brings the necessary calmness to the ferocious incarnation of Narasimha, who remained fierce and refused to return to his heavenly realm after fulfilling the divine role of vanquishing the demon Hiranyakashipu. It is through Lakshmi and conducting the marriage (kalyanam) of Lakshmi and Narasimha in temples that the social groups have related to Narasimha for millennia. Although vanquishing adharma and establishing dharma form the central aspect of the incarnation of Narasimha, it is through the relationship of Lakshmi-Narasimha that Narasimha tradition becomes an essential part of the cultural milieu of Narasimha tradition.

It is important to consider the theoretical perspectives that prevented these two stories from being considered together, the divine story of Lakshmi and the popular story of Chenchulakshmi as one. This is derived from two issues that scholars find unresolvable; the first is the refusal to consider classical Puranas and local Puranas as a single continuing tradition. The second is the theory that "marriage is a technique through which local religion is absorbed into Hinduism" (Shulman 1980; Sontheimer 1989) as previous scholarship worked on the assumption that Hinduism is a religion introduced into India by the invading Aryans.

Recent research has disproven the Aryan myth, establishing the indigenous origin and development of all aspects of Indian history and culture (Vemsani 2014; Shinde 2019). The multifaceted deity Narasimha is remembered through multiple sources and indicates gradual evolution rather than forceful absorption and assimilation imposed by occupational gangs invading Aryans.

Previous scholarship tended to divide the Hindu deities into two gods, or three gods based on different aspects of the deity. For example, previous scholarly works argued for three Krishnas based on different parts of the story of Krishna (Bhandarkar; Hopkins) even though that distinction is not supported in practice, which always considered Krishna as the singular most important deity of Hinduism. The increasing amount of literature only shows accretion and cultural evolution in connecting with Krishna rather than the existence of two or three different Krishnas who have been blended.

A similar tendency is shown in the case of early studies on Narasimha. The Narasimha of the classical literature and the Narasimha of regional literature are considered separate and seen as part of the Aryanization process (see Chapter 2). Hence, early studies on Narasimha exclusively focused on Narasimha from the classical texts and not on the regional tales of Narasimha. This indirectly affected Lakshmi, the divine feminine, depicted with Vishnu as his wife, since classical stories of Narasimha depict only the incarnation of Narasimha to vanquish the demon and not his worldly life following that cosmogonic event. The worldly life of Narasimha and his marriage to Chenchulakshmi, an incarnation of Lakshmi, come from regional literature and, hence, are missed by the discerning eye of modern scholarship, with its keen focus on classical literature. Secondly, even if the stories of Chenchulakshmi and her marriage to Narasimha are considered for examination, they merely form part of the traditional format of scholarly studies which considered marriage as a process of assimilation rather than a continuation of the original story (Debicka-Borek 2016).

For Indians, the stories appear in different sources but do not denote distinct deities or origins, but constitute a unitary thread of the divine play (*leela*) of the lord, Narasimha, in his multiple aspects. The Chenchulakshmi story is memorialized in the text Vasantikaparinayam composed by Sri Satakopa

Yatindra Desikan and sculptures represented at Prahlada Varada Narasimha Swamy temple in Lower Ahobilam and Ahobilam Narasimha Swamy temple at Upper Ahobilam. Two other sculptures of Chenchulakshmi and Narasimha have been noted at Kotikesavaram Narasimha temple in East Godavari district and Narasimha (Madabhushini 1989a; 1989b) temple in Pedda Mudiam in Cuddapah district (Adinaryana 2006). The two hills of Penchalakona are considered as representing Narasimha and Chenchulakshmi. At Penchalakona Lakshmi Narasimha temple is located on one of the hills, while the other hills have the temple of Chenchulakshmi. Therefore, overwhelming evidence is available in temples, sculptures, and literature from the fourteenth century CE. Therefore, the evidence for Chenchulakshmi from literature dates to the early fourteenth century, but the story might have been well known in the region to have been included in the sculptures and literature of this period. The modern temples of Narasimha in these places are noted from 1080 onwards based on inscriptions. The earliest inscriptions in the Ahobilam temple were issued by the Western Chalukya ruler Vikramaditya (1076–1106). This shows that there were Narasimha temples in this town before the tenth century, which indirectly indicates that the stories of Chenchulakshmi and Narasimha might have already been well known by this period. Female consorts of deities have been recollected in fragments. The story of Radha had also been not found in the classical Puranas but was widespread in local tales and well entrenched in the public memory. Similarly, it is difficult to know the original roots of the story of the marriage of Narasimha and Chenchulakshmi, but it was well entrenched in public memory by the fourteenth century to have been composed into a literary text of the region as Vasantika Parinayam composed in Sanskrit. Therefore, it is important to study the story of Lakshmi and also Chenchulakshmi to understand how Narasimha became part of the culture in the Telugu region within the Bhakti tradition and practice.

Lakshmi is the most important goddess connected with creation as the wife of Vishnu, who takes incarnations in the created world from time to time. Lakshmi's incarnation is not clearly noted in the prior incarnations of Vishnu, including those of Kurma, Matsya, Varaha, and Vamana. Although Lakshmi is not incarnated along with Vishnu during his Vamana incarnation she appears in the story to bless Bali (Harivamsa 250; Vamanapurana Saro 2.14b; 49). Lakshmi's incarnation is noted in the stories of Narasimha as his wife forms an important part of Narasimha tradition in practice. An enchanting image of Narasimha in the loving embrace of Lakshmi shared on the website of Sotheby's shows the special role Lakshmi plays in the episode of the avatara of Narasimha (https://

Figure 8 Narasimha seated with Lakshmi (Hoyasala era twelfth century CE), Somanathapura, Mysore Dt, Karnataka. Photo by Susan C. Huntington. Courtesy: John C. and Susan L. Huntington Photographic Archive of Buddhist and Asian Art.

www.sothebys.com/content/dam/stb/lots/N08/N08836/162N08836_69qsd.jpg .thumb.500.500.png). Numerous stone sculptures of this type are noted across Middle India. Another common depiction is Lakshmi seated beside Narasimha on the throne or sitting on the lap of Narasimha. These depictions indicate the central role of Lakshmi within the Narasimha tradition.

Even though the classical texts narrating the avatara of Narasimha merely include only a brief account of Lakshmi, her role is important in local tales and gains immense popularity among the masses and is represented widely in the sculptures, rituals, popular stories, and performing arts of the states of Andhra Pradesh and Telangana (Figure 8).

However, Lakshmi does not appear to have incarnated along with all incarnations of Vishnu. She only appears to incarnate along with Vishnu in certain important eras in which she plays a significant role alongside Vishnu. This is the case in her incarnation with Narasimha. She enriches the story of Narasimha in new ways and brings the deity closer to the devotees. There are three strands to the story of Lakshmi in the Narasimha legends of Andhra Pradesh and Telangana. These stories present her, primarily, as Lakshmi, the goddess of fortune, and secondarily as an incarnation of Lakshmi known as Chenchulakshmi, and thirdly remaining as Lakshmi, the first wife of Narasimha (Vishnu), while blessing a celestial maiden (Gandharva maiden) to become the second wife of Narasimha. I will examine the three traditional stories of Chenchulakshmi associated with Lakshmi in the latter part of the chapter.

It is only natural that when a great hunter symbolized by the Narasimha incarnation meets the most versatile hunters and residents of the forest, the Chenchus, he ends up as their son-in-law. Chenchus are mainly found in the regions where the temples of Narasimha are commonly prevalent in the Nallamala forest regions of Andhra Pradesh (Kurnool, Guntur, Prakasam) and Telangana (Nalgonda, Mahabubnagar) where early temples of Narasimha are found dating from the first to the third centuries CE (see Chapter 2).

Owing to the centrality of Narasimha in Telugu regions, it is in the Telugu literature that Lakshmi appears most elaborately, almost as an independent story, sometimes as an incarnation, Chenchulakshmi and at other times as the rival first wife accepting of a second wife. In most versions of Telugu stories, Lakshmi is considered to have been incarnated as a tribal woman, Chenchulakshmi, among the Chenchus (Sabaras in classical texts). The Sabaras of Aitareyabrahmana are identified with several tribes of central India including the Chenchus, Savaras, Gonds, Koyas, and Khonds, although Savaras due to the resemblance of their name claim to be direct descendants of the classical Sabaras. However, as the most ancient tribes of this region, all of these tribes might have shared an early relationship. Recent genetic research conducted in India showed Chenchus possessing early clades of the shared genetic heritage of all the living populations of India (Vemsani 2014).

Thus, this story depicts the tribes of central India, which regard Narasimha as their son-in-law, thus a member of the family, rather than a remote symbol of divinity. This brings the divine closer to the devotees. However, later Telugu texts try to keep Lakshmi and Chenchulakshmi as two separate individuals, thereby giving two wives to Narasimha, one divine and one human. Examining the stories of Lakshmi in the tales of Narasimha also helps us to understand the transitional nature of Narasimha that is his most defining characteristic.

Classical understanding of Lakshmi connects her with sovereignty and wealth/prosperity (Alf Hiltebeitel 1973: Chapter 14). I will begin my examination by analyzing the classical representations of Lakshmi followed by the analysis of the stories of Chenchulakshmi.

Analysis of the Feminine Divine and Marriage in the Stories of Narasimha

Narasimha tradition overturns the way Hinduism is understood. More information about Narasimha and symbolism comes from the stories preserved by Chenchus rather than texts. However, with an entrenched bias toward oral sources within the academic study, frequently, there is an overarching refusal to accept a variety of sources on an equal basis to understand the multifaceted nature, but to consider literary sources as primary evidence and oral sources as secondary of the tradition. These former scholarly methods are inadequate and only represent the predictably puerile manner in which Hindu deities are examined and their association with local people and goddesses is considered in academic studies as something secondary, which is also indicative of the prevalent mesogynistic attitudes towards studying the divine feminine (Vemsani 2021). The vanavasis, such as Chenchus, were only considered marginal despite the overwhelming evidence of prehistoric symbolism embedded in the stories they preserved and lifestyles of prehistory in addition to their association with sacred centers of Narasimha. The stories and practices associated with Narasimha are an example of how the early religion of India evolved by incorporating experienced religion of the prehistoric native populations of India in addition to the in conjunction with the mystical revelation and deep symbolism. Could it be that the Chenchus preserved early religions the same way they have preserved early lifestyles?

There are two strands to the story of Narasimha's marriage as Chenchulakshmi is depicted as an incarnation of Lakshmi and as a second wife in Vasantika Parinayam. It is this second marriage strand that attracted scholarly attention highlighting the theories of assimilation of local religion. It is noted that "considering the marriage to a second wife, the myth of Narasimha taking a human consort—A Chenchu damsel—is not exceptional within the Vaishnava tradition" (Debick-Borek 2019: 312). Marriage is frequently construed as a method of assimilation in previous scholarship (Shulman 1980; Sontheimer 1989). These theories of marriage impose the previous theory of Aryanization or invader vs. indigenous cultural assimilation in a new manner. They argue that the invader makes inroads into native culture through relationships, not war. However, this still preserves the concept of a higher culture slowly absorbing the folk culture through marriage. It is not clear why this story of incorporating Chenchulakshmi was given primacy or why the literary works chose to present this story. However, this shows the cultural adjustments taking place in fifteenth-century Andhra Pradesh, but not the original religious practice associated with Narasimha. When a story is superimposed precipitously onto an existing tradition, it often fails to depict the close association with a local family or social group of the region. For example, the arrival of Narasimha or incarnation of Lakshmi as Chenchulakshmi should appear grafted if it was imposed, but not organic, which is not true in the case of Chenchulakshmi. Numerous versions of both of these strands of the Chenchulakshmi story are well known and appear entrenched within the regional culture (Murty 1997: 179–88). This strengthens the conviction that this is the *leelasthali*, the place of the origin of Narasimha and Chenchulakshmi, which is intricately connected to this region through the symbolic stories. Therefore, the theories of assimilation or forceful reinvention seem forced.

With the availability of multiple versions of the story, it is difficult to accept the theory of assimilation, since it is too simplistic and places value on only one version of the story while ignoring the other version of the story, which is culturally rooted and intricately connected to the life of the region. This assimilation theory not only appears simplistic but also a bit misogynistic if one considers the first version of the story which is more popular among the Chenchu bards and the general devotees. This first version of the story of Chenchulakshmi has also been adapted as a film version (Subba Rao 1958). This first version of the story represents Chenchulakshmi as the reincarnation of Lakshmi, depicted as a more confident woman. This first version of the story adapted for the film version, *Chenchulakshmi*, which represents her as a confident woman testing Narasimha to see if he has the skills of a forest-dweller, such as collecting honey, climbing trees, and hunting. Other versions of this story represent Narasimha as approaching the father of Chenchulakshmi who tests Narasimha appropriately for his skills as a hunter-gatherer before acceding to his request (Murty 179). This first version of the story of Chenchulakshmi indicates that the story might have been preserved among the Chenchus for a long time before it was taken over and a second version was composed in Sanskrit in the fifteenth century.

It is important to consider the stories of the feminine divine as an important part of faith traditions. A well-entrenched story of Chenchulakshmi and her identity as an incarnation of Lakshmi indicates a strong prehistoric religion incorporating the goddesses and lion god and placing the memory of prehistoric lifestyles at the center. The central question of this chapter is if a prehistoric tradition organically evolved with cultural evolution over the millennia or an invading classical religion overtook local religion by imposing marriage on local people. The former hypothesis is supported by the internal evidence of the story as well as the practice of the Narasimha tradition in Andhra Pradesh.

The representation of Lakshmi in multiple forms in classical texts (Vedas and Puranas) and her affiliation with the Earth and the goddess Bhumi/Bhudevi help us to understand her incarnations as the feminine divine in numerous forms along with Vishnu. Therefore, I will consider the classical sources of Lakshmi in the following pages before embarking on the subject of Chenchulakshmi and her affiliation with Lakshmi.

Classical Understanding of Lakshmi

There are three notable aspects to Lakshmi described in the classical texts: First, she is depicted under two names, Sri and Lakshmi. Second, she is depicted as another form of the goddess of the Earth, the Bhudevi. Third, she is described as Srilakshmi and Bhulakshmi as a composite goddess of wealth and prosperity. While Bhumi is the physical manifestation of the goddess of abundance, her essential manifestation representing beauty, charm, wealth, and sovereignty is Sri.

It is this unique feature of Lakshmi to appear as a representation of two distinct goddesses or as a unified goddess representing multiple aspects of abundance that is represented in her multiple stories in the classical texts as well as the folk tales. The story of Chenchulakshmi represents this feature of Lakshmi in her ability to appear in multiple forms simultaneously. She remains the goddess Lakshmi while she also appears as Chenchulakshmi. It is this unique feature of Lakshmi to appear in multiple or single manifestations that is what makes her amenable to millions of her devotees who throng to her temples to worship her in her divine as well as earthly forms or composite forms without seeking difference, but unity between the various forms of her representations. This feature is again repeated in the numerous stories associated with Lakshmi in her incarnations along with Vishnu. For example, in the Srivaishnava tradition, she is important as the wife of Vishnu and appears with the earthly incarnation of Vishnu in her incarnation. Venkateshwara is worshipped along with Lakshmi and Padmavathi her incarnation in the central temple at Tirupati. Similarly, Lakshmi is also represented as the dual wife of Narasimha as Lakshmi and Chenchulakshmi in her incarnation with Narasimha.

Early depictions of Lakshmi are noted in the Vedic texts. Lakshmi finds extraordinary mention in the Vedas. In addition, it is also notable that almost all the important aspects of Lakshmi find mention in this early depiction, which shows that the forms as well as unique qualities of Lakshmi are well established at least before the first millennium BCE. Sri Lakshmi is noted as an important goddess in the Vedas, including Rigveda. Her stories, praise texts, and ritual compendium are aggregated in the later Puranas (Chaudhuri 1962; Tripathi 1976; Nayar 1994). Sri Lakshmi attains the position of central goddess not only in Hinduism but also in Buddhist and Jain traditions (Ghosh 1979).

Appearing as Sri and Lakshmi in the Vedas, Lakshmi features a long textual history besides strong popular traditions. Sri Sukta dedicated to the praise of Sri appears in the Rigveda (III.2.6.3). Sri Sukta is part of the Khila text of the third Mandala of the Rigveda. The Sri Sukta contains fifteen verses referring to and praising the goddess, while the first two verses and the last two verses directly address Srilakshmi.

Even though the Sri Sukta contains both names, Sri and Lakshmi, these names are used separately as well as together. Hence, these names appear simultaneously as a representation of the same goddess as shown by the attributes assigned to her. However, confusion persists among early scholarship. Sri is frequently attested in the Vedas while the name Lakshmi appears infrequently and her name as Lakshmi is also used as a name to represent other goddesses subsequently, which might have also caused further confusion among the early scholars. Sri/Lakshmi represents a number of qualities in the Vedas that are also represented by Srilakshmi in the later texts including Devi Mahatmya (Gonda 176–231; Coburn 165–9). Even though both names Sri and Lakshmi are interchangeably used to refer to common attributes, which indicate that these names are connected to a single goddess, some theoretical perspectives persisted in identifying the divine feminine represented by these two names as two different goddesses. My examination of early sources showed that the names Lakshmi and Sri are used synonymously to refer to the same goddess since the attributes of both goddesses represent the same qualities of prosperity, wealth, charm, and sovereignty. Therefore, these two names, Sri and Lakshmi, even though used separately, probably represent the dual manifestation of the feminine divine with the same attributes. Regardless of whether both of these names, Sri and Lakshmi, are either used separately or jointly, they refer to the same goddess whose attributes are the positive aspects of wealth and prosperity.

Hence, both of these names are joined later to form a unique name Sri Lakshmi to refer to the goddess denoting numerous positive attributes including prosperity, fortune, kingship, beauty, and health (Rigveda 10.125). The Vedic Lakshmi was represented in her auspicious aspect as Lakshmi, and as Alakshmi and Papilakshmi in her inauspicious aspect. This has caused some confusion, leading early scholars to speculate that Lakshmi might represent both auspicious and inauspicious aspects simultaneously (Coburn 1984: 157–8). However, the only incidence in later texts representing two different goddesses occurs with the representation of the positive and negative aspects of abundance. The goddesses Lakshmi and Jyeshtha are depicted as representing the positive and negative aspects of abundance, thus providing evidence that the concepts may have existed separately initially. However, for the positive aspects of abundance Lakshmi is the only representation whether named Sri, Lakshmi, or Sri Lakshmi. Although some scholars have speculated that Lakshmi and Sri might have represented two different divinities in the Vedas (Coburn 159), the evidence does not support it. Even though the names Sri and Lakshmi are sometimes used as adjective terms, the unity of the two terms representing a single goddess is obvious in the Vedas, especially the Upanishads (Gonda 214). Continued use of Lakshmi as an adjective to describe women in positive and auspicious aspects in later texts such as the Mahabharata had led scholars to identify many feminine divines and feminine heroics such as Draupadi and a myriad of other divinities with Lakshmi (Coburn 159; Hiltebeitel). The common depiction of Lakshmi with a reclining Vishnu in yoganidra (deep sleep) on the Milk Ocean occurs in the Vishnu Dharma Sutra (99.1–23) emphasizing the inseparable nature of their relationship. While Vishnu is in deep meditative slumber, Lakshmi stays awake ever-present in her watchful relationship with Vishnu. In fact, Lakshmi declares that "I do not remain separated from Purushottama for a single moment" (99.23).

There is no evidence for the existence of two separate goddesses by the names Sri and Lakshmi since both names even though used individually represented the same qualities. Although both of these names are used in separate instances they refer to the same attributes, such as prosperity and auspiciousness. Lakshmi seems to be a shortened form for the Sanskrit word, Lakshana, which roughly translates as attribute (Monier-Williams 1997: 892). It is not unusual for the last part of the term "ana" to change to "ma" or "mi" in some cases. For example, in the Mahabharata, the name of Bhima, originally named Devavrata, was derived from Bhishana due to his Bhishana pratijna (severe pledge), an attribute that gave him a memorable eponym (Vemsani 2021). Bhishana became his name Bhishma as a reminder of this event. In the case of Bhishma, the ending 'na' in the word Bhishana changed to 'ma' to form his name. In fact, the term Lakshmi is used in the Rigveda (10.71.2) in the sense of the Lakshana (mark/imprint) of special attributes of prosperity and good fortune and hence the derivation of her name is clear.

Even though there is no clear evidence for prehistoric invasions, early studies of Hinduism also focused on the dichotomy of Aryan and non-Aryan/pre-Aryan divinities, categorizing Lakshmi as a pre-Aryan divinity (Coburn 168; Gonda 213; Dhal 1978). However, the available evidence contradicts this view, since Vedic evidence and material evidence excavated from numerous archaeological sites support rather than oppose the early origin of goddess worship. Both types of evidence support the early origin and continuity of the worship of the goddess associated with prosperity, radiance, and fecundity depicted with similar attributes in Vedic texts as well as early iconic representation. Even though she is amply represented in the Rigveda, a supposed Aryan text in their conceptualization, this presented a problem for these early scholars, since it was theorized that Rigveda lacks female divinities to support its difference from the indigenous religion of India. The presence of Lakshmi in Rigveda contradicts this basic premise of the Aryan invasion theory. The original invasion theory is based on Rigvedic text. The later theory of absence of goddesses in Vedas might have been propounded to support another vague theory that Vedic religion does not have a significant feminine divine. This vague theory is later used to support the theory of "marriage as assimilation" in which the gods of Vedic origin marry the local goddesses to form part of the religion of India. However, the religion and practice associated with Narasimha and Chenchulakshmi prove the futility of these construed theories in understanding the true nature of the origin of religion of India.

Such categorizations rest on assumed notions of early Indian history that early Hindu practice of the Veda was male-centered and only assimilated female divinities as it spread in the subcontinent. The assurance of early scholars that the Vedas lack feminine divinities also falls under this category of colonial theories, which refused to recognize Indian classical texts as representing indigenous Indian faith. The earlier notions of history about Aryan invasion/migration are disproven (Vemsani 2014), and the mere fact that Sri and Lakshmi, as well as the numerous goddesses, appear in the Vedas rules out that these goddesses were assimilated into Hinduism from elsewhere or another religion or culture through marriage.

There are two stories of the origin of Lakshmi in the classical tradition. Both traditions portray her origin from the fundamental elements of nature, heat, and water. Both of the stories depict the a self-born independent origin of the goddess. I will discuss these origin stories below to show the special qualities associated with Lakshmi and how they continue to be carried forward in her incarnations.

Two Stories of the Origin of Sri/Lakshmi/Srilakshmi

The origin of Sri from Prajapati and her rivalry with other gods is discussed in Mitravinda yajna in Satapata Brahmana (11.4.3.1–18).

> Prajapati was becoming heated (by fervid devotion), whilst creating living beings. From him, worn out and heated, Sri (Fortune and Beauty) came forth. She stood there resplendent, shining, and trembling. The gods, beholding her thus resplendent, shining, and trembling, set their minds upon her (Satapata Brahmana 11.4.3.1).

In this account Sri originates from Prajapati, who was practicing tapas (austerities), while busy in creation. When Lakshmi originated she was born with numerous attributes, which were desired by the other gods. They were so enamored by the exceptional qualities she possessed and they desired so much to take her attributes that they were willing to embrace those, even at the risk of killing her. "They said to Prajapati, 'Let us kill her and take (all) this from her.' He said, 'Surely, that Sri is a woman, and people do not kill a woman, but rather take (anything) from her (leaving her) alive'" (11.4.3.22.).

Prajapati advised them against killing her and told them to get the attributes from Lakshmi without killing her. Her ten attributes were then taken by the ten deities, Agni, Soma, Varuna, Mitra, Brihaspati, Savitri, Pushan, Sarasvati, and Tvashtri. Agni then took her food, Soma her royal power, Varuna her universal sovereignty, Mitra her noble rank, Indra her power, Brihaspati her holy luster, Savitri her dominion, Pushan her wealth, Sarasvati her prosperity, and Tvashtri her beautiful forms (11.4.3.33). Therefore, it is clear that Lakshmi possessed many desirable special qualities such as food, royal power, universal sovereignty, noble rank, power, holy luster, dominion, wealth, prosperity, and her beautiful forms. These qualities appear consistently in her descriptions in her forms as Sri or Lakshmi and her numerous incarnations as well as sojourns on the Earth. This early story also makes it clear that Sri is not only the possessor of these special qualities but that these special qualities are desirable for all. The fact that all of her special qualities are desirable for the gods makes them even more desirable for the mere mortals the humans also.

Sri was shocked that all her special qualities were taken from her. Sri then approached Prajapati and complained to which he advised her to perform Mitravinda yagna to obtain her attributes back. Sri followed Prajapati's advice and the gods returned her special attributes to her at the end of the Priyamvada Yajna (Satapata Brahmana 11.4.3.4). This may indicate her role as an important goddess in the Vedas. Her exchange and re-exchange of her important attributes form the important part of this early narrative of Lakshmi, indicating the central role she had among the deities during this early phase. Possessing the qualities that are desired by the other gods, places Sri in a commanding position.

Her receiving special attributes from the divinities is compared to the goddess (Devi) obtaining the tejas of gods as described in the Devimahatya (Coburn 169). However, this comparison is misconstrued, since Lakshmi commanded the gods to return her qualities to her instead of taking anything from them. In this case, Lakshmi simply reclaimed her qualities rather than acquiring anything from them. This shows generosity rather than retaliation or dependency on the gods for her attributes. They had previously taken from her all her special attributes, so regaining her qualities is only an act of proving her authority rather than dependency. Sri did not receive anything from them that did not belong to her unlike Devi in the Devimahatmya, who received the tejas from all gods, thus becoming stronger. Here, the attributes that Sri received are her attributes. Therefore, it could be understood that Lakshmi and Sri are one. Close examination of this story reveals that Sri possessed exceptional attributes right from the time of her origin. These numerous special attributes were passionately desired by other deities, which indicates her special qualities and positive attributes that could influence the life of anyone touched by her as evidenced here. Those who are blessed with receiving her attributes from her become positive deities themselves and are able to pass on her positivity back to her. Although all goddesses are represented as givers and bringers of joy, Lakshmi is especially unique in that she is endowed with all the positive qualities with which she rules the universe. She blesses her devotees with the most sought-after qualities, wealth, prosperity, and success; hence she is the most worshipped goddess regardless of whether one follows Vaishnava, Shaiva, or Shakta practices of Hinduism. And so stories of the marriage of Narasimha indicate the return of prosperity and sovereignty to him.

The second account of the origin of Lakshmi also connects her to special attributes noted here, but with a connection to water. This story presents her as self-born independent nature unlike the Atharvaveda story of her origin from Prajapati.

Epic and Purana Tales of Lakshmi's Origin

The Puranas include a second story of the origin of Lakshmi, which also includes her marriage to Vishnu. The Ramayana (1. sarga 44) and the Mahabharata

(1.15.12) and numerous other Puranas include the story of Lakshmi's origin from the Kshirasagara (Milk Ocean). It is said that Lakshmi left her celestial abode due to a curse of Durvasa (Vishnupurana 1.9.1–149). She subsequently appeared at the Samudramanthana (churning the ocean) to produce the amrita (the drink of immortality). During the churning Vishnu acquired the form of Kurma serving as the base for the churning rod in the Kshirasagara. During the churning precious objects emerged from the ocean followed by the deity Lakshmi. After she was honored by gifts from gods, Lakshmi chose Vishnu as her partner.

Popular practices such as vows to and worship of Lakshmi are depicted in the ritual texts. Lakshmi is worshipped widely as she is the goddess of wealth, prosperity, and joy. Saubhagya Lakshmi Upanishad is dedicated to the narration of her story, special attributes, and central religious practices associated with her (Mahadeva 1950; Warrier 1931). Mahalakshmi Stotram and Mahalakshmi Stuti are also widely popular and include the praise verses addressed to Lakshmi used in vratras (vows) and worship (Rhodes 2011). Modern practices draw upon Vaishnava thought based upon Pancharatra and Srivashnava practices, which assert the centrality of Lakshmi to achieve the goals of spirituality as well as earthly prosperity (Kumar 1997: 21–49).

As Vishnu incarnated from time to time in various avataras Lakshmi is depicted as incarnating along with him. However, the full-fledged incarnation of Lakshmi only begins with Narasimha. I will examine the stories of Lakshmi in association with Narasimha prevalent in Sanskrit as well Telugu story traditions of the Telugu states, Telangana and Andhra Pradesh.

Srilakshmi and Bhulakshmi

Lakshmi represented as Srilakshmi is the goddess of wealth, while Bhulakshmi also known as Bhumi or Bhudevi is represented in a close relationship with Vishnu. The Varaha incarnation of Vishnu is depicted with Varaha raising the sphere of the Earth between his tusks or the Earth in human form sitting or standing with him. The relationship between the goddess Lakshmi and the goddess Bhumi but depicted in the early Vedic texts is complex. The wedding of the god Surya's daughter Suuryaa with Soma is noted in the Rigveda Book 10.85. 1–10. Verse 7 of this section (85) notes that her treasure was the Earth (Bhumi) when she married Soma. This also shows the identification of Bhumi with wealth, which is personified as Lakshmi.

The Bhumi Suktam in the Atharvaveda depicts the relationship in a subtle manner (Atharvaveda Book VII Hymn 1 Bhumisuktam). The essence of

Bhumi (Prithvi) symbolically represented as the flavor (scent) of the Earth also indirectly connects her to Lakshmi. The verse (Atharvaveda Book VII.1.24) notes, "that fragrance of thine which has entered into the lotus," and the verse continues "that fragrance, O Earth, which the immortals of yore gathered up at the marriage of Suuryaa,"[1] and then the verse ends with the request, "make me fragrant: not anyone shall hate us!" It is then noted as the charm and special quality of beings, men, and women simultaneously. The Bhumi Suktam (Atharvaveda Book VII.1.25) further notes the extensive presence of this among many beings of creation, "That fragrance of thine which is in men, the loveliness and charm that is in male and female, that which is in steeds and heroes, that which is in the wild animals with trunks (elephants), the luster that is in the maiden, O Earth, with that do thou blend us: not any one shall hate us!" This second verse indicates that the quality of the goddess Bhumi indicated here is not limited merely to the fragrance; but, it is also mentioned as "the loveliness and charm that is in men and women," and "luster that is in the maiden," which shows the unique features associated with Lakshmi. It is still common to refer to bride as Lakshmi or compare her appearance to Lakshmi. This fragrance is also described as loveliness and charm as well as luster. As the divine manifestation of wealth, Lakshmi is also identified as the essence of the Earth. The essence of the Earth described as fragrance entered the lotus (verse 24) and also spread into creation as manifold qualities, which are also the qualities associated with Lakshmi. Luster (shining) or being resplendent is one of the main qualities associated with Lakshmi. Srilakshmi and Bhulakshmi are depicted as the wives of Vishnu. This shows the close relationship Vishnu has with the goddess Prithvi and the essential wealth of the Earth, the goddess Lakshmi.

Chenchulakshmi in the Telugu Regional Texts: Marriage of Chenchulakshmi and Narasimha

The local stories of Chenchulaksmi are well known in Middle India including the states of Andhra Pradesh, Telangana, and eastern Maharashtra as well as eastern Karnataka. Chenchus were spread across central and southern India in prehistory, although presently they are notably found in the states of Andhra Pradesh, Telangana, Karnataka, and Odisha. The terms Chenchu and Sabara are used interchangeably in the local tales (Sthalapuranas) while discussing the tale of Chenchulakshmi and Narasimha. However, some differences can be observed within the lifestyles of these two tribes, which could be considered minor regional variations based on the wider regions their habitation in central India. The Chenchus are spread across the Eastern Ghats, forested mountainous regions in Andhra Pradesh and Telangana, and the Western Ghats in Karnataka and Madhya Pradesh, while they subsist on predominantly hunter-gatherer lifestyles (see Chapter 6). The Khonds, Gonds, and Koyas are spread in northern Telangana, Chhattisgarh, Maharashtra, and eastern Karnataka. However, the Chenchus holds the oldest genetic heritage shared among the residents of India regardless of caste and tribe (Vemsani 2014). It is possible that all these tribes might have originally related to a central tribal group from which these groups might have originated. Chenchus are known as fierce warriors noted for their skillful archery. They are also skillful at navigating dense forests, one of the reasons the British feared them, labeling some of the tribes as criminal tribes, arresting them on sight, and confining them to prisons for long terms under the pretext of reforming them.

Due to the similarities in name, the Sabaras noted in the classical texts are increasingly identified with the Savaras of Odisha and northern Andhra Pradesh, although I think use of the term Sabara at this early stage only indicates the common term to used designate tribes in general rather than any one or the other of the individual tribes spread in the region where the Narasimha tradition is practiced.

The story of Chenchitha and Narasimha is narrated as a loving embrace of two divinities in the original version of the story. This story is popularly known among the followers of Narasimha, which is widely narrated in theatrical traditions including but not limited to Yakshaganam, Oggukatha, and Harikatha ganam, and so on. This story also forms part of one of the early Telugu literary compositions. Tarigonda Vengamamba (1730–1817) is one of the well-noted devotees of Sri Venkateshwara of Tirupati and composed much poetical and dramatic literature. Incidentally, Tarigonda Vengamamba's first poetical composition was *Nrusimha Shatakam*, and she also composed *Chenchu Natakam*. This story is widely popular among the devotees of Narasimha in Andhra Pradesh, which also forms the basis for the Telugu film, *Chenchulakshmi*.

The regional story of the wedding of Narasimha and Chenchulakshmi differs significantly from the stories of classical Purana texts. Chenchulakshmi appears more composed and strong-natured in her conduct with Narasimha than she was depicted in the *Vasantika Parinayam*. I will discuss the oral traditions and how they differ from the *Vasantika Parinayam* narration.

Marriage of Chenchulakshmi and Narasimha

The marriage of Chenchulakshmi and Narasimha is one of the most popular stories in Andhra Pradesh. The first part of Narasimha story depicts the incarnation of Narasimha and the vanquishing of Hiranyakasipu while the second part of the story of Narasimha depicts his falling in love with a vanavasi (forest) woman and his marriage following which he lived in Ahobilam as a grihastha (householder). The story of Chenchulakshmi draws on the classical Purana stories that depict the event of Lakshmi leaving the celestial abode for the Earth.

The original story of the marriage of Chenchulakshmi and Narasimha begins in the celestial world. This story also served as the basis for a number of films in the southern languages of India. Two films were produced on this subject (1943 and 1958). The film produced in 1958 is called *Chenchulakshmi* (https://www.youtube.com/watch?v=FYSbMXM8fqk) and depicts the separate stories of Narasimha and Lakshmi and their marriage later.

The story of Lakshmi's incarnation as Chenchulakshmi spans two worlds. It so happens that the sage Durvasa was not invited to the wedding of Vishnu and Lakshmi. This enraged the sage Durvasa who cursed the parents of Lakshmi, Samudra and his wife, to be born on the Earth. Eventually, they were born among the Chenchus. Samundra became the leader of Chenchus known as Surasena, as the valiant leader Sura. Lakshmi was born as their daughter called Chenchitha. Vishnu incarnated as Narasimha and vanquished Hiranyakasipu, he did not come out of his fierce composition even after accomplishing the purpose of his incarnation. He roamed the forests around Ahobilam. One day while roaming in the forests Narasimha saw Chenchitha collecting honey. He immediately fell in love and transformed himself into a handsome young man Narahari. He approached Chenchulakshmi to propose to her. However, she refused, challenging him to perform a number of tasks, common to the Chenchu folk roaming in the forests. He had to prove his valiance as a fearless hunter in the forest and skilled collector of honey and other forest produce. Establishing himself thus he married Chenchitha with the permission of her parents and tribe. The relationship between Narasimha and Chenchulakshmi is represented as a relationship between two equals. Chenchitha was free to challenge Narasimha to prove his prowess, while Narasimha was polite enough to approach her family respectfully for his wedding with Chenchitha.

Representations of Chechita and Narasimha are found in the Narasimha temple of Ahobilam and at the Narasimha temple in Korukonda in East Godawari district in Andhra Pradesh. However, this narrative changes considerably later in Vaishnava theological literature. Here, Chenchitha becomes the second wife of Narasimha instead of being an incarnation of Lakshmi. I will discuss Vasantikaparinayam which shows this second version of the story.

Vasantika Parinayam

Vasantika Parinayam was composed by Sri Sathakopa Yatindra Mahadesikan seventh guru (pontiff) of Ahobilam Devasthanam. He introduced numerous innovations into the story. Introducing the dramatical theory of Bharata, and following the plot structure of Kalidasa, Satakopa wrote a five-act drama. I will also narrate the popular versions of the story, which differ from the Vasantika Parinayam, which I call the first version of the story of the marriage of Narasimha and Chenchulakshmi. I will compare below the story of the marriage of Narasimha from Vasantika Parinayam with popular versions of the story recollected in the oggukatha performances and later made into a film.

Act 1

Chenchulakshmi: Popular Narratives

This first act in popular narratives of Chenchulakshmi begins with the marriage of Vishnu and Lakshmi, a very happy occasion, which was attended by sages, gods, and other celestials. However, the happy occasion turns into a sad event as the sage Durvasa appears uninvited and curses the parents of Lakshmi along with Lakshmi to be born on the Earth. Distressed, Lakshmi and her parents pray and appeal to the sage Durvasa to spare them. To which Durvasa says, Lakshmi will marry Vishnu in her earthly life, which will help release them from their curse. This is similar to the narrative of Narasimha incarnation in the classical texts, which say that the brothers Hiranyaksha and Hiranyakashipu were the cursed doorkeepers of Vishnu, Jaya, and Vijaya

Vasantika Parinayam

This act introduces the main characters of the play. Mahendra arrives in Ahobalam with his retinue to honor the lord of Ahobala. They see the beautiful

Chenchitha proceeding to a forest temple. Mahendra explains that she was the daughter of a Gandharva king born as a tribal girl due to the curse of Lakshmi. While evesdropping on the conversations of the girls, they learn that she was the daughter of Surasena (referred to as Sura), the king of the tribe. In the meantime, Vasantika prays to the forest deity wishing to marry Narasimha. At the suggestion of Vidushaka Narasimha sends her a letter. Vasantika reads the letter; even though the letter is signed by Ahobalesa, Vasantika fails to make the connection between the handsome prince and the deity Narasimha she wished to marry.

Act 2

Chenchulakshmi: Popular Versions

This act depicts the birth of Chenchulakshmi. Vishnu gathers the eminence of Lakshmi and deposits it in a mango fruit on a mango tree he created. In the meantime the parents of Lakshmi born as Chenchu king and queen are concerned that they are not able to give birth to a child. Narada meets them and presents them with the mango fruit which contains the essence of Lakshmi. Narada informs the queen to eat the mango fruit to obtain children. The queen thus ate the mango fruit and gave birth to a beautiful girl. Hence, Lakshmi is born to them. The loving child is named Chenchulakshmi by the couple.

Vasanitika Parinayam

This act shows the women's world connected to Chenchitha. Through the conversations of an old attendant and Chenchitha's maiden, the love of Chenchitha's for Narasimha is revealed while also indicating that she was suffering from her separation from Narasimha. Vasantika wonders if her status was hampering Narasimha from accepting her as his bride. Thinking in this way she also suffers from her separation and loses her senses, becoming desolate. At this time Narasimha reveals himself to her in her dream as the handsome prince she had met in the forest temple. The old maiden consoles Vasantika, assuring her that Narasimha will marry her. Using her esoteric powers the old maiden visits the palace of Narasimha and finds out that Narasimha is also in love with Vasantika. The maiden then informs Vasantika that Narasimha is deeply in love with her too, but Vasantika still doubts and cannot trust the assurances of her old attendant.

Act 3

Chenchulakshmi: Popular Versions

This episode focuses on the appearance of Narasimha from the pillar to the prayers of Prahlada and the killing of Hiranyakashipu. Narasimha remains enraged even after killing Hiranyakashipu. None of the deities and sages are able to pacify him. Lakshmi also fails to pacify him, since Lakshmi lacks her essence, which was hidden in the mango fruit previously. Hence, Narasimha continues to roam the forests, performs yoga, and eventually transforms into a handsome prince.

Vasantika Parinayam

This act brings forward the world of Narasimha in both the celestial and earthly realms. Narasimha's attendants enter saying that Lakshmi has already learned that her husband Narasimha has fallen in love with a tribal girl. Narasimha suffers from lovesickness and forgets that his return to the celestial world is impending. A bird, another celestial in disguise, enters the palace of Vasantika to convey the love of Narasimha to her, which is chased by her, to convey. In the meantime, Narasimha also reaches the palace garden along with Vidushaka. He reveals himself as Ahobalesa to Vasantika and her attendants. Narasimha proposes to Vasantika, who, as we know, is already madly in love with him. This act ends with Vasantika leaving the palace garden as she is summoned by her mother.

The first version focuses on Narasimha's incarnation, while this second version presented in the Vasantika Parinayam focuses on the divine presence of Vishnu. In addition, the second story also brings in a celestial bird and other celestial attendants of Vishnu.

Act 4

Chenchulakshmi: Popular Versions

This episode narrates the wanderings of Narasimha in the forest and his meeting with Chenchulakshmi. Chenchulakshmi visits the forest to gather honey where she meets Narasimha, now settled as the young prince of the forests. The popular versions as well as the film version based on the popular stories describe this episode as a romantic encounter between a young and naïve Chenchulakshmi and the handsome prince Narasimha. As Chenchulakshmi rebuffs the advances of Narasimha, he tries to impress her. This episode is depicted in a romantic song sequence with the lyrics, "Chettulekkagalava O Narahari...," which continues to be a very popular musical composition in Telugu states.

Vasantika Parinayam

This act brings more activity into the play. This act also introduces a number of characters revealing the true the background of Narasimha and Chenchulakshmi and planning the impending wedding of Narasimha and Vasantika, the Chenchu heroine. Information comes from ancillary characters in this section. This section reminiscent of the Bhagavatapurana in which bees are depicted as messengers. Discussion of bees begins the act. The bees are busy in the garden and continue to discuss how the Gandharva king was reborn on the Earth in search of his daughter. A discussion of Narasimha's attendants reveals that Lakshmi had given her permission for the wedding of Vasantika and Narasimha. Narasimha meets the forest deity who tries to convince him about their wedding in her effort to calm him down. Narasimha meets Vasantika in Vanadevata's temple and assures her about their wedding.

This act brings out the independence and strong nature of Lakshmi represented in Chenchulakshmi. The second version represented in the Vasantika Parinayam decreases the role of Chenchulakshmi in favor of the Bhagavata symbols.

Act 5

Popular Versions

Popular versions bring two forms of Lakshmi together in this final concluding act. The divine Lakshmi is concerned that Narasimha has fallen in love with the Chenchu maiden and is getting ready to marry her. The parents of Chenchulakshmi are equally concerned that continuing with the wedding preparation might attract the wrath of the goddess Lakshmi and other celestials. At this juncture, Narada appears to reveal the truth of the incarnation of Narasimha and the birth of Chenchulakshmi from the glow (aura) of Lakshmi deposited by Vishnu in mango fruit. This revelation frees the parents of Lakshmi from the curse as Durvasa stipulated earlier that they would be relieved of their curse as soon as they learn of the true nature of his daughter and son-in-law as Vishnu and Lakshmi. The story ends with Lakshmi and Vishnu as well as the parents of Chenchulakshmi leaving for their respective abodes.

Vasantika Parinayam

Act 5 narrates the conclusion bringing everyone together. The act begins with a conversation between Narada and Prahlada expressing concern about how Lakshmi might react to the marriage of Narasimha with Vasantika. Surasena visits Lakshmi along with his daughter Vasantika, to seek her permission for the wedding. Lakshmi receives them well and informs them about their previous life as Gandharvas and her blessings to Vasantika previously to marry Vishnu. Lakshmi also informs Surasena that he would regain the celestial world as a Gandharva at the wedding of Narasimha and Vasantika.

The final episode of version 1 of Chenchulakshmi's wedding preserves the Vedic depiction of Lakshmi's appearance in dual forms, while the standardized version of Vasantika Parinayam missed this point, by incorporating Chenchulakshmi as an incarnation of another celestial woman. This second version also misses the self-determination and strong nature of Lakshmi noted in the first version of the story of Chenchulakshmi.

Each act of the *Vasantikaparinayam* is sprinkled with information about Vasantika's previous life as a Gandharva woman. The story written as *Vasantikaparinayam*, the marriage of Vasantika, in fact, serves the purpose of presenting Chenchitha as Vasantika and as a celestial being rather than a simple Chenchu maiden and an incarnation of Lakshmi, as she was in other simple popular versions of the story.

Numerous popular Yakshaganas are known to record the story of the marriage of Narasimha and Chenchulakshmi. Two popular versions of the story known under the title of Garudachala Yakshaganam, record the story of the marriage of Narasimha and Chenchitha. The earliest recorded version of Garudachala Yakshaganam is attributed to Obayya/Obamantri, who may have lived around the seventeenth century (Rao 1937: 443–5). The second Yakshaganam by the same name was composed by Yadavadasu of Bhadrachalam, which he dedicated to the central deity Srirama of the Srirama temple in Bhadrachalam (443). Both of these Yakshaganas present Chenchitha as the second wife of Narasimha, but the first version presents Chenchulakshmi as the incarnation of Lakshmi's radiance, while her depiction as the second wife seems to have been based on sixteenth-century Vaishnava culture of southern India rather than the earlier Chenchu version depicting Chenchulakshmi as the reincarnation of Sri Lakshmi.

Gender and Society in the Marriage of Chenchulakshmi and Narasimha

The first popular version of Chenchulakshmi, preserves the Vedic representations of Lakshmi as a dual-form goddess, in depicting Chenchulakshmi as the essence of Lakshmi born from the mango fruit. She remains as Lakshmi in her divine realm, while also incarnated simultaneously as Chenchulakshmi on the Earth. Chenchus are associated with the sacred location of the temple as well as the central stories of the temple. It is possible that the stories of the marriage of Chenchitha may have formed part of the cultural life of Chenchus along with the cave temples that they may have maintained for millennia, worshipping the deities and maintaining the sacred center. Chenchus may have been living within these regions since the Paleolithic period, which can be understood from their genetic heritage. The genetic heritage of current populations of the region shows a shared genetic heritage with Chenchus sharing the oldest genetic heritage of native populations of India (Vemsani 2014). The Chenchulakshmi story erases the social differences between the caste and tribe, which were placed at the center of academic studies of Hinduism theorizing the dichotomy of 'invader vs. indigenous'.

Nevertheless, vanavasis might have formed part of the original cultural fabric of the Middle Indian region and remained close to the roots holding on to the Paleolithic lifestyles; while the other population groups changed their lifestyles, Chenchus have remained close to their primal lifestyle of hunter-gatherer society, continuing to maintain mutual relations with their neighboring communities. The origin stories of Chenchus narrate their origin from Shiva and Parvati, the central deities of Srisailam, regionally known as Mallikharjuna and Bhramarambika. Narratives of tribal history are closely connected to numerous sacred centers located in Middle India. Their historical stories are closely interconnected with the regional stories of the temples. The oral stories may have been older than they were given credit for in shaping the historical accounts of this region. The original stories of the Chenchus might be as old as the sacred centers of Ahobilam and Srisailam around the first millennium BCE. Therefore, it is important to consider the oral sources to understand the nature of religion in Middle India. Exclusive focus on only one type of source, either literary or oral, might not reveal the true depth of the religious history and practice of the region. Without understanding the importance of Chenchulakshmi through considering the oral sources and religious practice, it is impossible to gain an in-depth understanding of the history and culture of Middle India.

Conclusion

Representations of the feminine divine in the stories of Narasimha are examined in this chapter. The stories of Lakshmi, Vishnu, and their incarnations of Chenchulakshmi and Narasimha as noted in the classical texts (Vedas and the Puranas) and popular stories reveal the cultural and social fabric of Middle India. Representation of Lakshmi under two distinct names as Sri and Lakshmi is noted in the Vedic texts representing the same special qualities associated with Lakshmi. Lakshmi also appears to imbibe the special qualities as the essence of Bhumidevi noted in the Vedas. Similarly, Lakshmi appears in dual forms in her incarnations accompanying Vishnu in each of his earthly sojourns. However, Lakshmi's appearance is brief along with the avataras before Narasimha, such as Matsya, Kurma, and Varaha. Similarly, Lakshmi's incarnation along with Narasimha is non-descript in the Puranas. However, her role is elaborate in the folk stories popular in the states of Andhra Pradesh, Telangana, and Karnataka, in which the popular tale of Narasimha's wedding with Chenchulakshmi forms the most important part of the local devotional practice. Examination of the classical stories of Lakshmi and the stories of Chenchulakshmi not only gives clearer understanding of the Narasimha tradition in Middle India, but also reveals ways in which folk tradition mutate and evolve, thus informing the development of indigenous religion of India. Examination of the classical as well as popular accounts of Lakshmi and Chenchulakshmi help clarify the complex process of the evolution of Hinduism in India, which was previously mistakenly theorized as Aryanization or Hinduization.

6

Narasimha in the Eastern Region
Odisha and Andhra Pradesh

The eastern part of Middle India is the most sacred place in connection with Narasimha as the *leelasthali* (land of divine play). This is the region where Narasimha lived and connected with the simplest people (the vanavasis) in addition to other significant people such as the sages, demons, and other devotees in general. Regional stories of the numerous sacred centers located in Andhra Pradesh and Odisha closely record these features noted in the classical texts. This chapter also considers the spread of the Narasimha tradition between Ahobilam and the sacred centers of Narasimha in Tamil Nadu. Therefore, this chapter examines the regional traditions associated with Narasimha in Andhra Pradesh and Odisha, two of the states located on the east coast of India, popularly known as the Coromandel Coast on the Indian Ocean. Andhra Pradesh contains the most important temples of Narasimha, located in Ahobilam and Simhachalam, connecting it to the classical accounts of the origin of Narasimha.

The regional legend of Ahobilam depicts the temple of Narasimha as the place of appearance of Narasimha and his subsequent life with his wife Chenchulakshmi in the Nallamala forests of the region. The temple of Simhachalam also depicts the places associated with the harassment of the child devotee Prahlada as described in the Vishnu Purana. This place is also associated with Urvashi and Pururavas,[1] who is said to have renovated the temple during the Dvapara Yuga. A comparative study of the common themes in the classical and regional mythology of Narasimha is undertaken in this chapter. This helps with understanding the classical Hinduism and regional practices associated with Narasimha.

One unique feature associated with Narasimha in the eastern part of Middle India is his close association with vanavasi social groups in addition to his affiliations noted with Shiva and the goddesses. The regional practice of Narasimha is associated with Lakshmi in her form as Chenchulakshmi, daughter of Chenchus, and so represents the association of vanavasi social group of Chenchus with Narasimha in Andhra Pradesh. The regional practice of the state of Odisha associates Narasimha with Jagannatha, the goddesses, and folk practice of the tribal groups, Sabaras and Konds, through regional tales and practice. This chapter examines the classical literature as well regional tales and practice in Andhra Pradesh and Odisha to understand the social and religious history in this region. This chapter focuses on understanding the feminine divine in tribal and classical traditions as well as at the intersection of the Shaiva (followers of Siva) and Vaishnava (followers of Vishnu) philosophical and theological traditions in connection with Narasimha (Figure 1).

Early evidence of the historical practice is consistently noted in this region (see Chapter 3). Sculptural representations and early temples are noted in Andhra Pradesh and Odisha. Early sculptures noted in Andhra Pradesh (Kondamotu and Motadaka) near Nagarjunakonda (see Figure 1) are datable to as early as the first to the third centuries CE, and historical evidence places the inscriptional sources of Narasimha in the eighth century in Odisha. Similar images of Narasimha datable to the Gupta era are noted in northern and northwestern India including Gandhara and Kashmir regions (see Figure 9). Even though these sculptures and inscriptions are dated to 300 CE for sculptures and 800 CE for inscriptions, they might indicate an earlier and well-entrenched religious practice in connection with Narasimha in the area at least two centuries before the construction of the temples. Therefore, the worship and construction of temples of Narasimha are traceable to the beginning of the first century CE in Andhra Pradesh based on sculptures, and to the middle of the first century CE in Odisha based on inscriptions.

Sacred centers of Narasimha, besides preserving the early inscriptions and sculptures, also preserve the original symbolic nature of Narasimha. I will discuss the central aspects of Narasimha represented in Andhra Pradesh and Odisha discussing select temples from both these states.

Transitional Geographical Points Representing Energy Centers

Narasimha is associated with distinct geography rather than a specific object in his representation at the sacred centers. The special geographical points indicate energy points (shaktisthanas) as well as symbolic features associated with Narasimha such as the middle and transitions. Narasimha temples are also located in the hills or other prominent geographical features of the land that mark the presence of Narasimha in a geographical location, distinct yet transitional features. Narasimha is also represented in composite forms.

Regional traditions of India have been studied with a view to supplying evidence for the preconceived theory of "Aryanization" (Kulke 1986), which was also later described by different words such as "Sanskritization," (Srinivas 1955: 30) and "Hinduization" (Eschmann 79–80) as if Hinduism was developed outside of India in its complete form. This also presupposes the view that a group, preferably Aryans, later identified with upper castes, were invaders bringing culture into India, while the lower castes and vanavasi populations were converted forcefully by the invading Aryans. However, this could not be supported by fact-based evolution noted in Hinduism. Aryans is a misconstrued racist colonialist term developed into an overarching theory imposed on India to divide the indigenous Hindu society of India. Due to the lack of evidence to support the theory of arrival or the historicity of Aryans (Vemsani 2014), it is impossible to sustain this invader vs. indigenous framework for understanding Indian religion, especially Hinduism. Mystical revelations noted in the Vedas depict the esoteric understanding of Hinduism, while practice-based Hinduism is derived from popular traditions noted since the late Mesolithic period in India.[2] The mendicants, mystics, and sages represented in the Vedas and classical literature of India might have come from the same society that had practiced the living tradition of the prehistoric religion noted since the Mesolithic period in India. Therefore, the classical texts and popular practices depict different modes of practice rather than different societies that are antagonistic to each other. It is difficult to know how or when the affiliation of different traditions took place to form the pluralistic Hinduism as we know it today. Although defined as "High" Hinduism, classical Hinduism/Vedanta Hinduism certainly incorporates popular elements of religious practice. This is evident in the practices in the countryside of India, which demonstrate the two-way interaction of popular as well as classical elements of Hinduism (Marriott and Beals 1955). The unity of Hinduism was noted and recorded (Singer 1972: 47) even though some scholars continue to define and divide Hindu practice by following disproven classifications of popular practice vs. classical practice. Confusion is generated by considering Hindus as separate from tribal and lower caste populations, which is not the case; since the Aryan migration theory is proven false, this theory stands on shaken foundations and needs to be discontinued in academic discussions. Due to the overwhelming evidence of practices and textual traditions it is important to consider the indigenous origins of Hinduism from practiced traditions dating as far back as the Paleolithic era at Ahobilam. Popular practice and the mystical revelations of classical texts complement each other rather than opposing or overtaking one another as theorized previously. It seems that the issue is not with traditional Hinduism and practice, but how the tradition began to be studied in the West. Academic examinations began with translating classical texts, considering them as the authentic practice, which is derived from the Western notion of text-based religious practice as central to a culture. Hence, the popular traditions and texts were only considered as secondary to the classical texts and popular practice considered as ancillary to the major religious practice. The problem is with retrofitting information to a century-old theory rather than considering the information on hand independently. However, Hinduism presents an anomaly to the established academic study of Hinduism, entrenched in textual studies, by presenting equally strong popular practice, which appears only remotely connected to the classical tradition on a cursory glance, but they are not mutually exclusive. Upon close examination, the complementary nature of popular traditions and the classical tradition comes to the fore and is beneficial in understanding the true nature of religion in India.

Therefore, it is important to focus on understanding Hindu tradition as an amalgamation of prehistoric indigenous traditions, prevalently noticed among the vanavasi (forest-dwelling population of India) social groups of India currently referred to as the tribal/Scheduled Tribal population of India. However, Hinduism is also indigenous to India, derivative of numerous practiced traditions of India in close conjunction with the mystical revelations of the Vedas. The Vedanta religion noticed from the first millennium BCE is a fusion of these multiple aspects of religion. Hence, it is futile to separate each aspect of religion practiced by different social groups as distinct. It is much more useful to focus on how many aspects of Hinduism find unique expression in each region. This is especially true in the case of the deity Narasimha, our focus of study in this book. It is unique that Narasimha, symbolizing the middle/transitional state within the established theology, certainly preserved multiple aspects of regional practices, which also find cryptic expression in classical traditions as well as practice (see Chapter 2 for examination of multiple aspects of Narasimha in classical sources). This chapter will focus on the unique traditions associated with Narasimha in the classical as well as vanavasi traditions of Odisha and Andhra Pradesh. Narasimha traditions in Odisha and Andhra Pradesh help us to understand the unique way in which multiple patterns of religion are preserved, while unique elements of each social group are also represented. Regional temples in Andhra Pradesh and Odisha represent these two aspects simultaneously.

The Narasimha tradition on the east coast represents three aspects: First, theologically, Narasimha is connected to Vishnu as a vyuha and also an avatara almost overtaking the representation of Vishnu. Secondly, the temples also highlight the connection to the tribal culture through the marriage of Narasimha to Chenchitha. Thirdly, the regional temples are located in symbolically isolated places, indicating Narasimha's association with transitional geographical locations such as hills or forests.

The Narasimha tradition in the Odisha region on the east coast of India is represented as part of the Vaishnava tradition, especially as part of the Vaishnava trinity, the Jagannatha triad. Here, Narasimha is also represented along with Shiva and the goddesses widely indicating the entrenched theological characteristic of Narasimha, which affiliates him with Shiva and Shakti simultaneously alongside Vishnu.

Temple traditions and rituals are firmly rooted in the Vaishnava tradition, although some exceptions can be noticed.

This chapter is divided into two sections for the convenience of examining the information from the states of Andhra Pradesh and Odisha. The first section examines the sacred centers, regional tales, and practices from Andhra Pradesh, while the second section examines the sacred centers, regional tales, and practices associated with Narasimha in the state of Odisha. The first section also examines the mutual relationship of sacred centers in Tamil Nadu with Ahobilam.

Regional Centers of Andhra Pradesh: Tradition and Practice

"*Utthistha Narasardula*," (wake up! Man-lion!)[3] begins the Suprabhatam in Venkateshwara temple, Tirupathi.[4] Narasimhamantra (see Chapter 9) is used in temple rituals in a number of Vaisnava temples.[5] Narasimha is one of the most popular Vaishnava deities of Andhra Pradesh.[6] The god Narasimha is one of the most widely worshipped deities in erstwhile Andhra Pradesh, now divided into two states, Andhra Pradesh and Telangana.

Early historic evidence of worship of Narasimha is noted in Andhra Pradesh datable to the early first millennium BCE (see Chapter 3). Early representations of Narasimha are noted in the Krishna river valley in Andhra Pradesh from Kondamotu and Motadaka. The Panchavira panel found at Kondamotu represents one of the earliest forms of Narasimha with the five Varshni viras, in the form of a seated lion, which is variously dated between the first century CE and the fourth century CE (Khan 1964; Vedagiri 2004; Vasantha 1991; Srinivasan 1979: 39–55). While the Kondamotu panel represents a rustic form of the deity, the Motadaka image represents a sophisticated form of Narasimha seated on a high chair (pitha). It is important to note that almost all of these early representations of Narasimha are located close to one of the important centers of Narasimha temples in Andhra Pradesh, Mangalagiri, symbolizing the early origin of this temple. The Narasimha temple in Managalagiri is unique in preserving early origins symbolically, while the temple is a unique cave formation of the hill, which indicates an early tribal origin. One side of the hill is worshipped as the svayambhu (self-emergent) form of Narasimha, while the temple rituals including the adornment of the central deity Narasimha with a garland of Salagramas, the aniconic representation of Vishnu might represent the early historical origin of this temple.

Mangalagiri

The central deity of Mangalagiri temple is known as Panakala Narasimha Swamy, for the favorite offering of this temple is Panakalu (brown-sugar (gud/bellam) water). The local story of Mangalagiri is known as *Totachala Mahatmyam* composed in Telugu by Sanjeevi Kavi based on the original story narrated in the Bhavanishakaragita. Mangalagiri is one of the Panchanrisimha kshetras in Andhra Pradesh along with Vedadri, Mattapalli, Vadapally, and Vethapuram, which were said to form a yoga circle representing Tantra (Vedagiri 2004: 165–95). The hill temple is in a cave on the hill marked by silver kavacham, and a second temple is at the base of the hill, which was renovated by the Vijayanagara emperors. Lord Narasimha is midway on the hill as swayambhu (self-manifested); a shape of a mouth, eyes, and nose are carved on the back wall of the hill. The preparation of Panakalu is poured directly into the mouth of the Narasimha icon, which emits the drinking sound and only half the amount of the offering is accepted as it is being poured into the mouth of the deity here. Despite the large amount of Panakalu in the temple, it is interesting to note that there are no flies or ants seen here. The connection between the Vedic tale of Namuchi and Narasimha is clearly expressed here. The Sthalapurana says that Narasimha killed Namuchi in Krita Yuga and installed himself on this hill (Ramesan: 97). Sri Chaitanya is noted to have visited this temple, which is memorialized by a verse and an imprint of a pair of feet. A week-long Tirunallu (festival) is held during the Narasimhajayanti in the month of April or May each year. The Tirunallu is celebrated by performances of theater and folk singing. The festival also hosts a trade and herbal exhibit of Ayurvedic products. Another week-long celebration is held during spring in February or March of each year known as the Brahmotsavalu, which celebrates the appearance of Narasimha here.

The symbolism of the middle and transitions is also noted in the hill, which is considered as Narasimha.

Penchalakona

The Sthalapurana (local story) of Penchalakona (near Nellore) is particularly indicative of how closely the natural geographical forms represent this geographical affinity of Narasimha through connecting it with the appearance of Narasimha. The temple is located on a hill identified with Narasimha (https://penchalakona.co.in/history/). The hill is made up of two hillocks, which almost appear to intertwine, seemingly representing Narasimha and Chenchulakshmi. The appearance of the hill is interpreted to resemble the lion. One of the hills hosts the temple of Narasimha, while the other hosts the temple of his wife Chenchulakshmi.

The local story states that one day a cowherd was grazing his cows near the hill when he saw an elderly man, who informed him that the hill hosted the god Narasimha in the form of a rock. The elderly man also instructed the cowherd to inform the others in the village. As the cowherd was leaving to inform the villagers, he noticed that the elderly man disappeared into the hill. He went and informed the villagers who later had a similar vision in their dreams in the night. The hill was therefore identified with Narasimha and a temple was built near the hill. Nearby flows the river Kandaleru, and a waterfall also called Penchalakona is here. The symbolic representation of the lord Narasimha as the hill of Penchalakona is clearly noted in this local tale. The hill located at the edge of the village near the river and waterfall represents a transitional zone, which does not form a zone of habitation or a river basin, but something in between these two distinct landforms.

Simhachalam

The Simhachalam temple is also located on the hills on the shores of the Indian Ocean on the east coast, commonly referred to as the Coromandel Coast. The temple is located on a part of the hill which is a natural formation which appears as an amphitheater (Ramesan 137).

The temple story indicates that the temple was built as a memorial for an event in the life of the devotee Prahlada. Hiranyakasipu ordered his guards to kill his son, Prahlada, by throwing him from the hill (Vishupurana 1.18.1–46). The guards threw him off a cliff, which happened to be the Simhachalam hills. As he fell to the ground, the goddess of Earth, Bhudevi, caught the falling Prahlada in her lap, hence preventing Prahlada from getting any injuries. So the temple of Narasimha at Simhachalam connects devotees to Prahlada in the primal tradition of devotion. Hence, this place holds significance in the incarnation of Narasimha as well as the demonstration of the Bhakti of Prahlada. Hence, as soon as Prahlada ascended to the throne, he built an impressive temple for Narasimha on this hill, Simhachalam. However, this temple does not just venerate Narasimha, but a combined form of Varaha and Narasimha referred to as Varaha-Narasimha (Sriramachandracharya 1991).

The combined form of Varaha and Narasimha is another unique icon of Narasimha in India. In other instances, Varaha and Narasimha are depicted together separately, mostly side by side. Important examples of such side-by-side depictions of Narasimha and Varaha are noted in cave temples such as Udayagiri, Badami, and Ellora.

However, the Shtalapurana of Simhachalam says that the temple built by Prahlada during the last part of the Krita Yuga fell into disuse and was lost in growing weeds and creepers on the hill. During the Treta Yuga the temple was rediscovered by Pururavas and Urvashi while traveling in the area. Shocked at the desolate condition of the temple they decided to revive the temple by renovating it and bringing it back into popular practice (Vemsani 2009: 35–52). Pururavas found the image of Narasimha hidden in an anthill as directed by Lord Narasimha. He cleared the anthill but was not able to remove the anthill from the foot of the image of Lord Narasimha. According to the Mastyapurana, Prahlada was informed by a celestial voice (akashavani) that the feet of the deity cannot be seen by anyone. The divine voice had also indicated that the icon of the Lord Narasimha cannot be seen except for one day of the year on which the image was discovered and cleared by Prahlada, seen in general and hence he covered the image in thick layers of sandal paste, similar to the number of clay layers he removed. The akashavani also informed him that the true form (nija swarupa) of the deity could only be seen on only one day of the year. Hence, the sandal paste is removed on only one day of the year. This is celebrated as a major festival of the temple called Chandanayatra, celebrated on Akshayatritiya day on the third day of Shukla paksha (bright half) of Vaishaka month, which normally occurs in May. The appearance of Narasimha as a joint form of Varaha and Narasimha as well as the image being covered in sandal paste throughout the year, which makes the image appear as Shiva, also indicates the transitional qualities associated with Narasimha. Narasimha's transitional quality is not separation, but unity. By representing three forms Narasimha, Varaha, and Shiva, united in one, the true transitional nature of Narasimha is clear here.

Simhachalam temple of Narasimha signifies the transitional middle associated with Narasimha in a geographical context. The hill of Simhachalam is located in a geographically unique location on the east coast of India distinctly separating the plains from the coast. Hence, the Simhachalam hills with their elevation stand out as a transitional zone from the surroundings, that differs from each other, on the one side of the hill is the coast and Indian Ocean, and on the other side is the fertile land and habitations.

Ahobilam Temples

The origin of the Ahobilam temples is lost as the monuments were destroyed successively during the early second millennium. Ahobilam is the central temple of Narasimha in India. The legend of Narasimha records the appearance of Narasimha in the hills of Ahobilam, and popular tales depict Narasimha as one among the Chenchus of the area. Numerous early studies have examined historical data recorded in inscriptions and literature (Vasantha 1991; Debicka-Borek 2016, 2019; Pidatala 1982; Madabhushini 1989a: Ramesan 1962: 24–32; Adluri 2019: 168–80). Although some inscriptional pillars have been rescued and are housed in the temple complex currently, there is no guarantee that these were the only inscriptions at that site, since many inscriptions might have been lost beyond recovery. However, scholars have been inclined to date the early structures of Ahobila to 300 CE, similar to the early sculptures and monuments recovered elsewhere in Andhra Pradesh (see Chapter 3 for historical information). The Sthalapurana of the temple, Ahobila Mahatmyam, said to have been derived from Brahmanda Purana, described the narratives and practices of the temple in ten chapters. The Ahobila Mahatyam brings together the classical stories of the Vaishnava and Shaiva Puranas, but still avoids the local stories, especially the marriage of Chenchulakshmi and Narasimha. The story of Narasimha and Chenchulakshmi is depicted on the temple sculptures of Prahlada Varada Narasimha temple in Lower Ahobilam and Ahobila Narasimha Swamy temple at Upper Ahobilam.

Ahobilam temple preserved the earliest remnants of practice associated with Narasimha even though the monuments may have been destroyed due to Muslim invasions and occupations. Who can decide if the popular legends and practice came first or the classical legends came first? Or is it that the earliest form of religious practice survived in fragments in different forms including oral and literary sources? It seems that the fragments of Narasimha legend preserved in different sources might refer to different aspects of life rather than different deities. The previous scholarship had separated the classical Narasimha from the folk Narasimha who married Chenchulakshmi and lived in the forests since references to Chenchulakshmi are lacking in the classical texts. As so frequently happens in Hindu classical texts, which are encyclopedic in nature, numerous elements of the sacred story of a deity are not recollected. For example, the story of Radha is not recollected in the classical Puranas in connection with Krishna, but Radha is central to the devotional tradition of Mathura. Similarly, Chenchulakshmi is not referred to in the classical texts, however, the classical texts mention the refusal of Narasimha to leave for his heavenly abode, choosing to live in the forests of Andhra Pradesh. Brahmanda Purana on which the regional stories mention that they were based does not mention the withdrawal of the Narasimha form (Brahmanda Purana II.5–29). Similarly, Brahmapurana also does not include the withdrawal of the Narasimha form and the return of Narasimha to the abode of Vishnu (Brahma Purana 213.44– 79). Shaiva Puranas and Sthalapuranas provide additional information on the earthly sojourn of Narasimha following the vanquishing of Hiranayakashipu. This abrupt end to the legend of Narasimha in the classical texts forms the basis for the regional stories connected with Narasimha in Andhra Pradesh. During his stay and wanderings in the forests and hills of Telugu states, Telangana and Andhra Pradesh, Narasimha meditates as well as meeting other sages, while also meeting the beautiful maiden Chenchulakshmi, finally marrying her. It seems that the regional legends of Narasimha are as old as the early monumental evidence of the Telugu states (100 CE), if not older. Therefore, according to the temples and the accounts preserved in connection with numerous temples in Telugu states, this region is the land of sacred wanderings of Narasimha, his *leelasthali*, chosen place of life, after he killed Hiranyakashipu. Similar to the Gopis and Gopas of Mathura, the Chenchus of the Nallamala forests became his friends and family, becoming part of his divine play (*leela*).

The first chapter is dedicated to outlining the kshetra mahatyam of Ahobilam,[7] highlighting its importance in the pilgrimage circuit. The second chapter presents information on the penance of Garuda for the special darshan of Lord Vishnu and relates the story of Garudachala in Ahobilam. The third chapter narrates the stories of the tirthas on the lakes and ponds in Ahobilam. The fourth chapter discusses the details of the nine temples (nana Narasimha) of Ahobilam. This chapter also discusses the penances of Bharadwaja, Gobhila, and Bhargava Rama. The fifth chapter relates the story of Jaya and Vijaya, their curse to be born as demons Hiranyaksha and Hiranyakashipu. The sixth chapter recollects the story of the birth of Prahlada, and his bhakti, which was opposed by his father and other demons. The seventh chapter continues with the Bhakti of Prahlada, the appearance of Narasimha, and killing Hiranyakashipu. The eighth chapter discusses the Sarabhavatara of Shiva and the defeat of Sarabha by Narasimha. The ninth chapter discusses the narrative of Bhairava as the Kshetrapala of the Bhavanasini river.

The early textual evidence of the most important sacred center of Ahobilam is noted in Errana's Narasimhapuranamu. The earliest Telugu *Narasimhapurāṇamu*, dated to about 1350 CE, was composed by Errapragada Erranna, popularly referred to as Errana, one of the three celebrated poets known as the *kavitrayamu* (poet trinity) of Telugu literature. He was born to Errapragada Surana and Potamma in the village of Gudluru in Prakasam district of Andhra Pradesh. Errana was associated with the court of King Prolaya Vemareddy of Reddy kingdom, to whom he dedicated his Telugu *Narasimhapurāṇamu* and his composition of the remainder of the fourth khanda of the Mahābhāratamu. Although considered translations from original Sanskrit texts, Erranna's compositions utilize Telugu regional tales, anecdotes, and native aphorisms, making his compositions reflect Telugu culture and literature.

Therefore, the Telugu *Narasimhapurāṇamu* of Errana is not a direct translation of the Sanskrit narrative of the incarnation of Narasimha, but a free composition utilizing the well-known regional tales of Narasimha popular in the Telugu region before the tenth century. Therefore, even though the Telugu *Narasimhapurāṇamu* follows the basic elements of the narrative of the Narasimha incarnation noted in the *Vishnupurāṇa* and the *Bhāgavatapurāṇa* (see Chapter 2), it also differs in numerous details, connecting Narasimha firmly to sacred centers in Telugu states of India. Errana explicitly stated the purpose of his undertaking the composition of Telugu *Narasimhapurāṇamu* in the preface. Errana noted that his grandfather Erapota Suri appeared in a dream vision in which he urged Errana to compose the account of "lord of Ahobala, Narasimha incarnation" (*Narasimhapurāṇamu* Preface. Verse 21). This regional tradition is further corroborated in chapter four of the Telugu *Narasimhapurāṇamu* (*Narasimhapurāṇamu* Chapter IV. Verse 121). Here, the god Narasimha voiced his decision to choose the Garudadri hill in Ahobilam as one of the places of his eternal residence. Hence, the Telugu *Narasimhapurāṇamu* places the incarnation of Narasimha firmly in Andhra Pradesh, as his chosen abode, thus connecting Narasimha intricately with Telugu land, as his chosen region.

Classical texts depict the Hindu deity Narasimha in his cosmogonic role as neither here nor there, which in practice is transformed as the transitional middle, represented in the classical tale of Narasimha. The states of Telangana and Andhra Pradesh, located in the middle land between the northern region (*Uttarapatha*) and the southern region (*Dakshinapatha*), are central to the religious traditions and practices based on Narasimha. The state of Telangana is located in the middle of India and is closely aligned with the deity Narasimha depicted as the lord of the middle in the classical Hindu texts. Although Narasimha is the central deity of Telangana (with a population of approximately 40,000,000) as well as one of the most popular deities in Andhra Pradesh (with a population of approximately 50,000,000), little research had been undertaken on this subject. The primary sources, Telugu *Narasimhapurāṇamu* and a number of *Sthalapurāṇas* connected with Narasimha, preserve unique aspects of the religious history, thought, and culture of Telangana and Andhra Pradesh. It is to translate important text such as Telugu *Narasimhapurāṇamu* into English with short, critical, and editorial notes, In addition, further research into inscriptional and monumental sources as well as regional practices must be conducted to supplement existing knowledge on the history, thought, and culture of Telangana and Andhra Pradesh states. Preliminary survey is attempted here in the following pages, but another study focused on this temple complex is necessary.

The *Narasimhapuranamu* text has five chapters of about 4,000 lines including poetical verses and prose. The central part of the story of the incarnation of Narasimha appearing in the palace of Hiranyakashipu, vanquishing him, is described in the fourth chapter of the book in Errana's impeccable literary style. This text preserves the most central aspect of Narasimha's connection to Andhra Pradesh depicting Ahobilam as the sacred center of the origin of Narasimha as well as the sacred center (Shaktipeetha) of Narasimha. Ahobilam is also depicted as the center of the larger *leelasthali* of Narasimha spread across the Middle India.

> Thus, spoke Prahlada in sweet, gracious, and joy-inducing words. Then the great sages and gods too, elated, delighting in the great affection of that supremely peaceful universal soul (paramātma), praised and congratulated the God.
>
> The Lord of the world, then, smiled at everyone assembled, and said,
>
> "This great place, so very auspicious, draws me to stay. Here, my heart is filled with loving joy. From now on I would reside on this great hill."
>
> You have praised my strength and called me by the title Ahobalam. Therefore, this sacred ford shall henceforth become auspicious in the three worlds by the name Ahobalam."
>
> This hill too, mounted by me, shall attain fame with the name Garudādri."[8]
>
> Thus spoke the Lord to those assembled in front.[9]
>
> (Errana. *Narasimhapurāṇamu* Chapter IV. Prose verse (*vacanam*). 122)

Ahobilam recalls the imagery of the middle through the location of the temple and marriage to Chenchulakshmi (see Chapter 5), and due to its location on the pilgrim circuit connecting the most popular Vaishnava sacred center (Tirupati) and Shaiva center (Srisailam).

Examination of the most important sacred centers of Narasimha in Andhra Pradesh, Mangalagiri, Ahobilam, Simhachalam, and Penchalakona brought forward the most important features associated with Narasimha. These four temples are located on hills signifying the symbolic nature of Narasimha located in a distinct geographical formation that does stand out from its surroundings, while also remaining transitional, but with no barrier. The temples at Ahobilam and Simhachalam are associated with the appearance of Narasimha and saving Prahlada indicating the special connection of Narasimha to Andhra Pradesh as the sacred zone of the appearance as well as Narasimha's earthly sojourn for the period until his return to his heavenly abode. Hence, this region acquires the significance of being the *leelasthali* of the avatara of Narasimha, not merely a center of his worship. The temples of Mangalagiri signify the early origin of Narasimha temples in this region supported by associated evidence found at Kondamotu and Motadaka (see Chapter 3). The Mangalagiri temple preserves the early origin of this temple by incorporating Salagrama into the worship of Narasimha. Penchalakona represents another form of the symbolic representation of Narasimha in this region, by appearing conspicuously in hills, a geographical formation, which are symbolically represented as Narasimha.

The Narasimha temple at Ahobilam is also known as the *Navanarasimha kshetram*, since Narasimha appears here in nine unique forms (swarupa/rupa).

Bhargava Narasimha Swamy

This is the first temple of Narasimha as one reaches Ahobilam known as Lower Ahobilam. It is situated about 2 kilometers from the town on a small hill near a pond known as Bhargava Tirtham. The temple legend is connected to Parashurama, another fierce incarnation of Vishnu. It is said that Bhargava Rama (Parashurama) performed penance here, hence the pond and temple are known by his name. Another meaning of Bhargava is Sun. As the first temple of the nine Narasimha temples, it might be called the Bhargava Narasimha temple also. Kevala Narasimha is the presiding deity established in the sanctum of the temple, and another form of Narasimha, the Varaha-Narasimha, is depicted on a pillar in the mandapa.

Yogananda Narasimha Swamy

This is the next temple in Lower Ahobilam located about 3 kilometers from the town. Yogananda Narasimha temple marks the spot where the deity Narasimha taught Prahlada yoga. Yoga is an important aspect of Narasimha. Yogananda Narasimha temples are commonly found across Andhra Pradesh and Karnataka. Narasimha is worshipped here seated in a yoga posture known as Yogananda Narasimha.

Chatravata Narasimha Swamy

This temple is also located about 3 kilometers from the town of Lower Ahobilam. The temple is located under a peepal tree forming a shade as the umbrella over the sanctum of the temple, and the form of the deity is known as Chatravata Narasimha. The deity is worshipped in a graceful form (Abhaya Mudra) in the seated posture. The deity's right hand is raised in Abhaya Mudra, while his left hand rests on his thigh. The raised hands hold the signature attributes of Vishnu Shankha and Chakra.

Ahobila Narasimha Swamy

This temple is located 8 kilometers away from the town of Upper Ahobilam. The Narasimha here is in ugra form (fierce) connected with the killing of Narasimha. The image of Narasimha is considered swaymbhu (self-emanatory).

Krodakara/Varaha-Narasimha Swamy

This temple is located about a kilometer away from the Ahobila Narasimha Swamy temple. The presiding deity is Krodha/Varaha-Narasimha, with the face of Varaha. Combined forms of Varaha-Narasimha are less frequent but found at some temples in the states of Andhra Pradesh and Karnataka.

Karanja Narasimha Swamy

This temple is located in Upper Ahobilam a little further on the way toward Lower Ahobilam. Here the temple is located under a Karanja tree, hence the temple is known as the Karanja Narasimha temple. Karanja is an important Indian herbal plant, which is used widely in Ayurveda.

The form of Narasimha combines the attributes of the incarnation of Rama, as the image of Narasimha is seen holding a bow in one hand. The presiding deity here is also known as Saranga Narasimha as he holds the bow, Saranga, commonly associated with Rama. Hanuman, the faithful devotee of Rama, is also seen standing in Anjali mudra in front of Narasimha. The temple faces the river Bhavanasini with the mountain Garudadri behind it.

There is a Mandapam with ornate pillars, which is partially ruined, which shows that the original temples might have been destroyed.

Malola/Lakshmi Narasimha Swamy

This temple is located 2 kilometers away from the central temple in Upper Ahobilam. Legend narrates that the deity appeared in the dream vision of Srimat Adivan Sathakopa Jeer, the first jeer of the temple. The deity Narasimha is seen in saumya form with the goddess Lakshmi.

Jwala Narasimha Swamy

According to the legends of Ahobilam, this is the exact spot where Narasimha killed the demon Hiranyakashipu. Hence, the central sanctum hosts the fierce Narasimha known as Jwala Narasimha. Narasimha is depicted here with eight arms as killing Hiranyakashipu. Numerous other images depicting the events of the Narasimha Purana connected with the appearance of Narasimha are also depicted here, such as Narasimha appearing from the pillar while Prahlada and Hiranyakashipu are standing on either side of the pillar. There is a small pond near the temple called Rakta Kunda. The pond appears a bit reddish since it is said that Narasimha washed his hands here after killing the demon.

Pavana Narasimha Swamy

This temple is known as Pavana Narasimha temple as it is near the stream Pavana. This is said to be the exact place where Narasimha saw Chenchulakshmi. This temple marks the loving relationship of Narasimha and Chenchulakshmi, a central aspect of the legend of Narasimha, which connects him to the land, life, and culture of the region.

There are also other spots marking the Ugra Sthambham and Prahlada Mettu. The cleft in the mountain is called the Ugra Sthambham, identified as the spot where Narasimha emerged. Prahlada Mettu is the temple of Prahlada, inside a small cave.

The Sthalapurana notes that it is derived from Brahmanda Purana. The Sthalapurana contains ten chapters that describe the appearance of Narasimha and sacred details of the ponds and sacred places in Ahobilam. Ahobilam was also subjected to raids and destruction by the armies of Golkonda in 1579. These raids brought numerous jewels, images, and manuscripts back to Golkonda (Eaton 1995: 59–81). Some of the manuscripts including a manuscript of Narasimha Purana are held at the library of Osmania University.

Narasimha Tradition in Tamil Nadu

The Narasimha tradition and its practices also spread to Tamil Nadu, which recalls their connection with Ahobilam, the central temple of Narasimha. Ghatikachalam (Sholingur) is one of the most important centers of the Narasimha tradition in Tamil Nadu in addition to Kanchi and Tanjore. The Ghatikachala Mahatmyamu was composed by Tenali Ramalinga Kavi, one of the well-known poets of the Vijayanagara empire.[10] The Kanchi Mahatmyam narrates the story which connects Ahobilam, Kanchi, and Ghatikachalam (Debicka-Boreck 2019: 159–64). The arrival of Bhagavata Melam artists at Melattur is well recorded (Guy 2016). Numerous Narasimha temples in Tamil Nadu form part of the pilgrimage circuit of Narasimha. Narasimha temples at Sri Rangam, Kanchi, and Sholingur represent important places in this sacred geography. Narasimha, while also located at Ahobilam, splits himself into two forms to protect sacred places in Tamil Nadu including Kanchi and Ghatikachalam.

Narasimha Tradition in Odisha

About 105 historical temples of Narasimha were noted in Odisha (Eschmann 103; n11), which were recorded in inscriptions with endowments datable from the fourth century CE onwards following the Gupta period in Odisha. There might have been many more temples as well as popular temples located in a temple complex with other major deities such as Jagannatha, which might not have been represented in inscriptional or literary records, but only in oral tales and popular practice. Hence, Narasimha also breaches this divide between classical temples and popular tradition by spreading equally among the traditional temples and non-traditional popular practice. However, the number of temples increased from the eighth century onwards. Narasimha is represented in three aspects in Odishan temples: (1) Vaishnava temples of Narasimha, Vishnu, and Jagannatha, (2) Shiva and Shakta temples, (3) aniconic popular temples and practice.

Narasimha is depicted as the lion or a standing lion (Kondamotu panel), the form of which was considered to be similar to the composite Bidala Narasimha depicted at Nrusimhanatha temple in Padampur, even though the facial depiction differs, which currently symbolizes the central concepts associated with

Narasimha. Hence, the Bidala-Narasimha image can be considered to indicate the early origin of the other more elaborate stylized sculptures found in this temple. Another composite feature noted in the eastern region of Middle India is the close association of two avataras of Vishnu, with Varaha and Narasimha. One of the most popular temples of Andhra Pradesh, Simhachalam, preserves the combined form of two deities, Varaha and Narasimha, known as Varaha-Narasimha as the central deity of the temple. Varaha and Narasimha incarnations appear in close succession to vanquish the demon brothers Hiranyaksha and Hiranyakashipu successively in that order. A combined Varaha and Narasimha form might indicate the combined powers and efficacy represented by the two incarnations of Vishnu.

Images of Mahavishnu (Vishwarupa) containing three faces of which the central face represents Vishnu, while the right and left faces represent Varaha and Narasimha, are noted across India (Gail 1984: 297–307). The three-faced images represent the avatara concept while the four-faced images represent the vyuha concept, even though the three-faced images may sometimes include a fourth face on the back.

Odisha also depicts Narasimha in close affinity with Matrikas (goddesses). Simhika (lion-faced) and varahi (Boar-faced) goddesses form part of the seven mother goddesses depicted as a group (Meister 1986: 97–112; Donaldson 1995: 155–83). Narasimha is also worshipped while the temple also hosts Varaha and Trivikrama as ancillary deities at Narasimhanath temple at Nuasasan (Mohapatra 2016: 96–9). The original temple here was built by Langala Narasimha of the Ganga dynasty, and was destroyed by the Muslim invader Kalapahada, and another temple was built in the seventeenth century (Mohapatra 2016: 96).

Narasimha and the Jagannatha Triad

The Jagannatha legend associated with the Jagannatha temple at Puri included in the Skanda and Narada Puranas presents the worship of the deities by Sabaras (Savaras) in the beginning (Tripathi 1987: 83–93). Sudarshana Chakra is identified as Narasimha following the Ahibudhnya Samhita (87). The male pillar here is identified as Narasimha, while the female pillar is identified as Sthambheswari/Skambheswari (89). The Narasimha mantra is used during the worship at the Navakalevara ritual. Balabhadra (Balarama) is also identified with Narasimha. Balabhadra worship forms the crucial part of the Jagannatha triad at Puri as established through early studies (Sircar 1982). This demonstrates the deeper understanding of the theological nature of Narasimha and his incorporation into the worship and ritual practices of the temple; even though the temple is dedicated to another form of Vishnu (Vasudeva, Baladeva, and Subhadra), worship and incorporation of Narasimha demonstrate the entrenched nature of Narasimha in this region.

An important early temple of Shiva near Baramba represents Shiva as Narasimha. This temple has been dated between 750 CE and the late eighth century CE. Similar representations are also noted in Narasimhanatha temple in Padampur and Samalai temple in Baragar in Sambalpur district. In these temples, Shiva is worshipped as Narasimha or incorporating Narasimha. In the Simhanatha/Narasimhanatha temple at Padampur, the iconic representation resembles Narasimha, while the presence of a trident, the symbol of Shiva, indicates the god worshipped as Shiva.

The Nrusimhanatha temple at Padampur might be much older than the eighth-century inscription attested here. A recent renovation (1983–4) at the temple brought out some old pillars, which were recovered and fitted to the pillars of the mandapa (Behera 2015: 116), which indicate that the original temple might have been built during the 800 CE under the Panduvamsi dynasty, most probably during the period of King Mahasivagupta Balarjuna of Sirpur as his mother was a devotee of Narasimha. However, the popular tales indicate that the sacred center might have been older than any of the structural temples in existence here. In addition to the popular tale of the appearance of Narasimha as Bidala (cat), popular tales also connect this sacred center to the Ramayana and the Mahabharata. The tale of the *Nrusimha Mahatmya* (Mahalik 1984: 20–5; 485–6) narrates that a sage Udanga was residing on the banks of Godawari with his daughter, Malati. A demon Ravan took a liking to Malati and proposed to her. Unable to consent to marry his daughter to the demon, the sage was disappointed, but soon after that, her father went missing. Malati started weeping and searching in the forest. She was approached by a mushika (rat) who promised to help her search for her father if she agreed to consummate with her. She trusted the rat and consented to the relationship as she was in deep sorrow at losing her father. Soon after she gave birth to Mushikaditya, a demon, who ate her soon after his birth and began tormenting the beings and the divine in the area. Then the gods prayed to Rama to help them, and he took the form of Nrusimha to kill him. But the demon assumed his original form of a rat and hid in the Gandhagiri hill. Nrusimha took the form of a cat to chase the demon Mushikasura and kill him. While Nrusimha was waiting hidden in the bushes he was accidentally hurt by a Khond woman searching for roots. As she ran away and informed her family they launched a search. However, Nrusimha appeared to inform them of the purpose of his appearance there and instructed the Khonds to worship him who has appeared and decided to stay on Gandhagiri hill. There is another version of the story that mentions that Nrusimha remained there waiting for the demon Mushikasura who never came out of the Gandhagiri. The Khond couple named Yamuna and Hari also had a vision of the deity Marjala-Kesari (cat-lion) form of Nrusimha. This is the form established in the temple of Nrusimhanatha as Yamuna and Hari began worshipping Bidala Narasimha here. Descendants of Yamuna and Hari continue to play important roles in temple worship. The symbolism of composite form as Bidala Nrusimha and connection with the tribe of Khonds and his appearance in the Gandhagiri hill indicate the symbolism of the middle noted in the classical accounts of Narasimha. One of the important festivals celebrated here is the Nrusimha Chaturdasi. This festival is celebrated for five days, from the eleventh day of the Baishakh to the full moon day (Purnima). This festival is also called Baishakh mela. Along with special celebrations at the temple, the arrival of the sages and saints of various maths (monasteries), the festival also includes the celebration of arts and sciences. An herbal exhibit (Ayurved mela) is held which showcases the many herbs native to the Gandhagiri hill. Legend has it that the Gandhagiri hill was a piece of the Sanjivani hill, which was carried by Hanuman for reviving the life of Lakshmana earlier. One of the ponds here is also named Sitakund. A natural fountain and pond here are named Bhimdhar, which were created by Bhima by hitting the ground with his mace (Gada). Another special feature of the Nrusimhanath temple and the Nrusimha Chaturdashi celebrations is the close affinity displayed with Shiva, located on the opposite side of the hill, located in the temple of Harishankar Dham. Both temples are connected through hilly terrain, and devotees visit both temples during the Bhaishakhmela celebrations. This also indicates the Shaiva and Vaishnava affiliation of Narasimha noted in the classical texts (see Chapter 2).

The association of Narasimha with hills is indicative of his symbolic affiliation with the middle, as hills are isolated, frequently located at a certain distance from habitations as well as deeper forests. However, Narasimha's affiliation with hills has been misinterpreted as evidence of a "Girija," "hill born" aspect of his origin (Eschmann 106) while examining the Narasimha temples in Odisha. However, Narasimha is not hill born; none of the classical tales of Narasimha mention his appearance from the hill, while noting the appearance of Narasimha in the palace of Hiranyakashipu, while Bhagavatapurana (VII) unequivocally notes the appearance of Narasimha from the pillar. Therefore, the basic conceptual theory of "Girija" (hill born) denoting a hill born origin of Narasimha does not find textual support and hence this theory remains unsupported by evidence. Hills/hilly regions are indicative of the symbolic nature of Narasimha representative of the middle (transitional middle), which stands to separate distinct yet connected landforms, the forests, and the habitations.

Narasimhanatha temple in Padampur (Sambalpur) hosts a svayambhu (self-born/revealed) stone face worshipped as Narasimha. It was probably an ancient temple protected and maintained by the Khond tribes of the region. However, on the rock surface is applied a silver iconographic representation of the deity Narasimha, which was interpreted by some scholars to represent a cat face due to vague representation, which depicts the wide face of a lion with thin strokes, which might be interpreted to resemble whiskers and hence a cat. This composite depiction had been interpreted to support the theory of the "Girija" form of Narasimha (Eschmann 107). Composite forms of representation of Narasimha are not uncommon in the eastern region of Middle India as noted here in Simhachalam temple, which is home to the composite form of Varaha-Narasimha. Such composite representations might indicate the fluidity and flexibility of Narasimha avatara, which is also representative of the middle/transitional aspect of Narasimha.

Odishan oral tales preserve stories of the appearance of Narasimha as the cat to Khond social groups. The Khond family priests of the temple narrated the story of Narasimha's appearance (Eschmann 107). It is said that Narasimha intended to kill a demon who haunted the hills and assumed the form of a cat and hid under the cover of plants. A Khond woman digging for roots accidentally hurt the cat and ran away out of fear. However, learning about the incident, male members of her family came looking for the cat and began performing an exorcism considering the cat to be an evil spirit. However, the Bhagavan appeared to them and informed them that he was not a bhut or evil spirit, but Bhagavan, who appeared to the lady due to her bhakti. He informed them he should henceforth be worshipped on the hills in this revealed form of the cat. Therefore, the image depicts a combined form of lion and cat, with cat whiskers sketched on the silver iconic form of the lord represented in the Narasimha temple in Padampur.

Eschmann considers this temple story as well as the fact that the temple is served by the Khond family, who call themselves Aranyaka brahmins (forest brahmins), as evidence for the hilly or forest origin (Girija) of Narasimha (Eschmann 107–8). But the appearance of Narasimha from the hills or being worshipped by tribes is not uncommon for Narasimha. Narasimha is represented in composite form and as a hill surface in numerous temples in Andhra Pradesh. The association of Narasimha with hills as well as tribal populations represents the transitional middle, the most important symbolic feature of Narasimha, which connects the habitations with the forests by being in the middle.

However, this temple story only indicates a variation within the bhakti traditions associated with Narasimha. Similar tales of the appearance of Narasimha are also noted elsewhere in stories as well as iconic representations (see Chapter 2). Citing the evidence of the Bhumija tribe's worship of Narasimha, Eschmann tries to emphasize her theory that Narasimha might have tribal origins later assimilated into Hinduism (108). Without clear evidence, she continues to identify the depiction of Narasimha in the Kondamotu panel as "Girija" form representative of this early forest (tribal) origin of Narasimha. She also cited the worship of Narasimha in svayambhu form at Mangalagiri, which is also called the Salagrama Narasimha, in support of this theory of the forest origin of the deity. However, the worship of Narasimha in these temples represents the symbolism of the middle, indicating the transitional nature of Narasimha, which had been known from classical texts noted from 300 BCE. However, she notes the futility of theory, remarking that "the idea to worship Narasimha in an uniconical form seems so common that it is done even where there does not seem to be an apparent necessity in terms of a tribal cult to be Hinduised" (Eschmann 109), as she noted the worship of Salagrama Narasimha as Salagrama stone beside the bronze icons of the deity at Narasimhanatha matha in Aska. Here, theriomorphic and aniconic representations of Narasimha are worshipped simultaneously beside each other. Both these traditions of worshipping the hill face with silver iconic representation and Salagrama Narasimha are noticed in Mangalagiri, another important early Narasimha temple in Andhra Pradesh, which does not show any tribal affiliation, but Vedic affiliation (Vemsani 2009). Differentiation between tribal and Vedanta religions is non-existent as seen here in the simultaneous representation of Narasimha in iconic and aniconic forms of the deity. Other than the difference in practice, the conceptual understanding of Narasimha as representing the transitional middle is overarching.

Narasimha in Jagannatha Tradition

Narasimha plays a central role in the temple of Jagannatha at Puri as well as the larger Jagannatha tradition in Odisha (see Chapter 3). Odisha preserves one of the important Narasimha traditions along with tribal affiliation. The Jagannatha temple at Puri is dedicated to Jagannatha, Subhadra, and Balabhadra. However, the Narasimha tradition is intertwined with the worship of Jagannatha in numerous ways. During the Navakalevara ritual, Narasimha is worshipped in each stage of the ritual in his divine form as well as his symbolic form as a lion. I discuss the rituals of Narasimha as a deity and Simha (lion) next.[11]

The *navakalevara* ritual performed as part of the consecration of new images every twelve years involves *vanayaga* (forest rituals), a series of oblations, involving mantras. Once the tree is selected sacred ash as well clarified butter and water are sprinkled on it to begin the consecration. The process involves the dedication of the first nine oblations to the Vedic gods and accompanied by Vedic mantras, while most of the subsequent oblations are dedicated to Narasimha and accompanied by the Narasimha mantra except for the last few which address the deities of Jagannatha temple, Jagannatha, Balabhadra, and Subhadra. Thus, the most important part of the Vanayaga involves worship of Narasimha including the *acarya* meditating on Lakshmi-Narasimha reciting the Patala-Narasimha mantra while making offerings to the sacred fire following which the ritual of a thousand oblations is offered to the Simha (lion) accompanied by the *Anushthubha* Narasimha mantra.

During the Pratishta phase of the Navakalevara ritual, a log is carried to the prathishthamandapa. Here, the log is worshipped by the *acarya* through worship of Narasimha and identifying the log with Simha (lion). After the pratishtha ceremony, worship of the deities of *Chakrabjamandala* is performed followed by placing the four parts of the Anushthubha mantraraja on different parts of the log. It is only following this ritual of placing the mantraraja that the nyasas of the Puri divinities are performed.

The next ritual of *Navakalevara*, the fire sacrifice, also includes worship of Narasimha. In this phase, Narasimha is worshipped with the *Anushthubh* Narasimha mantra for five days and oblations are offered to the Simha (lion).

The association of Narasimha and Jagannatha is close, almost overlapping. The Purushottama Mahatmya (Ch. 38–69) describes the importance of Narasimha following that of Jagannatha. The *Patala-Narasimha* mantra is also described in the context of yogic (Tantric) accomplishments, which bestows a worshipper with superhuman qualities. Numerous Shaktipithas (energy centers) of southern Odisha and Andhra Pradesh (especially in the Krishna and Godawari basins) are dotted with Lakshmi-Narasimha temples, which memorialize these yogic affiliations of Narasimha (Vedagiri 2004: 175–206).

The affiliation of Narasimha with Jagannatha in the Puri temple had been ruled out as purely tribal (Stietencron 1986: 73), which is again based on the assumption that tribal religion might not have been Hindu. However, tribes practiced Hinduism, which included elements of tribal religion based on early historic lifestyles preserved by the tribes. The tribes preserve the practiced aspects of Hinduism, while Vedas preserve the theological and symbolic aspects of this early religion. Narasimha could be understood through a combination of Vedic symbolism and tribal practice.

In addition to the rituals noted here, Jagannatha temple also contains a Narasimha temple within the Jagannatha temple complex, which is contemporaneous with Jagannatha temple, as one of the first inscriptions from the Narasimha temple is dated to 1111 CE, which suggests that the temple might have existed at least 200 years prior to this inscription (Joshi, A. 1990: 2–4; Behera 1991: 168).

Conclusion

This chapter examined the Narasimha traditions in the eastern part of Middle India, the states of Andhra Pradesh and Odisha. While the earliest historical evidence in the form of sculptures is available from Andhra Pradesh, the regional stories also located the appearance of Narasimha at Ahobilam in the Nallamala forests in the Eastern Ghats. Regional tales also inform of the spread of the Narasimha tradition to Tamil Nadu, connected with protection and vanquishing demons.

The most important popular legend of this region is the marriage of Chenchulakshmi and the god Narasimha. Hence, the Nallamala forests surrounding the Ahobilam temple become the home of Narasimha, while the Chenchus, an early vanavasi social group of this area become his family and friends. This region is depicted as the *leelasthali* (land of divine play), the place of origin as well as the life of Narasimha, thus forming one of the central zones of Hindu sacred geography in India.

The most important feature of Narasimha legends from this region is that the temples identified with the life of Narasimha. Sacred space is identified with the places where Narasimha appeared and vanquished his enemies, as well as married and lived. Andhra Pradesh is the *leelasthali*, the region of the divine play, of Narasimha. Thus, Andhra Pradesh forms the most important region for understanding the sacred centers of Narasimha as well as the historical religion of this region.

Examination of temples, literature, and practice showed that the Narasimha tradition in this region is the earliest historical practice in this area datable at least to the beginning of the first millennium CE. Composite forms of Narasimha and the aniconic form of Narasimha, as well as Narasimha temples affiliated temples with Jagannatha (Odisha) and Venkateshwara (Andhra Pradesh) are noticed in addition to Narasimha's close affiliation with Shiva and the Matrikas. The special aspects of Narasimha, of transitions and the middle, are represented not only in the composite form but by identifying the hills and hill surfaces with Narasimha in this region. This is also the region which preserved the historical stories of Narasimha, noting the close affinity of Narasimha with the vanvasis of the region, the Chenchus, and Khonds. Numerous temples of the region are still served by the descendants of the founders of the temples of Narasimha in this region belonging to these tribes. Hence, this chapter successfully outlined the historical religion of the eastern region of Middle India which incorporates the foundations of Narasimha tradition here, through the symbolic elements of the stories, which connect it to the origin of Narasimha. The historicity of Narasimha in this region is also established through historical evidence as well as the popular practices and legends preserved in some of the original inhabitants of the region, the Khonds and Chenchus who continue to practice the prehistoric lifestyle of hunters and gatherers.

7

Narasimha in the Central Region

Madhya Pradesh, Chhattisgarh, and Telangana

This chapter examines the regional stories and practices associated with Narasimha in the central part of Middle India, specifically in the states of Telangana, Madhya Pradesh, and Chhattisgarh. The regional stories of Narasimha in the states of Telangana connect Narasimha with the classical textual stories as well as oral stories. The state of Telangana is in the middle of the middle region noted here and hence naturally represents most of the central features and traditions associated with Narasimha. Central India (Madhya Pradesh and Chhattisgarh) preserves copious amounts of data on prehistoric religion, which continues in practice. The goddess temple at Baghor in Madhya Pradesh is dated to about 9000 BCE (Kenoyer at al. 1983: 88–94). The cave shelters at Bhimbedka in Madhya Pradesh include depictions of lions and hence preserve symbolic religion datable to the Paleolithic era. Similarly, the earliest evidence of the Narasimha tradition is also noticed from excavations near Vidisa in Madhya Pradesh datable to the middle of the first millennium BCE.

Examining the history, regional practices, and temples of Narasimha, this chapter contributes to understanding the emergence of Narasimha as the most popular deity of the state, thus contributing to the evolution of the unique tradition of Telangana. Regional practices associate Narasimha with health and healing, especially at the central temple of Telangana, in Yadadri. Swamy Narayana Tirtha, the author of Krishnaleela Tarangini, connects Narasimha to health and healing practices. Narayana Tirtha also composed a new dance style, known as Andhra Natyam, to perform Krishnaleela Tarangini, in reverence of Narasimha, once he was cured of a stomach pain (Vemsani 2016a: 147–61). Hence, artistic and devotional practices coalesce together within the Narasimha devotional tradition. This chapter focuses on yoga, health, healing, and performance traditions associated with Narasimha. Similar practices are also noticed in the states of Chhattisgarh and Madhya Pradesh, which will also form part of the discussion in this chapter.

Occurrence of Narasimha images in prehistoric painting of caves and caverns in the middle region of India preserves the symbolic connection of Narasimha to the middle as well as his connection with the prehistoric origins of the Narasimha tradition. The prehistoric paintings must preserve some profound symbolic meaning rather than childish scribbles. The vanavasi social groups are known for preserving prehistoric modes of life including religion as well as the symbolic prehistoric traditions. The continuity of prehistoric sacred sites and the central place noticed for vanavasis within the temple traditions inform about the prehistoric continuity of religious life of this region, being in the middle, distinct, yet not separating but joining the regions, the north to the south. Hence, the nature of the middle can be observed in the traditional practice, which is the unique quality of Narasimha traditions.

Telangana state was formed in 2014 even though the region has been referred to by this name since the seventeenth century. This state is located in the central region of India along with the state of Chhattisgarh formed in the year 2000. These two new states are located roughly in the central region of India. Geographically, these states contain a forested region, commonly referred to as the Dandakaranya, including caves and rock gorges. Numerous natural locations in forested and hilly and rocky outcrops are associated with Narasimha.

The earliest information datable between 300 BCE to 300 CE is noted from the eastern part of Middle India (see Chapter 3), which is not too far from the central temple of Narasimha at Yadagiri. The most important site for early historic India is Vidisa, which had seals, coins, and early historic monuments considered pre-Ashokan in nature. Hence, one of the seals depicting Narasimha seated on a high seat (pitha) indicates a well-entrenched tradition of religious practice surrounding Narasimha. Evidence datable between the first century and the third century CE is noted in Gupta era ruins and other ruins in Andhra Pradesh and Telugu in the area of Telangana, indicating the early continuous religious practice based on Narasimha in central states of India. Monumental and inscriptional evidence increases gradually beginning from the sixth century onwards. Due to the historical wars and numerous invasions that Middle India endured between the twelfth century and the middle of seventeenth century numerous monuments faced destruction and only partly survived. Early monuments located on the hills were abandoned due to issues with desecration and destruction of these Islamic invasions as new temples were built in the vicinity as noticed in the Narasimha temples at Dharmapuri, Koyilakonda, and others in the state of Telangana. Even though the older temples have been renovated and brought back into the religious landscape, this nonetheless indicates the disturbed religious landscape of the central part of the middle region of India. Therefore, I will survey the background of Narasimha traditions in the states of Telangana and the states of Chhattisgarh and Maharashtra in the following pages by examining select temples to understand the practices and conventions associated with Narasimha in this region.

Being located in the center of the region in the middle region (Madhya Desha) of India, Telangana consists of numerous temples of Narasimha. Close to a hundred temples were surveyed in earlier research on Narasimha in this area (Madabhushini 1989b), which indicates the historical importance of the Narasimha tradition in the state of Telangana. In fact, deriving from this historical background, the Telangana State Endowments Board chose the seat of Narasimha at Yadagirigutta (Yadadri) as its headquarters and central administrative post for the state of Telangana. State governments directly administer the Hindu places of worship through appointed government officers and other staff. No Hindu temple is administered independently of the government boards.

As the central region, this state also incorporates the central theories of Narasimha in regional representations as well as the regional Puranas (Sthalapuranas). The most notable features associated with Narasimha are his appearances in forested regions, hills, and caves. In addition, Narasimha is associated with yoga as well as health and healing in this region. I will explore the regional stories in the following pages to understand how these stories link to the most commonly noted features of Narasimha, that of being neither-here-nor-there as well as his transitional nature.

Narasimha Tradition in Madhya Pradesh

The central part of Middle India brings to light evidence of early worship of Narasimha through pre-Mauryan seals and coins which depict Narasimha from at least 400 BCE. if not earlier. The earliest historical evidence of Narasimha is noted from the archaeological excavations at Vidisa (see Chapter 3). Gupta era sculptures of Narasimha are noted across northern and northwestern India including Gandhara and Kashmir regions in addition to central India (see Figure 9). This indicates the widespread worship of Narasimha during the Gupta era. An early temple complex datable to the Gupta era (300 CE) at Eran contains one of the earliest temples of Narasimha.

Figure 9 Yoga Narasimha (third century CE) Sri Pratap Singh Museum, Srinagar. Photo courtesy: John C. Huntington.

The Eran temple complex had been badly damaged. Even though it has been declared a protected site as a Monument of National Importance by the Archaeological Survey of India (ASI), it remains in ruins and no renovation had been undertaken. The broken Narasimha image is left lying on the remainder of the pedestal in what might have been the original garbhagriha. The original Murthi (image) of Narasimha might have stood more than 10 feet tall as the image measures 7.5 feet in length and it was established on a high pedestal of 3–4 feet, which is partially damaged now. The original image standing on its platform might have looked quite majestic during its heyday during the Gupta era (third to fourth century CE). Another image of Nrivaraha (Narasimha-Varaha) connected to the Eran temple complex is housed at Sagar University. The Udayagiri caves show one of the best preserved of the earliest depictions of Narasimha. The earliest depiction of Narasimha in Madhya Pradesh is noted at the Udayagiri caves, dated between 200 BCE and 400 CE. The lion capital of the Ashoka pillar was also discovered near the Udayagiri caves indicating the popularity of (Simha) lion symbolism in this area.

Eran is also located at 78 degrees eastern longitude and 24 degrees northern latitude. Seventy-eight degrees longitude is important for the Narasimha tradition as most of the significant Narasimha temples are located in the central region and Andhra Pradesh and Maharashtra are also located at and between 78 and 79 degrees eastern longitude. Here too, once again the symbolism of middle or center is enshrined within the sacred geography of Narasimha as the most important temples are located in the center of the larger sacred zone, the *leelasthali*, of Narasimha.

The Narasimha Tradition in Chhattisgarh

Chhattisgarh contains numerous early temples including early temples of Narasimha (Stadtner 2004: 157–66; Cunningham 1884). A Narasimha temple is located in the Rajim temple complex in the northwestern corner of the complex. The Rajiv Lochan temple in the Rajim temple complex is dedicated to Vishnu, which also contains temples of Vishnu, and temples for the incarnations of Vishnu including Narasimha, Varaha, Vamana, Rama, and others. Rajiv Lochan temple was dated to about the seventh century CE although historians speculate that there might have been an earlier temple at the site. The Narasimha temple here faces east and is built in the Pancharatha style.

The Lakshmana temple (600–700 CE) in Sirpur, Chhattisgarh, depicts Narasimha in high relief on the wall. The Lakshmana temple was built by Queen Vasata, mother of Mahasivagupta Balarjuna. She is also known to have built many Jagannatha and Narasimha temples, including the Nrusimhanatha temple at Padampur in Odisha. The Rajim group of temples located in Rajim dedicates a temple to Narasimha, considered to have been built during this period. It is a Panchayatana temple with a central temple surrounded by four temples on its four sides. The central temple is dedicated to Vishnu as Rajivalochana, while Narasimha temple is on the northwest corner, and temples of Vamana, Varaha, and Badrinath are on the other sides. The incarnations of Vamana and Varaha are frequently depicted with Narasimha during the early phase of the sixth to the seventh century CE. One of the early inscriptions in the temple complex is dated to the late seventh century CE, attributed to the Nala dynasty.

Chhattisgarh is an important center of the Narasimha devotional tradition. A large number of devotees visit temples in Chhattisgarh as well as nearby states. The Papanasini tank at Nrusimhanatha temple in Odisha is named Chhattisgarhi tank due to the large number of devotees from Chhattisgarh who visit this temple.

Devotees from Chhattisgarh also visit Narasimha temples in nearby states including Odisha, Maharashtra, and Telangana. The Papanashini pond at

Nrusimhanatha temple in Padampur, Odisha, is called Chhattisgarhikund on account of numerous visitors from Chhattisgarh (Behera 2015: 114).

The Narasimha Tradition in Telangana

The state of Telangana contains numerous temples across the state. Even the small towns in this state have Narasimha temples. Therefore, the number of Narasimha temples if surveyed would run into many hundreds. The Narasimha temple at Vadapalli in Nalgonda district shows an inscription dated to the seventh century, while other temples contain inscriptions datable from the tenth century onwards. The Narasimha temple at Alampuram describes the repairs undertaken in 1093 CE. However, it is notable that all the inscriptions mention only repairs rather than the founding of new temples, which indicates an existing tradition in the area.

Yadadri Narasimhaswamy Temple

Yadagiri (also known as Yadadri) Narasimha temple is the central temple in Telangana state, which also is the seat of the Telangana State Endowments Board. The temple is located at 78 degrees eastern longitude and 17 degrees northern latitude. Sthalapurana of Yadagiri (Govardhanam 1978; Sadhu 1968) describes the origin of the temple and the five forms of iconographical representation of Narasimha. This Sthalapurana also includes information from Narasimha Purana, Skanda Purana, Brahmanda Purana, and Padma Purana.

After the vanquishing of the demon Hiranyakashipu, Prahlada praised the terrifying god Narasimha. Numerous gods and other celestials also descended on the Earth and congratulated Narasimha on his divine feat (Bhagavatapurana VII.8.40–50). Gods and other beings thanked Narasimha, and Brahma washed the feet of Narasimha, which formed the pond (Vishnu Kunda) at Yadagiri.[1] Prahlada requested Lord Narasimha to remain on the Earth and bless him. The god Narasimha informed Prahlada that he would manifest on the hill at Yadagiri. Therefore, the temple is connected to Prahlada and the original appearance of Narasimha at Ahobilam (see Chapter 6). This pond is believed by the devotees to be a healing tank of water. Hence devotees undertake vows to obtain health, usually referring to Narasimha as Vaidya Narasimha or Arogya Narasimha.

The most important feature associated with Narasimha in central India is yoga. Representations of Narasimha as Yoga Narasimha are widespread in temples.

As an extension of yoga, health and well-being form part of ritual and practice.

The Narasimha temple at Yadagirigutta is considered the abode of Yoga Narasimha in Telangana state. One of the most important rituals undertaken in connection with Yoga Narasimha is Mandala Deeksha which involves forty days of austere living with limited food and comforts. The Mandala Deeksha is performed for the fulfillment of wishes with regards to health or marriage, childbirth, or academic and career success. The Yoga Narasimha is also considered the Arogya (health-giving/healing) Narasimha. Numerous anecdotes of Narasimha instructing devotees in their dreams about cures for their long ailments are recollected at the temple. The *Yadagiri Kshetra Darshini* by Sri Govardhanam Narasimhacharya records the personal stories of followers cured of a variety of illnesses.

The Yadagiri temple is also considered the Rishi Aradhana Kshetra since numerous sages performed austerities on the hill near Narasimha temple.

Four forms of Narasimha are represented here denoting the special qualities associated with Narasimha: Lakshmi-Narasimha, Gandabherunda Narasimha, Jwala Narasimha, Yogananda Narasimha. However, three forms of Narasimha are unique to this temple: Gandabherunda, Jwala, and Yogananda. Close to the main entrance is located the Hanuman temple with Panchamukha Anjaneya Swamy. Behind this Hanuman temple, a big boulder is identified as Gandbherunda Narasimha. The garbhagudi is a natural formation of a cave on the hill. The cave is 30 feet high and 12 feet wide. The garbhagudi (sanctum) has three formations regarded as Narasimha in addition to the silver images of Narasimha used for daily worship in the temple. The first is a rock formation on the left which is considered a non-iconic formation of the Lord Narasimha called the Jwala Narasimha; on the face of the rock is depicted naga (serpent) indicating the face of the deity Jwala Narasimha. On the other rock is the seated Narasimha in mediation (Ramesan 166–7). This is considered the Yoga Narasimha, the central feature associated with Narasimha. On the opposite rock is the icon of Narasimha in yogasana (seated in yoga posture). At the other end of the cave is the image of Lakshmi-Narasimha, seated on the throne. There is also a Shiva temple within the Narasimha temple compound. The temple is being renovated and rebuilt currently.

Nearby Yadagiri Narasimha Swamy temple is Someswara Narasimhaswamy temple in Peddireddigudem, at a distance of two kilometers from Yadadri

(Yadagirigutta). This Narasimha temple is called the pata Lakshmi-Narasimha Swamy temple as this was considered the original temple. There are two other temples nearby, one for Shiva, called Someshwara temple, and another for Narasimha called Lakshmi-Narasimha Swamy temple. The garbhagudi, sanctum, is built into the hill, which forms the roof of the Narasimha temple, upon which was built a shikhara. The annual festivals of Someshwara and Narasimha are celebrated together on Shivaratri (Madabhushini 297–8).

Narasimha temples depict the god in multiple forms, as Jwala Narasimha, Yoga Narasimha, Lakshmi-Narasimha, Gandabherunda Narasimha, and Someswara Narasimha Swamy, indicating the multifaceted nature of Narasimha as well as his relationship with other deities including Narasimha and Hanuman.

Girirupa Narasimha at Inugurthi

Another temple of Narasimha is noted in the natural formation of hills in the village of Inugurthi located 11 kilometers from Kesamudram in the Warangal district. The Lord appeared in the dream of a devotee and informed them about his manifestation on the hill. The temple also has an inscription of Ganapatideva, which demonstrates that this temple might have been in use before the twelfth century CE (Madabhushini 287–9). The temple is on the lower part of the hill. The garbhagriha contains a larger rock which is regarded as the manifestation of Narasimha. There is a small mouth on the rock, which is adorned with the tripundra mark, the three vertical lines, of the Vaishnavas.

Numerous temples located Narasimha on a rock surface, regarding Narasimha as the swayambhu (self-emanated) form representing his nature as appearing the transitional form in nature, neither the forest nor the plain, but the hill in the middle represents him.

Narasimhaswamy Temple at Khammam

The hill in Khammam is referred to as Narasimhaswamy gutta (hill) designating the hill as Narasimha and is considered auspicious by the devotees. The name sthambhadri is the original designation of Khammam, which is derived from Kambham, a Prakrit word for sthambham, the original Sanskrit word for pillar. Even though the origin of Narasimha from a pillar is attributed to a hill in Ahobilam, the hill in Khammam is considered to be the original place of his appearance, while he killed Hiranyakashipu on the hills at Ahobilam. References for Sthambadri (Madabhushini 1989b: 148–9) are noted in Haribhattu's Narasimhapurana (Uttara Bhagamu) and another work *Sthambhadri* written by Kodamasimha Satyanarayanacharya. The temple was established during the early Kakatiya era but fell out of use. The temple was rediscovered and brought back into service about a hundred years ago. The local legend notes that a local landlord's wife Venkamma from Astnagurthy village about 32 kilometers' distance from the hill had a vision in her dream about the temple of Narasimha on the hill (Madabhushini 1989b: 148). The lady Venkamma accompanied by a number of villagers came to the hill and rediscovered the cave, the temple of Narasimha.[2] The back of the cave is considered the self-manifest form of the Lord Narasimha. Narasimha here is known as the form of Sthambodhbhava Narasimha. Numerous idols of deities are consecrated and installed in the antarala. Images of Lakshmi-Narasimha, Bhudevi, Neeladevi, Chakra perumallu, and Andalu are installed here.

The Narasimhaswamy gutta and the cave temple of Narasimha on the hill and the name of Khammam deriving from the classical story of Narasimha's origin from the pillar indicate the symbolic connection of Narasimha with the hill and the middle.

The Narasimha Temple at Narsimlapalle

The Narsimlapalle Narasimha temple also indicates Narasimha's connection with caves and hills. In Narsimlapalle (Nandagiri-Kotla) the central image of Narasimha is considered swaymbhu as it is carved out of a large rock boulder, which is sacred representation of the god, this again represents the girirupa form of Narasimha, another swaymabhu (self-emanation) aspect associated with Narasimha. The image of Narasimha here is the Ugrarupa (fierce form of Narasimha. The image of Narasimha contains Panchamukha (five-faced) with sixteen arms as he is attempting to kill Hiranyakasipu. Panchamukha Narasimha is an important representation of Narasimha incorporating Vaishnava theology and symbolism (Kalidos 1987). Although the Panchamukha Narasimha form is very popular in central India, especially the state of Telangana, this image is rarely depicted in southern India, although it can be seen on the Kesavaperumal temple chariot in Sri Perumbudur, Varadarajeswara temple chariot in Kanchi, and Vatapatrasai temple chariot in Srivilliputtur (Kalidos 195–7).

The temple is built right into the cave. The original sculptures may have been much older than the outer constructed structures (the mukhamandapa).

The mukhamandapa is added to the cave, which directly leads into the temple garbhagriha, the sanctum, which is a naturally formed cave on the hill. The right side of the cave contains the back wall of the hill designated as the representation of Narasimha. The back of the cave shows large images of Sanka (conch) and Chakra (the wheel), and a representation of the mouth of Narasimha. On the left side of the cave are installed the idols of the nine alvars. One can also climb up the hill from the mukhamandapa (front pillared hall) to reach the top of the hill which is directly above the sanctum. Here on the boulder is depicted the large Panchamukha Narasimha with five heads and sixteen arms killing the demon Hiranyakasipu.

The local story recorded here notes that (Madabhushini 1989b: 95) a certain local official had a vision in which Narasimha appeared and informed him that he was manifest on the hill and informed him to clear the outgrowth and build a temple there. Hence, the cave temple and the sculptures might be much older than the outer mukhamandapa and other structures built in the past couple of centuries.

Overall, the representation of Narasimha as the hill here is notable through the representation of the mouth of Narasimha in the cave, and the larger representation of Panchamukha Narasimha on the hill. This temple of Narasimha is in line with the convention of Narasimha and his association with thick forests and hilly regions.

The Narasimhaswamy Temple in Yelgandal

This temple is another important historical temple located on the hill with part of the hill identified as Narasimha. However, an inscription was discovered in a tank near the town, known as the Chintamani tank, which records a donation of land to maintain the Angaranga vaibhogam (the daily ornamentation and service) of Narasimha (Madabhushi 99–100). The inscription mentions the date of 1203 CE which shows that there was an existing and ancient temple on this hill at least a couple of centuries prior to this inscription. The temple is not atop the hill, but close to the top of the hill, even though the hill is identified with Narasimha. The temple contains a central sanctum in which the back is marked with srinamalu (Vaishnava sign) indicating the presence of Narasimha as the hill.

The Lakshmi Narasimhaswamy Temple Bejjanki

The Lakshmi Narasimhaswamy temple is located on a hillock spread about a hundred acres wide on the hill located close to the town. The rock formation upon the hillock contains a naturally occurring cave, which is the garbhagudi, the central sanctum, while the entire rock containing this cave is identified as Narasimha, and hence it is regarded as sacred hill, housing the girirupa Narasimha as the rock and the archarupa (worshipful form) Narasimha in the cave temple. Therefore, Narasimha appears in three forms here, the natural form of girirupa, and archarupa in the cave temple, and swaymbhu (self-emanating) form of rock boulder on the inside wall of the cave sanctum. There is also a Shiva temple here (Madabhushini 1989b: 102). There is also a koneru (water tank) on the hill. There are about 108 stairs cut into the side of the hill to help reach the temples on the top of the hill. The main structure of the temple contains the garbagudi (sanctum), antarala (attending room), and mukhamandapa (front mandapa). The mukhamandapa is ornately decorated with numerous sculpted pillars. The garbagriha is a cave, and the inner wall of the cave is a boulder, which is regarded as the svayambhu form of the god Narasimha. The rock has a pair of footprints considered to be the symbolic representation of Narasimha.

The Lakshmi-Narasimha Swamy image was installed later in 1974 in the temple. This temple also indicates the symbolic association of Narasimha with hills and other uninhabited places.

Koyilakonda Narasimha Temples

Numerous temples of Narasimha have been established by the tribes living within Andhra Pradesh and Telangana. The Ahobilam temple is connected to Chenchus. The Narasimha temple in Koyilakonda about 21 kilometers from Mahabubnagar is connected with Koyas, another tribe of this region. Local legend informs that the original temple of Narasimha was located inside the hill fort (Madabhushini 160–1). The village is named after the hill fort of Koyas as Koyala Konda (Hill of Koyas) slightly changed over time to Koyila Konda. The fort along with the temple was attacked and looted. During numerous successive Islamic raids beginning with Malik Kafur during the early thirteenth century, which conquered the region marks the beginning of continued occupation and destruction. The Narasimha temple and fort were destroyed while numerous local people including the Koyas were killed, captured, and maimed. The fort remains occupied for the next five centuries, changing hands continuously as successive Islamic rulers raid and occupy this region such as Taimurids (Mughals) and the subsequent Nizam of Hyderabad in the seventeenth century, founded by Quli Qutub Shah (AP State Gazetteers 216; Sherwani 1974: 23). The temple was partly destroyed to build a mosque, and the main idols of the temple were moved to the town and another temple was built there (Madabhushini). However, the original rock temple of Narasimha remains on the hill. There are two ponds on the hill called Konerulu. The rock is decorated with the tripundra (three vertical lines) marking the presence of Narasimha. There are two pillars constructed out of stones and mortar marking the sanctity of the hill and the presence of the central deity Narasimha. The worship of Narasimha in an aniconic form, like a hill, boulder, or rock surface in a cave, is noted in at least twenty other temples in the state of Telangana (Madabhushini 1989b: 365). Interestingly, the aniconic form of Narasimha is widespread, forming the most important rupa (form) representation of worship, which is only second to the image of Lakshmi-Narasimha, which is the most commonly worshipped form (archarupa) of Narasimha. This is emblematic of the recognition of girirupa (hill form) of Narasimha, which is sometimes confused as girija (hill born) form of Narasimha (Eschmann 1978). The state of Telangana is located roughly in the middle of the sacred zone of Narasimha, the Middle India. It is also natural that a number of temples in this state depict the appearance of Narasimha in his symbolic natural form, swayambhu, as hills and rock boulders. This is consistent with the sacred symbolism associated with Narasimha as described in the Mahapuranas and the Sthalapuranas.

The Narasimha Temple at Dharmapuri

The Narasimha temple at Dharmapuri had received royal patronage from the ruling dynasties in Karimnagar since the Vemulawada Chalukyas, Kakatiyas, and later Nayaka rulers. However, the temple had been also attacked and destroyed repeatedly and rebuilt between the fourteenth and seventeenth centuries. A new temple was constructed behind the earlier temple in 1448. A Subedar of Aurangzeb converted the temple into a mosque in 1693. Another temple of Narasimha was constructed in 1724–50. Even though the Nizams took over as independent rulers in the seventeenth century, this continuous occupation was not condusive for improving the desolate condition of the temple. The temple was later rebuilt, but still contains Islamic structures within the temple walls, as a reminder of this Islamic occupation previously.

Dharmapuri is on the banks of the Godavari, which has ghats, known as Brahmagundam, Chaktrateertham, Yamagundam, Vasishthagundam, Satyavathiteertham, and Gopikateetham. The town is dotted with many temples in addition to the Narasimha temple. A number of inscriptions of ruling dynasties dating from 930 onwards belong to Vemulawada Chalukyas, Kalyani Chalukyas, Kakatiyas, and the Vijayanagara empire. This is one of the most historically well-developed temples of the state of Telangana.

The earliest manuscript of the Sthalapurana of the temple composed in Sanskrit is dated to 950 CE (Madabhushini 1989b: 119–20; 1989a: 211) and is based on the Brahmanda Purana. Another manuscript of the Sthalapurana of the Dharmapuri Kshetra Mahatmyam composed in Sanskrit is dated to 1767 attributed to the Skanda Purana. A Telugu version of the Dharmapuri Kshetra Mahatyma was edited and published by K. Sadasiva Sastri in 1956 and 1979. Another Telugu version of the Dharmapuri Mahatmyam is by Shyama Sundara Sastri published in 1970. The story of the Dharamapuru begins with the classical tale of Narasimha and Hiranyakashipu (see Chapter 2). However, the Sthalapurana narrates that when Vishnu arrived in his incarnation as Narasimha, Hiranyakashipu requested Shiva for help, who sent Sharabha. However, Narasimha vanquished Hiranyakashipu and Sharabha too who was trying to save Hiranyakashipu. After that Lord Narasimha wandered the forests of Dandakaranya (the areas of Dharmapuri) and the gods did not know how to pacify him and have him return to the world of the gods (svargaloka). Brahma performed meditation and requested Prahlada and Narada to pacify the god Narasimha. They were able to pacify him, and he subsequently appeared in his saumya (graceful form) at Dharmapuri.

The Dharmapuri temple complex contains four temples, the Kottha Narasimhaswamy temple, the Patha Narasimhaswamy temple, the Venkateshwara temple, and the Venugopalaswamy temple.

The patha (old) Narasimhaswamy temple is the most important temple in Dharmapuri. The presiding deity of the temple is Yogananda Lakshmi-Narasimhaswamy. This temple also has eight Hanuman temples surrounding Narasimha known as Hanumadashtadi Bandhana, since Narasimha is established in his terrifying aspect. The legend and temple of Narasimha with the establishment of eight Hanuman images surrounding the temple of Narasimha as well as the presence of deep forest known as Dandakaranya show the symbolic nature of Narasimha.

Another temple in this complex is known as Satyavati temple, but in reality, this is also a temple of Narasimha established in the sthambha form. There is a 20-foot-tall earthen pillar here in the temple which is known as the sthamba form of Narasimha. However, there is another couple also established in the temple for worship known as Satyavati and Chitrangada (Madabhushini 1989b: 136). A story recollects that Satyavati's husband was a naga, and he turned into

Chitrangada when they took a holy dip in the river Godawari. The tirtham where they took a bath on the Godawari is known as Satyavathi Gundam.

It is interesting that the Kotta Narasimhaswamy temple also had the image of Narasimha with four hands along with Chenchulakshmi and other ancillary deities. Lakshmi is also established nearby in a seated posture.

The Narasimha temple complex in Dharmapuri hosts three temples of Narasimha along with numerous deities including Chenchulakshmi. This is an important temple where Chenchulakshmi is established within the sanctum. Narasimha is established here in three well-known forms, Yoga Narasimha, Sthambha Narasimha, and Lakshmi-Narasimha. The town is clearer now, but when the original temple was established during the late first millennium CE, this region might have been thickly forested. The affiliation of Narasimha with thick forests and hills is known. More than twenty temples of Narasimha in Telangana represent an aniconic form of Narasimha (Madabhushini: 365), in the form of a hill, boulder, or cave, which indicates the impressive inculcation of the nature of Narasimha within the Narasimha tradition in the state of Telangana. The representation of Panchmukha Narasimha on a boulder at Narsimlapalle in Karimnagar district is an interesting blend of the nature of Narasimha. The image depicts Narasimha on the boulder indicating his central nature and association with the middle or transitions as girirupa Narasimha, while also depicting his universal form identifying him with Vishnu simultaneously. Representing Narasimha in Vishwarupa (universal form) with sixteen hands and five faces, identifies of Narasimha with Vishnu. Similar to Krishna, Narasimha is depicted as the full (purna) incarnation of Vishnu as Narasimha functioned within the creation and beyond the creation while straightening the cosmic cycle, of the Yugas, correcting the course of the Earth (see chapter 2).

In the state of Telangana Narasimha is the central deity of Hinduism representing Vishnu, and not merely an avatara or minor deity. The marriage of Chenchulakshmi and Narasimha also forms a central aspect of the Narasimha tradition recollected in popular arts such as Oggukatha here in the state of Telangana. Telangana also preserves important strands of yoga, health and healing traditions associated with Narasimha.

Conclusion

The earliest data of the existence of reverence of Narasimha is noted in the central part of Middle India in the form of seals excavated near Vidisa. Hence, the worship of Narasimha can be noted from at least the middle of the first millennium BCE in this area. The sacred geography of Narasimha as well as sacred tales and practices associated with Narasimha in the central region of the Madhya Desha of India are examined in this chapter. Narasimha traditions in the states of Madhya Pradesh, Chhattisgarh, and Telangana are central to understanding the symbolism and theological concepts associated with Narasimha. Madhya Pradesh preserves the earliest evidence of Narasimha in the form of a seal datable to the sixth century BCE, while other early temples of Madhya Pradesh at Eran are datable to the Gupta period. Narasimha temples in Chhattisgarh and Telangana are datable from the ninth century onwards. As is specific to the Narasimha temples the temples are located on hills or deep forests near rivers. The legends of the temples preserved in the Sthalapuranas further confirm the theological aspects associated with Narasimha, which are also established in the classical texts. A comprehensive study of Narasimha in the central region established the antiquity of the religious practice associated with Narasimha. Temples in the state of Telangana also show the affiliation of Narasimha with vanavasi social groups seen in the association of Koyas and Gonds with the temples of Narasimha in this region.

8

Narasimha in the Western Region
Maharashtra and Karnataka

Each of the parts of the middle region of India shows typical features of Narasimha in temples and practice. The western region of Middle India is currently divided into the states of Maharashtra and Karnataka. The symbolic nature of Narasimha as middle and transitional is also represented in the overall depiction of Narasimha. The western part of Middle India shows unique representations of Narasimha indicating his association with Shiva, while the central part shows the most characteristic features of Narasimha representing his symbolic forms (girirupa) and appearance and the eastern part shows Narasimha in affiliation with Vishnu, and Krishna/Jagannatha tradition. Narasimha shows his swayambhu, girirupa, and vishwarupa forms in central part of the middle India (see Chapter 7), while his close affiliation with goddesses and multifaced nature in association with Krishna (Jagannatha) is represented in eastern part (see Chapter 6) along with original incarnation imprinted on the sacred geography (Andhra Pradesh) through identifying the events of the incarnation of Narasimha, thus becoming the *leelasthali* of Narasimha. Overall, each region contains temples and sacred lore expressing in its unique way significant aspects of Narasimha and highlighting the symbolic nature of Narasimha.

The most important temples of Karnataka associate Narasimha with Shiva, the symbol of Kala, Time. As a deity beyond time, Narasimha is closely connected to Shiva in classical texts, which is also represented in the regional tradition of Karnataka. Narasimha is also connected with Mallanna/Mailer, a folk deity with connection to Shiva, in these regions, especially Maharashtra. In this chapter, I will also examine the regional practices of the state of Maharashtra, an adjoining state of Karnataka, which also demonstrates similar regional practices associated with Narasimha. Southern Maharashtra as well as parts of Maharashtra adjoining Chhattisgarh and Andhra Pradesh have important traditions of Narasimha.

Maharashtra had important traditions of regional practices that were studied in a work in the early 1980s (Sontheimer 1974–5) even though the deities were called Pastoral Deities, thus limiting their scope. However, this work makes an effort to understand landscapes in connection with religion through collecting oral tales, which were subsequently interpreted to make connections that were not fully evident through the oral tales. The oral tales are helpful for understanding the religious landscape of the society, connecting it to the physical landscape; however, interpreting gods and demons beyond their representation while connecting the so-called Pastoral Deities to certain modern castes is problematic. This work also made bizarre connections between the deities which are not supported by adequate evidence such as identifying the leader of herds, Mhaskoba, with Mahishasura (Sontheimer 1989: 180). Sontheimer's efforts to use the physical landscape of Maharashtra, but the literary poetical understandings depicted in Tamil classical poetical landscapes, to expose the inner meanings of the physical landscape of Maharashtra through connecting castes to particularly popular deities of the area is very limiting in character and does not yield an understanding of the religion of Maharashtra, but confuses it through applying unconnected paradigms. However, the researcher misunderstood the concept of literary landscapes here in his enthusiastic application of these expressions to real landscape of another unconnected region. Literary landscapes are metaphorical and as such, they do not represent physical landscapes of a region, but they represent poetry that might incorporate certain characteristics of a physical landscape. In addition the poetical landscape represents and understanding of the Tamil landscape located on the east coast of India, which is very different from the landscape of Maharashtra, which is located on a tangent far from the Tamil region, on the West Coast of India and in Middle India. Such flawed methodology of applying disparate elements from different regions and periods to a twentieth-century religious practice collected through an ethnographic fieldwork and subsequently analyzing a set of collected oral tales is bound to lead to a failed understanding of religion overall, Hinduism in this case. Even though the gods, goddesses, and practices analyzed are Hindu the book avoided naming Hindu or Hinduism unless it was useful to theorize that the religion under the study was shown to have been assimilated by Hinduism. However, on the basis of what evidence, when or how these folk deities were absorbed into Hinduism was left as an open-ended question.

Inserting elements from other regional aspects, such as the literary landscapes of one region on another tangentially opposite region, to understand the religious practice of another region might not be fruitful to illuminate the subject at hand.

One of the major issues with numerous early studies on India conducted during the twentieth century is the predominance of colonial frameworks of understanding India, which were barely feasible, but accepted as fact. It includes the central assumption that Hinduism was brought from outside by a small group of invaders-occupiers, who imposed their religion on the large native population of India. Although there is a lack of basic evidence to support this assumption, it continued to dominate academic studies like the one discussed here. Therefore, the author works his oral tales into proving the framework of the invading brahmins and how they changed the local stories and practices of native tribes in the book *Pastoral Deities of Western India* (*Pastoral Deities* from now onwards). However, the problem is that the brahmins as well as the others were all equally natives. What the author referred to as tribes (pastoral tribes) in this book were not tribes but loose social groups with flexible occupations and mobility. The earlier theories depicted the Vedic Aryans as herder-pastoralists and nomadic which is similar to the lifestyle of the folks described in *Pastoral Deities* rather than the brahmins that the author holds responsible for bringing Hinduism to these folks. How and when these imaginary pastoralist Aryan invaders became brahmins or how they assimilated other pastoralists (noted as pastoral tribes in this work) and taught them to change their religion and practice it in a different form from the original is questionable. The original and the subsequent thread of Indian religion and practice evade clear understanding when the study is focused on theoretical construction rather than subject on hand.

Besides, there is no evidence to show that the Aryan gods are different from the so-called pastoral gods, or that the pastoral gods were worshipped by only a limited number of castes from which the stories were collected. These gods were worshipped by the folks of the region regardless of caste/race. It is not unusual for the god to appear familiar and become part of a social group, the one most prevalent in the region. Multiplicity is one of the most prevalent characteristics of Hinduism; further, having multiple names and forms as well as appearing in new forms to a devotee is not an aberration, but a common trait of the gods, in Hinduism. If the folk connection could be made at all it could be made concerning all gods within the region as well as the supposed Aryans, who are equally native and the original pastoral folk of the region.

Therefore, our goal in this book is to understand the regional religion on the merit of its practice utilizing the classical textual data as well as the practice from local tales. However, in the present book, *Hinduism in Middle India: Narasimha in Text and Practice*, our goal is not to fit disparate elements from literature, oral, and practiced aspects to a theory of "invader vs. indigenous," but to truly assess the impact of the religious practice on society and its role in the social and religious life of Middle India. It is not unusual for Narasimha to be connected with Shiva and Vaishnava avataras; however, this is more widespread in the western region. One special feature of Narasimha in the western region is his early association with the vyuhas in addition to the avataras. Another prominent feature of Narasimha in this region is his association with Shiva.

Narasimha Traditions in Maharashtra

In western India, Narasimha is depicted among the vyuha and avatara panels. The earliest depiction of Narasimha is noted in the Nasik caves, while the Nanaghat inscription of Naganika (Nayanika) begins with offering invocation to Samkarshana and Vasudeva (Vemsani 2006: 11; Trebold 1970: 49–88). Samkarshana identified with Balarama bears resemblances to Narasimha represented by a combined lion-elephant motif and bearing a lion-capped plow, Simha-langala (Vemsani 2006: 1–11). There are twenty-three caves known as the Pandav Leni caves in the Nasik caves group. The sculptures in the Nasik caves are dated to various periods between the second century BCE and the fourth century CE. The Narasimha and Hayagriga panels along with the Naneghat inscription of Shatavahana queen-regent Naganika are dated to the early Shatavahana period in the second century BCE. The Shatavahanas began their rule at the end of the third century BCE and are considered a clan of the Andhrabrityas (Fergusson 1880: 263, 264–5, 275). However, the Buddhist caves at Nasik are attributed to the first century CE based on the inscription of Shatavahana queen Gautami mother of Gautamiputra Satakarni noted in cave III of the Nashik caves dedicated to Buddha. Hindu sculptures at Nasik are dated earlier to the rule of Satakarni I and Queen Naganika. Hence, the Narasimha sculpture in the Nasik group of caves represents one of the earliest sculptures of Narasimha in western India. Shatavahanas also issued coins bearing the lion motif, along with an elephant, horse, and bull. The lion motif is one of the early motifs and displays their affiliation with Narasimha during the early phase of the Shatavahana dynasty. Therefore, the earliest representation of Narasimha was noted from 200 BCE in western India. However, it could be expected that the tradition of Narasimha might have continued during the rule of the Shatavahanas between 200 BCE and 200 CE. The next important piece of historical evidence comes from the third to fourth centuries CE. Another important sculpture of Narasimha is noted from Ramtek Narasimha temple examined in the following section.

Ramtek Narasimha Temple

A large temple and city ruins now identified as Pravarapura (in Mansar), the capital city of Pravarasena II, Vakataka ruler, was noted near Nagpur city, in Mansar, in the town currently known Ramtek. This town is also known for numerous early archaeological remains including Megalithic monuments of stone circles, and excavations at Nagardhan revealed early artifacts belonging to Vakatakas (third to fifth century CE). Nagardhan shows continuous habitation and a fort belonging to the Gonds, as well as early modern and modern constructions. Excavations at Nagardhan revealed ancient fortification walls attributable to the period of Queen Prabhavati Gupta, wife of Pravarasena I, on which was found a seal bearing Prabhavati Gupta's name and a copper plate grant, which show the rule of Queen Prabhavati for a decade following the demise of her husband Pravarasend I until her son Pravarasena II succeeded her.

Temples of Kevala Narasimha, Rudra Narasimha, and Varaha were identified along with the inscription of Queen Prabhavati ordering the construction of the Narasimha temple. Historians proposed numerous theories proposing that Vaishnavism was introduced here due to Gupta influence, since the Vakatakas were Shaivite; Queen Prabhavati's construction of the Vaishnava temple complex might show Gupta influence (Bakker 1990; Jamkhedkar 1987). However, this notion is misconstrued, since early depictions of Narasimha in Nasik caves indicate the well-established practice of Vaishnavism, especially the traditions centered on Narasimha.

Historians also theorized that Vaishnavism was introduced through the worship and rituals of Narasimha at Ramtek, and even proposed that the worship of Vishnu began in this region with the construction of the Ramtek temple complex and spread in Maharashtra (Jamkhedkar 1987). Religions did not function in water-tight compartments in ancient India. It was not unusual for ruling families to support all the religious traditions such as Buddhism, Jainism, and various traditions of Hinduism. Therefore, this view of Gupta influence on the religion of Middle India comes from a misunderstanding of the nature of the god Narasimha and the practice of religion in ancient India. The region of Middle India is affiliated with Narasimha as his *leelasthali* imbibing the symbolic features associated with Narasimha. Moreover, Narasimha is a deity known to share an equal affinity with Shiva and Vishnu. Therefore, the construction of a Narasimha temple and Rudra Narasimha temple along with a Varaha temple merely demonstrates the understanding of the sacred geography of the region and the divine nature of Narasimha rather than Queen Prabhavati's enthusiasm to introduce Vaishnavism in this region; she was merely following an established tradition. Queen Prabhavati Gupta's inscription was studied in detail to understand the construction of temples in Ramtek (Bakker H, Isaason H. 1993: 46–74; Bakker 1990: 62–85; Baker 1989: 79–102; Jamkhedkar 1986: 335–41; Jamkhedkar 1987: 217–23). Maharashtra is noted as the zone of Prahlada's visits and Agastya's asrama. The asrama of Agastya is identified here not too far from the Ramtek temple complex.

The inscription issued by Prabhavati Gupta was discovered in the Kevala Narasimha temple hidden under thick layers of wall paint (Jamkhedkar 1987). The cluster of temples is dedicated to the avataras of Vishnu, Vamana (Trivikrama), Varaha, and Narasimha (Kevala Narasimha and Ugra Narasimha). It is dated to 415-25 CE based on the reign dates of Prabhavati Gupta.

Another important Narasimha temple is located on the borders of the town of Narasimhapur near Nagpur. Even though no inscriptions could be located local legends indicate the new temple was built in the seventeenth century CE by the Jat kings relocating the Narasimha image from the old temple. The original Narasimha here is in the form of a boulder, girirupa, worshipped as the representation of Salagrama form of Narasimha represented, which indicates the early origin of this temple.

Nira Narsimhpur-Narasimha Temple

The temple of Narasimha is located at the confluence of the Nira and Bhima rivers. Although considered the location of an ancient temple, the historical temple is dated to the Vijayanagara and Maratha empires. The current temple was expanded during the Peshwa era. It was built in black granite and contains a very tall shikhara built on a high platform.

The Nira Narasimha temple is associated with Narasimha through Prahlada, the primary devotee of Narasimha. Local tales mention that Prahlada was born in an asrama at Nira Narsimhapura. Located at the confluence of the rivers Nira and Bhima was serene and an auspicious place where asramas might have been built in the previous era. Local tales also mention that Prahlada also practiced asceticism on the banks of the river here.

Besides these three Narasimha temples (Nasik, Ramtek, Nira Narsingpur), which are noted as ancient temples, there are numerous Narasimha temples in Maharashtra, which highlight the early origin of the Narasimha tradition in this state at least since 400 BCE since the earliest image of Narasimha is dated to 200 BCE. The tradition must have been practiced long before temples and images were carved for the deity. The most important historical temple is dated to 415–

25 CE in Ramtek, which shows continuing influence and worship of Narasimha in this region beginning in 400 BCE.

One of the important aspects of Narasimha noted here in the Maharashtra region is the association of Shiva and Narasimha. Although this association of Shiva and Narasimha is not unusual and found in other states of the middle region, its expression is central to the Narasimha tradition. Even the historical temples of Narasimha on Ramtek are located in a large complex, which also dedicates a temple to Shiva. Another important aspect is the yoga noted in the Nira Narasimha temple, which identifies the place of Prahlada's ascetic practices. Texts say that Prahlada was imparted knowledge by the god Narasimha. The aspect of yoga and the representation of Yoga Narasimha defy state borders, and are commonly noticed across the middle region of India.

I will examine in the following section some Narasimha temples of the Karnataka region to understand the major features associated with Narasimha.

Narasimha Tradition in Karnataka

Karnataka is home to numerous Narasimha temples. The largest image of Narasimha carved in stone is at the Hampi Historical City and Fort. A website hosted by the Tirumala Tirupati Devasthanams (TTD) lists more than a hundred historical and well-known temples of Narasimha in the state of Karnataka. This represents the largest number of Narasimha temples besides the states of Andhra Pradesh and Telangana, which also contain more than a hundred temples each. Understandably, numerous smaller temples might not have found their way into this list, which would have made the number of Narasimha temples in the state of Karnataka even larger. This shows the centrality accorded to Narasimha in the religious landscape of this state. It is impossible to survey all of them here; hence I decided to survey a few temples here to understand the typical features associated with the Narasimha tradition in the state of Karnataka. Historical rulers of the Chalukya and Vijayanagara empires built Narasimha temples as well as renovating numerous existing Narasimha temples (see Chapter 3). It is also important to note that the Chalukya and Vijayanagara empires included Andhra Pradesh, Telangana, and Karnataka; hence numerous traditions found in these states evolved simultaneously demonstrating overlap here such as Yakshaganam and ritual practices.

The stories of Chenchulakshmi and Vasantikaparinayam Yakshaganam are also important stories connected with Narasimha in Karnataka (see Chapter 9).

Narasimha tradition in Karnataka and parts of Andhra Pradesh also involves presenting Narasimha with new clothes on Narasimha Jayanthi as he is regarded as the son-in-law of social groups of the region, including Chenchus (Sontheimer 2004: 136–56). It has been proposed that "marriage represents the final stage of the god's incorporation into the circle of the deities of established settlements in areas with regular agriculture. This incorporation also moved him close to the all-India Brahmanical pantheon. At this stage there appears a mahatmya or charitra based on the Puranas and ascribed to some Purana" (Sontheimer 1989: 203). It is further theorized that "the marriage of the god of the forest and pasture area moves him out of the ascetic life of the forest, where, according to Brahmanical ideas (*Hinduism*), the only fourth stage[1] of life is to be spent" (Sontheimer 203). Although this theory is proposed in connection with Kalabhairava, "marriage as a trick" is one of the most commonly used theories in Hindu studies to dismiss beliefs of common folk as superficial that somehow developed to incorporate Hinduism, as though Hinduism was a foreign faith brought on the common folks using the trick of marriage. Another factual error in Sontheimer's statement is that only ascetics live in the forests. It is noted that vanavasi (forest-dwellers) folk now categorized as Scheduled Tribes have always stayed in the margins of the society on the edges of the forests. Hence, the concepts forests, pastures, or farms merely denote lifestyle changes. All of us might have once have been forest-dwellers living in the caves as prehistoric hunter-gatherers; it is only the evolving culture that separated us and brought changes among the lifestyles of part of the society, while part of the society continued with the primary modes of food production of prehistoric life. There is also an implicit arrogance embedded in this theory, that the forest-dwellers are passive receivers of culture, which underestimates their capacity to maintain the oral tales and a longstanding tradition. The problem here is not misunderstanding a single tradition, but the inability to comprehend the multiplicity that collapses into the singularity, which is the central feature of Hinduism. The god Vishnu appears in numerous incarnations and his wife Lakshmi also appears along with him as his partner in numerous incarnations, which is considered another form of the deity, thus Vishnu and Lakshmi are worshipped not in one form or name, but many forms and names. It is important that the frameworks for considering religion in India must adapt to this new paradigm rather than evaluating every new aspect associated with a deity not found in classical texts, but found in regional practice, as a trick. It is natural for any healthy natural object on this Earth to grow and multiply, which is the phenomenon noted with regards to religion also. Hinduism is not an exception to this phenomenon of change and continuity. Symbolic cryptic concepts of the Vedas appear elaborated in the Puranas. The accounts of the deity Narasimha appear in detail in the Mahapuranas. Further details are provided in the local stories (Sthalapuranas) and folk tales. Should information from one source be used to counter the information from another source? For example, should the accounts of Narasimha from classical texts be considered in opposition to Sthalapuranas and folk tales of Chenchulakshmi? Or can we consider the classical texts, Sthalapuranas, and the folk tales of Chenchulakshmi as enriching the tradition and practice associated with Narasimha?

Narasimha in the Badami Caves

The Narasimha and Varaha images in the Badami caves were considered one of the earliest specimens of Chalukya art (Lippe 1972: 273–331). Although the Chalukyas adapted Shaivism, they continued to support Vaishnava festivals and temples. The Badami cave temples are recognized as a UNESCO heritage site. These unique temples are natural formations with stairs and walls added as necessary. Some smaller caves were excavated further to make room for the temples. There are five large cave temples, most of which are dedicated to the ten avataras of Vishnu. The temples are dated between the fifth and sixth centuries BCE. The temples do not receive worship and no rituals or festivals are hosted now as they are maintained by UNESCO. The caves were explored by Thomas Biggs in 1855, and the numerous photographs he took during this exploration are now preserved and exhibited on a British Museum online exhibit (https://www.bl.uk/onlinegallery/onlineex/apac/photocoll/b/019pho000000208u00009000.html). The Badami cave temples are full-fledged temples built in the Nagara and Vesara styles of classical architecture depicting the events associated with the ten incarnations of Vishnu. Cave 3 contains large images of avataras of Vishnu Trivikrakama (Vamana) and Varaha depicted on the walls of the temple. Cave 3 is the largest and finest temple of Badami consisting of large high-relief images of Vishnu in numerous avataras. This cave is attributed to Pulakeshi I of the Eastern Chalukya empire (578 CE) based on the inscriptional data noted here. A Narasimha image is noted here. These images might be the largest natural cave depictions of Narasimha and Varaha. Cave 3 also shows images of Vishnu along with Shiva in the form of Harihara. Cave 4 is dedicated to Jain temples and Cave 5 is dedicated to a Buddhist temple. Overall, the temples are dedicated to the ten avataras of Vishnu and might have received regular adoration and worship during the first millennium CE. An image of Narasimha is located in the ornately carved front mandapa of Cave 3. The image shows Kevala Narasimha

Figure 10 Yoga Narasimha from Harakere (twelfth century CE). Courtesy: Wikimedia Commons @CC.

in a standing posture in Abhayamudra (graceful posture). The large mandapa with ornately carved pillars and walls leads into the temple of Vishnu. These cave temples might have served as precursors to the Kailasantha temple at Ellora which was constructed by excavating a large mountain. On top of the hill are the fort of Chalukyas and one of the earlier temples of this complex, the Malegitti Shivalaya.

Badami is, therefore, one of the earliest Vishnu temples depicting Narasimha in Karnataka and shows the well-established tradition of Narasimha in Karnataka (Figure 10).

Torvi Narasimha Temple near Bijapur

The Torvi Narasimha temple near Bijapur town exhibits the central features of Narasimha with hills and caves. One of the special features of the Narasimha temple here is that the garbhagriha (sanctum) is inside a cave and is considered a very ancient temple. The mandapa is at ground level as one enters the antarala, but soon as one enters it drops lower leading through a narrow passage to the garbhagudi. The cave temples of Narasimha indicate the well-known accounts of Narasimha which associate him with caves, hills, and other esoteric locations.

Karumgad Narasimha Temple

Narasimha temple is located on a tortoise-shaped island, appropriately named Tortoise Island/Kurumgad, near Karwar in Karnataka (kurum derived from the Sanskrit term Kurma). The large Narasimha temple built in the Chalukyan style is located on the top of the hill. It is reached by climbing about 300 stairs. The annual festival of Narasimha, Yatra, is held in January (Paushya Paurnami), held to be the day of the foundation of the temple on which a sage found Salagrama Narasimha in the river Kali. The island can be reached by boat on the backwaters of the Kali river. The festival attracts large crowds. This is another hill temple of Narasimha located on the island symbolizing the central features of Narasimha, of being the middle, but not part of any landscape exclusively. Narasimha is worshipped here in the forms Salagrama Narasimha, Ugra Narasimha, and Chakra Narasimha. The Salagrama Narasimha and the location of the temple on the island connect to the most primal features of Narasimha representing the middle and transitions.

Devarayanadurga Narasimha Temples

The hill here is known as Pushpagiri or Karigiri, the elephant hill. This hill is said to mark the sacred location where the god Narayana killed a demon called Pundalika. There are two temples dedicated to Narasimha, the Bhoga Narasimha temple at the bottom of the hill and the Yoga Narasimha temple at the top of the hill. There are also numerous other temples dedicated to other Hindu deities including, Sanjivaraya temple (Hanuman temple). The rivers Jayamangalai and the Shimsha rivers originate in these hill ranges. There are sacred ponds here called Narasimha Tirtha, Parashara Tirtha, and Pada Tirtha. The location of the temples and the hill represents the transitional qualities of Narasimha.

Melkote Yoga Narasimha Temple

Another important Narasimha temple is located on the top of the hill known as Yadugiri or Yadavagiri in Melkote. The temple is more located at a height of more than 1,000 meters above sea level, and it takes about 400 stairs to reach the temple. The temple is constructed in the style of Hoyasala architecture and should be dated to the eleventh century, but the inner temple appears to be older than the modern exterior of the temple, which might have been added later. The legend of the temple notes that the original temple was constructed by Prahlada installing the image of Yoga Narasimha. This temple memorializes the event of Narasimha imparting divine knowledge to Prahlada (Bhagavatapurana VII.5–6). Located on top of the hill this temple reminds one of the symbolic features of Narasimha, the middle and/or transitions.

Sthambha Lakshmi Narasimha Swamy Temple at Billur

Another important temple of Narasimha is seen in the town of Billur in the Chickballapur district of Karnataka. The Sthambha Narasimha form of Narasimha is rare and signifies the symbolic representation of the appearance of Narasimha. The legend notes that the sthambha, the representation of the central deity, Narasimha, was still growing, and it destabilized the temple structure, so the temple sthapati (chief sculptor) decided to place a hammer at the top of the sthambha to stabilize the structure. This also shows the classical story of the symbolic appearance of Narasimha from the sthambha. The sthambha stands about 16 feet tall on which the image of Lakshmi-Narasimha is installed. Another Sthambha Narasimha temple is noted in Dharmapuri in Karimnagar district of Telangana (see Chapter 7). Another important Sthambha Narasimha temple is located in the central temple complex of Narasimha at Ahobilam (see Chapter 6). Images of Yoga Narasimha represented along the pillar are also seen in the museum in Srinagar datable to the Gupta era (see Figure 10). This Narasimha temple memorializes one of the central events of the classical story of the appearance of Narasimha as he emerged from the pillar. This temple symbolizes the appearance of Narasimha which is marked by the sthambha (pillar).

Lakshmi-Narasimha Temple Javagal

The most impressive temple complex of Narasimha in the state of Karnataka is located here. The Lakshmi-Narasimha temple in Javagal is currently under the protection of the Archaeological Survey of India (ASI). Lakshmi-Narasimha temple at Javagal is a Hindu temple located about 50 kilometers from Hassan city and about 20 kilometers from Halebidu in Karnataka, India. The primary deity worshipped here is Narasimha, a form of Lord Vishnu. This temple is a protected monument by the Karnataka Archaeological Survey of India. This is an impressive temple built during the Hoyasala period (1250 CE) by Vira

Someswara (1235–63). A compound wall with a majestic entrance door was added during the Vijayanagra period. This temple is near the Chennakeshava temple of Halebidu, another important Hoyasala era temple. This is a trikutaka temple (triple sanctum) with a temple dedicated to Vishnu, Narasimha, and Venugopala. As one of the most well-preserved temples of Middle India, this region shows the well-preserved long-established tradition of Narasimha in the state of Karnataka.

Sri Bhuvaraha Narasimha Temple, Halasi

The Bhuvaraha Narasimha Swamy temple is one of the earliest Narasimha temples in Karnataka datable to the Kadamba period around the fourth to fifth century CE. A Kadamba inscription found here also establishes this date. The temple continued to be updated until the twelfth century, which is seen in the art and architectural features of the temple. A Bhuvaraha image was installed in 1169 CE based on the inscription found here. As is noted the Varaha and Narasimha incarnations of Vishnu are worshipped together in certain unique sacred sites. There are two garbhagrihas in this temple. The first garbhagriha has Vishnu, Mahalakshmi, Narasimha, and Suryanarayana. The other garbhagriha is dedicated to the god Bhuvaraha. The image of Varaha is depicted holding the goddess Bhulakshmi upon his tusks, one of the most admired forms of the god Varaha. The image of the god Varaha was installed by Vijayaditya III (1186–7) as noted from the inscription on the temple. The original temple dedicated to Narasimha earlier indicates the Narasimha tradition in this region by the third century CE. The addition of another garbhagriha with the deity Varaha also indicates the practice of worshipping Narasimha and Varaha simultaneously in a single sacred center, which was noticed in the temples at Ramtek and the Badami caves. This aspect of worshipping Narasimha and Varaha is also noted in the Simhachalam temple of Andhra Pradesh in which a combined form of Varaha and Narasimha, is the central deity.

Sri Narasimha Jharni Temple

The Narasimha temple in Jharni is located inside a cave. To reach the sanctum the devotees walk through a cave tunnel, which is always full of water up to 4–5 feet deep. The temple is under the Manichoola hill range near Bidar. Narasimha temples are generally located on the top of the hill, but in Jharni, the temple is located under the hill inside the cave. There is a special legend to explain the temple being located here under the hill. There is also a sacred spot dedicated to Shiva within the temple represented by the Shivalinga. The local story of the temple says that Narasimha killed another demon here called Jalasura (water demon), who turned into the water upon his death. The cave remains in flood, which is seen as the reminder of this demon killed here. The temple marks the sacred spot of Narasimha vanquishing the demon Jalasura in Jharni. This temple represents the symbolic nature of Narasimha as it is located inside a temple in the water. This temple also symbolically indicates the special relationship shared by the gods Narasimha and Shiva.

Nuggehalli Lakshmi Narasimha Temple

This Narasimha temple is located in Nuggehalli, near Hassan. This is an ornate trikuta temple built by Bommanna Dandanayaka of the Hoyasala empire. The three temples within this trikuta are dedicated to the gods Lakshmi-Narasimha, Kesava, and Venugopala. The temple follows Vaikhanasa Agama rituals. The temple is very similar in construction to the most popular temple styles of Hoyasalas in the state of Karnataka, seen at Halebidu and Belur. There is a Sadashiva temple near the Narasimha temple complex. These temples also show the overarching relationship of Narasimha with the gods Venugopala and Kesava. This temple also recognizes the unique relationship of Narasimha with Shiva.

Hampi Ugra Narasimha Temple

Hampi is part of the capital complex of the Vijayanagara empire, also known as Vijayanagara, the city of victory (Srinivasachar and Satyan 1995). A number of temples are located here on Hemakuta hill. There are three temples on the south side of Hemakuta hill, the Balakrishna temple, Shiva temple, and Narasimha temple. The Balakrishna temple is partially ruined, and the Shiva and Narasimha temples are drastically destroyed, leaving the central images open without the walls and temple exterior. The mandapa and walls and shikhara of the temples are destroyed. The four arms of Yoga Narasimha are also destroyed. This image of Narasimha is the largest image of Narasimha carved from a single boulder. The image of Yoga Narasimha is in seated posture atop the seat of Shesha; the hoods of Shesha are also partially destroyed. The Narasimha image is almost 10 feet high; despite the destruction inflicted on the temple and image, it still is the largest and most magnificent image of Yoga Narasimha in the world.

The temples and traditions of Narasimha examined here in Karnataka represent Yoga Narasimha and Narasimha who appear to kill demons (Jharni Narasimha). It is also notable that Narasimha temples in the state of Karnataka are also symbolically located on hills, in caves (Badami), at the edge of the forests, or on islands (Kurumgud), landforms known to be associated with Narasimha commonly in Middle India. The Narasimha temples are also located near Shiva temples at most of the locations, symbolizing the unique relationship Narasimha shares with Shiva.

Conclusion

The western part of Middle India has one of the earliest temples and practices associated with Narasimha in the Nasik caves and Badami caves. Therefore, this region shows the early origin and continuing tradition of the deity Narasimha in Middle India. Narasimha traditions in the states of Maharashtra and Karnataka are studied in this chapter through an examination of the well-known centers of Narasimha. Early Narasimha centers in the Nanaghat and Nasik caves as well as Narasimha temples on the Ramtek hill are connected to important dynasties, which ruled most of Middle India, the Shatavahanas and the Vakatakas. Contrary to some scholarly hypotheses this evidence also shows that the Vaishnavism of Maharashtra was not derived from the influence of Guptas, but was a long-established tradition in Maharashtra, at least noted from the period of the Shatavahanas. For the traditions to have been written down and mentioned in the inscriptions they may have been in constant practice at least a few centuries earlier. This puts the beginnings of the Narasimha tradition in the middle of the first millennium BCE. Therefore, evidence in the western part of Middle India shows that the historical continuity of the Narasimha tradition is known since the middle of the first millennium BCE. The early worship centers continued to flourish while more temples were added later to the sacred landscape of Narasimha in Maharashtra. One of the special features noted within the Narasimha traditions is widespread popular practices associating Narasimha with the culture of Maharashtra, connecting him with the popular deities Khandoba and Mallar, the forms of Vishnu and Shiva popular in Maharashtra.

The state of Karnataka records much more widespread practice of the Narasimha tradition due to the large number of temples spread across the state even though the early evidence is dated to the middle of the first millennium CE. Karnataka has managed to preserve impressive historical temples of excellent cultural architecture constructed by the Chalukya, Kadamba, Hoysala, and Vijayanagara empires, for example the largest image of Narasimha at Hampi and the largest temple of Narasimha at Hassan. The Narasimha tradition in the state of Karnataka connects the sacred centers of Narasimha to the appearance of Narasimha, Prahlada, or reappearance of Narasimha. The largest image of Narasimha even though partially damaged depicts the deity Yoga Narasimha seated in yogic posture.

Since the vanavasi social groups including Chenchus and Konds are spread between Andhra Pradesh and Karnataka, common practices can be seen spread between the states. The specific features associated with Narasimha, such as yoga and the association with hills and caves, are noted at most of the sacred centers of Narasimha. The Yakshaganam, Harikatha, and numerous regional storytelling traditions are also spread across the state of Karnataka.

9

Narasimha in Popular Culture, Performing Arts, and Devotional Practice

The popular practice represented in the performance arts and literature, as well as ritual both in community and individually represents the living religion. Hence, the numerous rituals and performances taking place each day in the villages and remote corners of India in connection with Narasimha provide an important link for understanding the Narasimha tradition in practice specifically and religion in Middle India in general. Important festival and ritual traditions are associated with Narasimha in Middle India. Narasimha is associated with the theater and performing arts of India, especially in southern India. Week-long theater festivals are organized across Middle India on the occasion of the Narasimha Jayanti festival each year. The examination of festivals, rituals, and theater as well as performance traditions associated with Narasimha also helps inform the historical and social as well as cultural traditions of Middle India. Numerous folk artistic traditions such as Oggukatha, Harikatha, Yakshganam, and Jamukula Katha present the story of Narasimha. Art, whether in the sculptures on the temples or the performance arts connected with the stories of Narasimha, is not merely art, but encompasses much more than that. The artistic representations and performances bring to life the metaphysical, theological, and cosmogonic concepts of the texts. This chapter examines the folk and theater festivals as well as the rituals and festivals associated with Narasimha to understand the practice of the Narasimha tradition in Middle India.

One of the major issues with studying practice, that is, performing arts and oral sources, is that these sources are frequently preserved in oral format within the families of performers, either itinerant or attached to temples. Therefore, the dating of the oral texts is not fixed and attributed frequently to a much later date than their original composition. The performance texts, as well as oral texts containing regional stories, were systematized and committed to writing from the twelfth century onwards in Andhra Pradesh and across most of Middle India. It is plausible that the stories and theatrical and other performance traditions might have been practiced much longer before they were committed to writing. First, the established modern wisdom dictates that the orality is based on backwardness, and hence there are concerns about its trustworthiness. Second, there is a prevailing notion among the scholars of Middle India that Telugu Sthalapuranas and other oral texts were only written following Muslim invasions in the south (Madabhushini 1989b: 15), although evidence does not support these early assumptions. Oral as well as literary traditions worked concomitantly rather than in opposition. The oral traditions continue to enrich written tradition, as continuity of oral traditions indicates, despite lack of modern sponsorships or support.

The first point has affected modern research which categorized written sources as opposed to oral sources, thus creating a dichotomy in understanding the sources as well as religion and culture of India. This process of considering sources as dichotomous rather than unitary source derived from the consolidated sources available historically is seen in a number of modern scholarly works on which, has shown that oral texts or poetical compositions are independent of writing traditions (Nagy 2001: 532–8). This was used to buttress the theory of Aryan invasion and occupation, because the oral tradition is seen as lesser tradition that was overtaken and changed, even though the evidence proves the contrary. This introduced a dichotomy of invader vs. indigenous within the analysis of religion and culture of India, thus leading to confusion and wrongful assumptions. Orality and literacy are seen as successive modes of cognitive ability rather than variants (Ong 1982). This theory has pushed the living traditions of oral poetry/compositions to the background since these expressions are considered to be not conducive to scientific thinking and hence may hamper progress. The prevalence of this type of thinking has also prevented the inclusion of oral poetry and performance practice in the modern education system, which prevented these subjects (oral poetics and performances) from being included in the school curriculum or even in the theater programs of higher education in the Telugu states of Andhra Pradesh and Telangana. Sadly, this has adversely affected the practice of the popular folk arts of Andhra Pradesh and Telangana, which also includes the Oggukatha, Harikatha, and Yakshaganam traditions whose practices have become rare, if not completely extinct.

The second point that the Sthalapuranas began to be composed following the Muslim invasions ignores the contexts of religious performances with which these oral traditions might have been involved in an earlier era. It also ignores the fact that literature in the regional languages only began during the second millennium. The literary compositions in Telugu only began in the late eleventh century with the translation of Sanskrit literature. Literary writing was not composed or known in Telugu, which might have also been the case of oral literature which was not set to writing in Telugu earlier. It is important to remember that Telugu literature began in oral compositions long before they were written and preserved, and the writing of Sthalapuranas is contemporaneous with the classical texts in the Telugu region.[1] The foundation of strong Telugu empires supporting the writing of books in Telugu is an important event, which brought about the writing of Sthalapuranas and other classical texts in Telugu rather than Muslim invasions. Muslim invasions seem to be secondary to the beginning of large-scale translations and writing activity undertaken from the twelfth century onwards, which could be largely attributed to the regionally located empires of the Chalukya dynasties and Kakatiyas. Even though the textual and inscriptional evidence is noticed only from the beginning of the eleventh century (1093 CE in Alampuram and 1080 in Simhachalam), these inscriptions only mention donations to an already existing temple, which helps us establish that the temples and associated traditions might have been in existence long before the inscriptions, since the middle of the first millennium CE, as the early sculptures and temples are dated to at least the third century CE.

The traditional practice of Narasimha blends textualities, local stories, and the represented theophany as well as the theogonic understanding of Narasimha reflected in multiple sources. Multiple sources came together as the practice evolved over the millennia, and the accounts and festivals of Narasimha continue to enchant millions of followers of Narasimha. Almost all of Vishnu's incarnations connect with simple and guileless folks while also accomplishing the task of ending adharma and restoring harmony. However, the avataras beginning with Narasimha are connected uniquely with their devotees, revealing divine truth (jnana) and connecting with simple folks by belonging to them by being one of them.

The classical stories of the appearance of Narasimha connect him to specific features, representing the middle, in form and actions, which are then taken over into local tales connecting him to the land, life, and culture of the middle region of India. These unique features that connect him to the people are also the features that reveal the divine truth to the folks. Parallels of divine revelation in the legends of Narasimha are consistent. Although scholars noted the divine revelation within the classical accounts of Narasimha in comparison with Krishna (Soifer 1991: 150–4) the focus was on clarifying which revelation might have occurred first, either the Purana or the Mahabharata, rather than the holistic analysis of divine revelation noticed through the avataras of Vishnu.

Relationship of Narasimha with Other Gods and Beings:

The devotional traditions center on Narasimha's relationship with other gods and beings. As soon as Narasimha vanquished the demon Hiranyakashipu he was met by beings from the divine as well as the earthly sphere. The Bhagavatapurana mentions lists of divinities who came down to visit Narasimha overcrowding the space with aerial chariots (VII.9.33; VII.9.37–9). Prahlada notes the relationship of Narasimha with his devotees (VII.9.10). Prahlada then requests Narasimha that he wishes enlightenment and moksha for all rather than for himself, "Oh, Lord! Sages desirous of self-emancipation, generally meditate on you silently in solitude. But they are indifferent to the interests of others. Leaving aside these helpless creatures, I do not long to attain the final beatitude for me alone. Nor do I see any refuge other than you for these, who are wandering in samsara" (Bhagavatapurana VII.9.44). Prahlada also lists the modes of connecting with Narasimha (Bhagavatapurana VII.9.50):

> Therefore, Oh Most Worshipful Lord! How can a person cherish devotion to you who the goal of the highest order of ascetics (*paramahamsas*) without the (following) six constituents of worship: 1. Paying Obeisance to the Lord, 2. Singing his glory, 3. Offering all acts to the Lord, 4. Waiting on you (seva/ worship in the form of service), 5. Meditation on the feet of the Lord, and 6. Listening to the recital of stories of the Lord.

All the activities listed here form part of the practices of devotees and the temples of Narasimha.

The divine revelation of Narasimha is very clearly narrated in the classical texts, while the local tales take it a step further in describing his life with the common folks of Andhra Pradesh, in Middle India. Even though the appearance of Narasimha is clearly described in cosmological terms and the symbolism of divine revelation is unmistakable, it was the Mastyapurana (161–3) and the Harivamsa (228) that clarified the occurrence of this unique revelation to Prahlada through divine eyes (divyena chakshusha) similar to the revelation of Krishna to Arjuna in Mahabharata. The immensely large group of spectators remain oblivious to the appearance of the god except for the one person for whom the revelation is intended. As Narasimha appeared in the court of Hiranyakashipu in a form that had never been seen by anyone, they remained oblivious to the true appearance of the god. However, Prahlada was able to see that it was Vishnu, and in the Mastyapurana and the Harivamsa Prahlada received the special vision (divya chakshuh) of the divine revelation of Vishwarupa (universal form) of the god, Vishnu. In the Bhagavata

Purana (VII.9.5–7) the event of divine revelation is described briefly. The Bhagavata Purana narrates that (VII.9.5) "seeing the child fallen at his feet, the Lord was thoroughly overwhelmed with compassion. Raising him, he placed on his head, his lotus-like hand which dispels the fear of those whose minds are fraught with the fear of the serpent in the form of Time (Death, Time, the Destroyer)." Immediately unknown to the other spectators' the divine knowledge is revealed to Prahlada. "At the touch of his hand, all the inauspiciousness (in the form of impressions left by past actions) in Prahlada was washed out, and the highest knowledge of the Supreme Brahman instantly dawned upon him" (Bhagavata Purana VII.9.6).

While the classical texts inform of the appearance and divine revelation of knowledge through the incarnation of Narasimha, local tales help bring it close to the social groups of Middle India, which is symbolically affiliated with specific symbols of the middle associated with Narasimha. The Narasimhapurana of Errana records the story that had already identified Narasimha with the land for centuries before it was finally composed in Telugu in the 1300s. Errana's introduction to the Telugu Narasimhapuranamu shows that the story might have been known orally for a long time before it was set into writing. The Telugu Narasimha Puranamu identifies the place of the appearance of Narasimha as the Ahobilam hills, which now host Nava-Narasimha (nine Narasimha) temples, one of which is known as the Sthambha Narasimha temple, marking the pillar of appearance of Narasimha (see Chapters 6 and 7). The Narasimhapuranamu depicts the hills of Ahobilam obtaining the name from the divine grace of Narasimha upon the request of Prahlada. Narasimhapuranamu describes that the sacred site of appearance of Narasimha came to be known as Ahobilam from the cries of happiness and praise that emanated there as the gods screamed "Ahobala" (great strength) praising Narasimha.

Thus, it is clear that Narasimha's appearance and revelation are located in the land of Ahobilam, and the other stories linked him to the common folk of the region. The Vasantikaparinayam and Chenchulakshmi narratives depict how the god Narasimha continued to live in the forests even after the divine purpose of vanquishing the demons and restoring harmony was met. During his many roamings and hunting trips in the forest, Narasimha meets the woman Chenchulakshmi and proposes to marry her. She agrees, but not before testing him in his hunting and food gathering skills. This last tale of Narasimha in the Nallamala forests of Andhra Pradesh depicts the complete *leela* of the avatara of Narasimha. Narasimha not only vanquished the demon here but stayed here identifying himself with the most common folks of the region, living among them as one of them, similar to Krishna, who lived among the cowherds of Vraja. Therefore, the Telugu regions, the states of Andhra Pradesh and Telangana constitute the *leelasthali*, the land of the divine play of Narasimha.

However, there were concerns among the scholarly studies in Hindu studies, which considered the classical sources and local tales as distinct and separate from each other rather than considering both as multiple sources indicating different aspects of culture as noticed here in our examination of Narasimha. Considering classical stories and local stories as representing different cultures rather than a single culture in multiple expressions only led to a partial understanding of Narasimha previously (Marriott; Sontheimer; Eschmann). Earlier studies exclusively focused on one aspect of the Narasimha story, either classical (Soifer; Hacker; Biardeau) or folk (Eschmann; Sontheimer). However, comprehensive study of Narasimha in this book has revealed that for a tradition that remained central to Hindu practice for millennia all these disparate aspects of written and oral sources come together in practice, which incorporates elements from all the sources. Therefore, I will examine in the next section the religious practice associated with Narasimha along with the social groups associated with Narasimha. The *leela* of Narasimha is revealed in his association with land, life, and culture.

Popular Hindu culture is seen in three strands: First, temple-related festivals, arts, and traditions. Second, popular arts, literature, and oral tales were preserved among the common folk. Third, individual vows and pilgrimages are undertaken by the common folk. With regard to the deity Narasimha, both of these above-noted traditions have been strongly maintained over the millennia even though some overlap is commonly noted between the temple-related traditions as well as the popular traditions preserved among the common folk. I will first examine the temple-related festivals, arts, and traditions followed by the popular arts, literature, and oral tales preserved among the common folk as well as individual vows and pilgrimages subsequently.

Temple Festivals, Arts, and Traditions

Narasimha is an incarnation of the god Vishnu; hence most of the Narasimha temples follow Vaishnava traditional rituals prescribed under the Pancaratra system of worship and rituals practice. The Madhva tradition (smarta system) as well as the Vaikhanasa tradition are noticed in the temple rituals. However, some Narasimha temples are maintained by priests from non-Brahman communities (Madabhushini: 166), even though they too celebrate and conduct worship and rituals according to the Vaishnava conventions. The deity Narasimha is worshipped simultaneously in popular rituals as well as traditional Vaishnava practices. Narasimha surpasses the traditional boundaries of society, which is also in tune with the transitional nature of Narasimha, which defies all known boundaries of life. Therefore, even though the temples are dedicated to Narasimha and follow Vaishnava practices, there is diversity in the worship and ritual practice of each temple.

The most important festivals celebrated in the Narasimha temples are the annual festival (referred to as Brahmotsavalu) and Narasimha Jayanti. In addition, each of the Narasimha temples may choose to celebrate a number of calendrical festivals in addition to birthdays of Alvars (Vaishnava saints) and kalyanam of Lakshmi and Narasimha or Chenchulakshmi and Narasimha. There are also numerous daily pujas (worship rituals) conducted on an everyday basis in almost all the temples of Narasimha.

As part of the annual festivals and other large festivals, performances as well as art exhibits are organized in which Harikatha and Burrakatha are performed narrating the Sthalapuranas and stories related to Narasimha.

Festival and Ritual Traditions of Narasimha

Temples conduct two types of festivals with their incorporated rituals. First, the Nityapujas are daily rituals conducted in the temple. Second, festivals of different varieties, known under titles such as Tirunallu, Melas, or Jataras, fall into the category of the annual festival, which is conducted in each temple although some festivals like Narasimha Jayanti are a common annual festival for all Narasimha temples.

Nityapuja

Most of the Nityapujas (daily rituals) are standardized currently even though previously they might have shown differences between temples located in different areas. Inscriptions datable to the early eleventh century describe numerous rituals conducted at the Simhachalam temple (Mukunda Rao 1987). Inscription as Ahobilam not only list the festivals and rituals, but also describe the specific food preparations for certain festivals (Adluri 2019). Currently, all the temples are run by the State Endowments Board, which is headed by an executive officer drawn from the ranks of highest civil administrators of India known as Indian Administrative Service (IAS) appointed by the state government as well as the Board of Trustees nominated by the state government, since the 1950s. Their pay and benefits are drawn from the temple exchequer and costs close to half or more of the temple revenue each year even though they belong to the government administration and not the temples directly. Between the tenth and eleventh centuries CE Ramanujacharya widely traveled throughout the region introducing standard ritual practices across all the Vaishnava temples which included Pancharatra rituals along with the recitation of Vedic mantras and verses of Nalayira Divyaprabhandham. However, local practices derived from Sthalapuranas remain unchanged. For example the layer of sand paste cover on the image of Varaha-Narasimha in the Simhachalam temple is derived from the Sthalapurana of Simhachalam temple. It is said in the Sthalapurana that the sacred image was covered in a thick layer of mud and hence the deity continues to be worshipped in the same form he was found, only difference is that the image is covered in a paste of Sandal instead of the layer of mud and clay that covered the image originally.

Nityapujas are standardized across all the Narasimha temples as the Endowments Board standardized the tickets for each type of service offered during the day in which the devotees participate. Nityapuja involves three pujas including archana and special Aradhana in the morning, afternoon, and night each day. All the services are ticketed including the sarva Darshanam. The ticket sales generate a substantial amount of income for the Endowments Board. Most Narasimha temples begin morning service (abhishekam) at 5:00 a.m. in which devotees participate. Prior to the archakas, awakening rituals are performed with the recitation of Suprabhatam at 4:30 a.m. Following the morning Aradhana (prabhata seva) Naivedyam is offered to the deity. Devotees purchase special expensive tickets to participate in this early morning seva. Following this, devotees are allowed to see the deity called sarva darsanamu from 6:30 a.m. to 10:00 a.m. The darsanamu tickets are nominal, but the devotees are also encouraged to purchase other seva tickets along with them such as Ashthottaram or Satananamam, which involves the archakas reciting the namas (names) of the deity. Afternoon Archana (Madhyandina seva) and offer of Naivedyam is performed between 11:00 a.m. and 12:00 p.m. noon. Sarva darsanam resumes after that until 2:00 p.m. Some temples close between 2:00 p.m. and 4:00 p.m., but busy temples like Narasimha temples at Ahobilam, Simhachalam, and Yadagiri continue the Sarva Darsanam throughout the day. Evening Aradhana and archana are conducted between 7:30 p.m. and 8:30 p.m., including the offering of Naivedyam. Sayanotsavam is performed between 9:00 p.m. and 10:30 p.m. The temple doors close at 11:00 p.m. and open again the next day at 4:00 a.m.

Festivals and Fairs (Tirunallu/Mela/Yatra/Jatara) of Narasimha

Some festivals are celebrated commonly across all the temples of Narasimha across Middle India such as Nityapuja, Brahmotsavalu, and Narasimha Jayanti. There are also special pujas performed in the temples depending on the special traditions incorporated into temple culture due to the unique local tales and culture represented in the Sthalapuranas.

Narasimha Jayanti

Narasimha Jayanti festival is celebrated on the fourteen days (Chaturdashi) of the bright half of the moon in the month of Vaishakha, generally occurring in the middle of May each year. It celebrates the appearance day of the god Narasimha. This festival is celebrated for three to five days with rituals and festivities, as well as shows of arts, crafts, and herbal products. This festival is celebrated as the appearance of Narasimha.

Brahmotsavam

The Brahmotsavam is a nine-day festival celebrated with much fanfare each year in almost all the Vaishnava temples. Brahmotsavalu is an annual festival celebrated in almost all Vaishnava temples. Narasimha temples celebrate Brahmotsavalu at the beginning of the Dvadasi during the Phalguna month (February–March) for nine days. The deity Narasimha and Lakshmi are taken in procession on decorated temple chariot adorned with different mounts such as hamsa, horse, elephant, lion, and so on, pulled through the temple street each day of the nine-day festival. The festival concludes with Teppotsavam (boat show) or a large final chariot procession. During these nine days, cultural and arts festivals are held which showcase musical and theatrical performances.

Other festivals that are regularly celebrated on an annual basis include Dasara, Deepavali, and Ugadi, and so on.

Popular Arts, Literature, and Oral Tales

The most important feature of popular arts is that they are sung in the regional language spoken by the people of a region and the stories are also improvised with details according to the singing prowess and time allotted. Oggukatha is a traditional form of Telugu singing similar to rap in rhythmic and rapid singing, while it also involves simple dance-steps, and is a popular performance of the countryside of Telangana.

Sabara, Koya, Gond (Kond), and Chenchu tribes stand in close relationship with Narasimha. Numerous ancient temples may have been established and maintained by these tribes, although due to the oral nature of the tribal tradition not much information has survived. However, some temples still contain information that provides important connections between the deity Narasimha and the tribes.

Stories of Narasimha and Chenchitha

Similar to the stories of Radha, the stories of Chenchitha are well known in popular lore. She is lovingly recollected in songs, folk arts, and literary classics, but she is missing from the classical Puranas, although ever-present in the local Puranas. Local stories of Narasimha haven't been studied extensively in relation to other contextual information. Even if they were studied they were studied in isolation. One of the common themes that predominate these studies is to examine the "insider" and "outsider" identities of tribal Hindus versus other Hindus even though there is no historical evidence to identify them as rival social groups (see Chapters 6 and 8). The differences among various social groups are merely in lifestyle rather than religion. The popular nature of the stories of the marriage of Chenchitha and Narasimha as well as the prevalence of this story in folk performance traditions shows that the original progenitors of this story may have been Chenchus rather than other social groups.

The Chenchus follow an ancient style of Hinduism with animistic practices similar to the early Vedic religion in which forces of nature such as the Sun, Moon, and stars are regarded as gods and elements of nature such as water, air, fire, and so on, are similarly regarded as symbols of the divine. It was also said that the Chenchus originally worshipped some jungle deities (Sontheimer 1987), in an utter disregard for the religious practices of the Chenchus including Narasimha, even though the stories and foundations of cave temples of Ahobilam are dated at least to 300–400 CE (Vasantha 1991: 70), which helps establish the fact that the cave temple may have been maintained by the Chenchus along with their sacred story traditions before their renovation and reconstruction in the second millennium under the Kakatiyas (eleventh to fourteenth century) and Vijayanagara (thirteenth to seventeenth century) rulers much later. As the

Vijayanagara emperor Narasimha Raya was betrayed by a section of his Muslim battallions at the battle of Talikota changing to the side of Golconda Sultans, leading to the fall of Vijayanagara empire (January 23, 1565). Following this many families associated with arts and Narasimha traditions were displaced. Many subsequently moved to Tamil Nadu finding support from the Nayaka rulers of Madurai, Tanjore, and Gingee, who continued to support the traditional culture of the Vijayanagara empire (Guy 2016).

The scholarly analysis presents Chenchus as if they were passive participants in the cultural evolution happening within their cultural centers utilizing their traditional tales. This cannot be far from the truth. Close examination of the traditional lore associated with Chenchus and their traditional practice shows that they continue to preserve ancient Hindu belief systems more symbolic of the ancient practice. The Chenchus follow strict endogamy through which they were able to preserve the most ancient genetic heritage of India. Similarly, they may have been able to preserve numerous ancient cultural traditions, noticed in the religion, arts, and dress of the region. Scholars have theorized that the outsiders introduced the story of Chenchitha to somehow influence the Chenchus when the case might have been the opposite as one examines the religious and cultural practices of the Chenchus.

Marriage is construed as a theme of assimilation in the early scholarship (Shulman Sontheimer) even though it might only be a symbol of the symbiotic relationship of numerous social groups of India (see Chapters 7 and 8). Like Radha, Chenchulakshmi is absent from the classical Puranas, but omnipresent in all local traditions, literary, folk, as well as temple practices.

Gonds

Gonds are residents of the Nagpur region and rulers of the areas in the premodern era. Hence, the monuments of Ramtek, an important center of the Narasimha tradition, continued to be protected from destruction during the premodern era. The Gonds seemed to have formed part of the Kakatiya military and were known to have been originally residents of northern Telangana. They founded republics within the Gondwana region of Middle India which included parts of Maharashtra, Chhattisgarh, and Telangana. Gonds resisted the incursions of the Delhi Sultanate and subsequent Mughal rulers of India. Hence, numerous monuments located in these regions survived, including the temples of Narasimha.

Khonds

Khonds are noted in the hill tracts of the Eastern Ghats in the states of Odisha and northern Andhra Pradesh, although some Khonds have adapted to living in the plains leading to divisions within the tribe, known as Hill Khonds and Plains Khonds. The Khonds are seen in the foundation and services offered at numerous temples in Odisha. The Padampur temple Nrusimhanatha temple is closely associated with Khonds.

Yakshaganam

Yakshaganam is an important dance-drama tradition spread in Andhra Pradesh and Karnataka. Singers and actors dressed in bright costumes bring stories to life with the help of live singing, musical instruments, dancing, and verse recitation. The narrative of Narasimha is one of the earlier oral tales noted in the Yakshaganam tradition. Although it is a popular art form known since the twelfth century, Yakshaganam found the support of the Vijayanagara empire which helped its historical growth in Karnataka and Andhra Pradesh. The mela connected Narasimha Jayanti in Tamil Nadu is known as Bhagavata Mela, which includes performances (Yakshaganam) based on the legend on Narasimha, more specifically the Hiranya Natakam and other subjects as Prahlada Vijayam and Chenchunatakam. The name of the town Melattur comes from the term Mela as it is associated with performing the Bhagavata Mela and found support from the local Nayaks. Lack of scholarly attention to Bhagavata Mela is noted, "as a village-based tradition, the Bhagavata Mela never attracted the scholarly attention or patronage of the urban elite that the early 20th-century revival of the Bharatanatyam dance tradition has enjoyed. Rather, it has survived to modern times as a village-sponsored communal act of worship, devotional in both intent and meaning" (Guy 2016: 34). This is true of the traditional practice associated with Narasimha in general. The Melattur tradition preserves a style of Yakshaganam, which is performed with large wooden masks.

Oggukatha

Oggukatha is a truly important pop singing tradition of ancient Telangana. In Oggukatha the singer is central to the storytelling performance. The central singer wears layers of anklets which make a rhythmic jingling sound of ankle bells as he moves around singing his story in simple sentences composed in Telugu easily understood by the audience. Scholarly studies of this popular genre bring out notable aspects of the popular culture of central India (Emigh 1984). However, this popular art form is still well received and adapted to modern subjects. Oggukatha was recently utilized in a Telugu film, *Pressure Cooker* (https://www.imdb.com/title/tt10801196/; https://en.wikipedia.org/wiki/Pressure_Cooker_(2020_film)), demonstrating its continued acceptance within the popular culture of Telugu regions.

Chukka Picchayya is one of the most popular Oggukatha singers of Telangana. The versions differ based on the singer. It is notable that in most of the popular stories narrated Lakshmi is actively involved in protecting and supporting Narasimha. Another important feature of the features of popular stories is that missing elements from textual and traditional narratives are highlighted.

The focus is on Prahlada's difficulties with punishments meted out by his father Hiranyakashipu and how Lakshmi/Bhulakshmi protected him and saved him even feeding and taking care of him appearing as his mother Leelavathi when he was imprisoned for fourteen days for his transgressions of praising Vishnu as a young child, so young that Lakshmi had to change his diaper when he was in the prison, so indicating that he was only a toddler at that time, when his father's torments began, in one of the versions sung by Chukka Sattayya hosted on YouTube (Sri Laxmi Narasimha Swamy Oggukatha by Chukka Sattayya: https://www.youtube.com/watch?v=hmlqkWYYCKY). Classical texts describe how the difficulties of Prahlada began as he began chanting Vishnu's name in school, which brought concern as Sukracharya the asura guru complained to his father Hiranyakasipu, the demon king. As numerous punishments are meted out to Prahlada Vishnu appears as Narasimha to rescue Prahlada (see Chapter 2). However, the popular traditions of Oggukatha and Yakshaganam bring the events to life through narrating the events with human connection. The oral and popular performance traditions are brought to life in the current society even though the legends happened millennia ago.

Individual Vratas and Pilgrimages

Individuals participate in the temple festivals, jataras/melas, and also form part of the popular traditions such as performances, storytelling traditions, and pilgrimages. In addition, individuals also undertake their vratas and celebrations at home. Individuals are part of celebrations conducted at the temple, as a social group, but individual vratas and celebrations form a crucial part of religious practice in connection with Narasimha.

Narasimha Manthra and Yantra

The most frequently used mantra addressed to Narasimha is included here:

Ugram veeram mahavishnum jwalantham sarvatho mukham|
Nrisimham bheeshannam bhadhram mrityumrityum namaamyaham||

"I bow to Lord Narasimha who is ferocious, heroic, and the great Vishnu, as well as terrifying, auspicious, and death on to death." This mantra of Narasimha includes the nine forms of Narasimha (Nava Narasimhas) as follows: Ugra (ferocious), Veera (heroic), Mahavishnu (Narasimha), Jwalanta (Jwala Narasimha), Sarvatomukha (multifaceted/universal form), Narasimha (Kevala Narasimha), Bhishana (terrifying), Bhadra (graceful), Mrutyormrutyum (death on to death—Kalanta). This is the most frequently used mantra during worship as well as meditation centered on Narasimha (Vemsani 2016a).

The Narasimha mantra is praised in texts such as Narasimha Purva Tapani Upanishad (1.1) as the Mantraraja (mulamantra) (Jena 19; 301–2). The Narasimha Purva Tapani Upanishad mentions that the god appeared to Brahma as Narasimha first and gave him the Narasimha Anushtup mantra with the help of which he was able to realize the Vedas and begin creation. The Narasimha Tapaniya Upanishad is one of the numerous Upanishads connected with Atharvaveda. The Narasimha Purva Tapani Upanishad and the Narasimha Uttara Tapani Upanishad explain the story, theology, and rituals. The Narasimha Purva Tapani Upanishad includes three sections explaining the meaning and importance of the Narasimha mantra. This Upanishad explains the series of mantras to be recited with the Narasimha mantra (4.1–2). The Narasimha mantra is to be accompanied by (1) Pranava, (2) Savitri, (3) Yajurlakshmi, and (4) Narasimha Gayatri.

The first mantra, Pranava is Aum, as known in the Vedas, which represents the world. The meaning of Aum is explained here in the Narasimha Purva Tapani Upanishad similar to the Vedic texts (Atharvasikha Upanishad). The second mantra is the Savitri mantra of the Rigveda, also known as the Gayatri mantra. The Gayatri mantra is foremost of the mantras recited in Hindu households and rituals, which is also included here with the Narasimha mantra. The third mantra is the Yajurlakshmi mantra, the 24-syllabic veneration of Lakshmi. Inclusion of this mantra within the list of mantras to be recited in the worship

Figure 11 Yoga Narasimha (tenth century to twelfth century CE), Chola Panchaloha. Image courtesy: Metropolitan Museum of Art, New York.

of Narasimha signifies the importance of gender and feminine divine noted as the consort of Narasimha (see Chapter 5). The fourth mantra is Narasimha Gayatri[2] (Narasimha Purva Tapani Upanishad 4.2. Om Nrisimhaya Vidmahe| Vajranakhaya Dhimahi|| Tanno Simhah Prachodayat|||).

One of the most common practices centered on Narasimha is yoga practice. Numerous temples are also associated with Tantrayoga of Narasimha at specific temples such as the Narasimha temple at Mattapalli (Vedagiri 2004). Yoga schools centered on Narasimha are also noticed across the world (Figure 11).

Narasimha Yantra (Chakra)

Yantra is used for meditation and marking sacred points (shaktipithas) in the temples. The Yantra is the visual representation of the mantra. The Narasimha Purva Tapani Upanishad (5.2) provides a very helpful representation of the Narasimha Chakra. While the center is inscribed with om, it contains sections on the circle similar to an eight-petaled lotus. It has six circles of expanding measurements; on the outer circle is inscribed the Narasimha mantra, one word on each section.

Narasimha Mudra and Narasimha Salagrama

Mudras and Salagramas are used for worship and meditation. The Garuda Purana describes the Narasimha mudra as that of bending three fingers ending with the little finger of both hands and keeping both hands bent down (Garuda Purana I.11.30). Salagramas are ammonite shells generally collected from the Gandaki river. The shapes of the stones as well as the rings noticeable from the small opening in the center of the stone help determine the representation of deity with the stone. The Narasimha temple at Mangalagiri hosts a number of Salagramas, connected with many deities in addition to Narasimha. Puranas (Garuda Purana I.45.17-18; Padma Purana V. Patalakhanda 78-31; Agni Purana 46.5) describe Narasimha Salagrama as a stone with a stout chest and with three or five dots. Its color is described as tawny. Agni Purana (47.2) further says that the triad of Salagramas of Varaha, Narasimha, and Trivikrama should be worshipped together to attain liberation. Salagramas are worshipped in the temples and homes. An important collection of Salagramas denoting a number of gods are housed in the Narasimha temple at Mangalagiri.

Narasimha Vratas

Numerous vratas have been undertaken for the purposes of obtaining a select goal. A number of Narasimha vratas are discussed in the Caturvarga Chintamani (Vratakhanda I). The Narasimhashthami (Ch. 12), Narasimha Dvadashi (Ch. 15), Narasimha Trayodashi (Ch. 17), and Narasimha Chaturdashi (Ch. 18) are most commonly celebrated by devotees. The vratas are undertaken by individual followers at home, which involves rules of purity, fasting, and abstaining from certain foods and activities. Vratas involve self-discipline as well as devotion.

Individual pilgrimage is undertaken to participate in festivals of the temple as well as to fulfill personal wishes such as seeking marriage, children, good health, and prosperity. Individuals might also undertake a pilgrimage to the temple upon worldly success in tasks undertaken, such as wars in the ancient period, but other challenging tasks in the modern world.

Vratakhanda of *Caturvarga Chintamani* of Hemadri (Ch. 12) discusses Narasimha Ashthami also called Narasimha Vrata which is described as an important vrata for obtaining success in battles by vanquishing the enemies.

Narasimha Chaturdashi (Padma Purana VI. Uttarakhanda 174.1-98; Naradiya Purana I.123.8-13; Skandapurana. Purshottama Mayatmya Ch. 16.63-6) vrata is most commonly observed festival in connection with Narasimha; it and is also known as the Narasimha Jayanti (day of origin of Narasimha), the most important day celebrated in connection with Narasimha. As these vows and rituals are discussed in detail in the Puranas and Chaturvarga Chintamani, it is notable that no restriction of caste or sect is mentioned. Each individual is encouraged to undertake the vows due to his/her own choices. Hinduism is a living tradition, and how the legends and devotional traditions are brought to life through the modes of practice discussed in this chapter indicates the invigorating religious life, even though no strict rules other than the basics are laid down in the texts.

Conclusion

The classical traditions and popular traditions may preserve numerous traditions, but it all comes together in the practice and the arts performed in the temples as well as individual practice. The rituals of the temples, the forms in which the deity appears, and the festivals celebrated at the temple, the stories narrated and the personal practice of individual devotees, all somehow connect with the symbolism and narratives associated with the deity. Major festivals celebrated at the deity Narasimha temples such as Narasimha Jayanti and Brahmotsavalu reveal the opportunities when the arts, rituals, and narrative traditions come together. Arts, literature, ritual, and celebration are brought together during the Narasimha Jayanti. The festival celebrated for five to seven days involves showcasing arts, such as Yakshaganam, Harikatha, and Chenchunatakam (Vasantika Parinayam). It also involves a crafts market with herbal (Ayurveda) shows. The temple organizes special rituals and the followers complete or undertake vows upon their visits to the temple. The individual, temple, and public rituals (chariot festival, processions, boat festival) coalesce, informing the theological debates of the texts and the public displays of faith.

10

Conclusion

Narasimha in Totality

Life and religion are intermixed in multiple ways in the spiritual land of India. Life is inseparable from the land, which is expressed in numerous ways through the cultural practices. Numerous practices of religion, literature, and performance arts studied in this book bring this forward even more explicitly. As emphatically noted in the Rigveda (1.154.2) "living in the mountains and roaming wherever he wants," the sacred geography marks Narasimha's presence in the mountains, and other unique geographical land formations which are consecrated with temples across Middle India noting the presence of Narasimha; thus emerges the *leelasthali* of Narasimha, etched on the memory of the people.

As the book draws to a close, this chapter provides the results of research presented in the previous chapters on the central themes of symbolic association of Narasimha with the middle, along with the representation of this concept in the land, literature, ritual, and theatrical practice of Middle India in association with Narasimha.

A comprehensive examination of Hinduism in Middle India (Madhya Desha) is undertaken in the previous pages of this book through an examination of the deity Narasimha from classical texts, historical resources, and oral tales. Historically Narasimha is imbibed in the life and culture of Middle India in its religion, arts, and culture. Any examination of the religion of Middle India is incomplete without including an examination of the deity Narasimha. Hence the present book contributes to a holistic understanding of the Narasimha tradition and a broad understanding of religion in Middle India. This book also contributes to the methodological study of the history of religion by incorporating oral sources along with literary and historical sources.

Therefore, this chapter, Conclusion, briefly discusses the common themes, methodical issues, and results, in addition to copious information on Narasimha available in connection with Middle India discussed throughout this book. It draws from the analysis of Narasimha contained in the previous nine chapters of the current book to present a comprehensive summary of the subject under study here. This chapter also emphatically presents the unique affiliation of Narasimha with not only Vishnu, but also Shiva, and the goddesses.

This chapter also uncovers the special nature of Narasimha's appearance in Middle India, precisely at Ahobilam in Kurnool district of Andhra Pradesh, identifying and establishing the sacred geography of the region as the *leelasthali* (zone of divine play) of Narasimha. Almost all the temples of Narasimha in the central part of Middle India are connected to the appearance and visit of Narasimha, while most of the temples in the peripheral zones of the east and west of the middle region are connected to Prahlada establishing the temples (Simhachalam) or the miraculous appearance of Narasimha to devotees (Padampur, Mangalagiri, Penchalakona) in reincarnation or dream vision.

This book fulfils the need for a holistic examination for the conceptual understanding of Narasimha, which is currently lacking due to the cursory nature of studies on Narasimha, since no comprehensive examination had been previously undertaken to bring together disparate sources and practices. Even though the land of Middle India is connected to Narasimha symbolically it is persuasively expressed in his symbolic connection to his sacred geography. Andhra Pradesh is designated as the land of Narasimha through his divine incarnation followed by numerous events depicting his divine play (*leela*), thus designating Andhra Pradesh as the *leelasthali* of Narasimha certainly clear. The whole area of Middle India (Madhya Desha) is connected with Narasimha as the zone of his divine play symbolically acquiring the symbolic qualities represented by him as the middle (see Chapters 1 and 9). Geographical landmarks bearing the transitional qualities are symbolically identified with Narasimha.

It is always the case that in each of the incarnations Vishnu accomplishes his tasks of vanquishing the demons and re-establishing dharma. Part of re-establishing dharma is revealing his special nature as well as connecting with his most devoted followers. As Krishna, the god revealed himself to the most simple folks he lived with in the region of Braj, the Gopis and the Gopas. Similarly, as Narasimha, the god revealed himself in Ahobilam and attached himself to the simplest folk of the region, the forest-dwellers, Chenchus, Khonds, and Sabaras (see Chapter 2 and Chapter 9). Middle India could be called the Narasimha Mandala for the way the traditions of Narasimha are intimately affiliated with the land and the people of the region.

Even though completely embraced by the folk traditions of the forest-dwellers, the regional practices (Mahatmyas) associated with Narasimha preserve Vedic antecedents, which form the undercurrent of symbolic representations of Narasimha in connection with the Namuci story indirectly. Therefore, one of the areas containing the early evidence of Narasimha in Andhra Pradesh, Mangalagiri, preserves the affiliation of Narasimha with the Namuci story more explicitly in practice as well as in symbolism through iconic representation and preservation of salagramas within the temple (see Chapter 6). The Sudarsana Chakra atop the Mangalagiri hill in which Narasimha is symbolically represented is the representation of the chakra that vanquished the demon Namuci.

Examination of the Narasimha tradition in Middle India shows that the current methods of studying a tradition (religion) focusing exclusively on a single aspect, involving either literary texts or folk practices, is proving to be inadequate to fully fathom the depth of religion in India. Oral traditions hold as much information as the literary sources for understanding Hinduism. Similarly regional texts contain as much important information to enrich our understanding of Indian history and religion as the classical texts. According primacy to Sanskrit literary sources and then constructing a theory of occupation and superimposition of culture by relegating oral and regional traditions to a secondary position merely represents a misunderstanding of the intricate workings of religion among the academic studies concerning a long-standing indigenous civilization. Contrasting classical literary and regional sources as opposite sources, that of belonging to invading occupiers vs. the native people projected a non-existent historical conflict into the cultural life of India. This did not help understand but resulted in a grave injustice to the understanding of religion of India. In addition, the presumed dichotomy between classical and oral literature is misconstrued and led to mistaken understanding of Hinduism. This introduction of perpetual conflict has placed hurdles in the way of the examination of Indian culture resulting in partial understanding leading to outlandish claims about Indian religion and culture.

Therefore, the study of Narasimha traditions in this book brings forward newer methods of examination for the understanding of Hinduism through considering oral resources and literary sources on an equal footing. This study contributes to a comprehensive understanding of religion in Middle India, and this also helps us to re-examine the methods of study of Hinduism, which displayed partisan interpretations and a one-sided understanding of Indian sources. It is important to move away from these colonialist frameworks based on Aryan invasions to arrive at a true understanding of India. This is important to maintain the trust and responsibility reposed in academia to bring truth to the forefront.

Introduction: Narasimha, the Lord of the Middle in Middle India

This book begins with an examination of previous academic work on Narasimha along with a discussion of the methods and plan of the current study. Since the past academic studies on the deity Narasimha is studied isolation separated by outdated criteria based on the nature of available resources, either the classical texts or the folk tradition, the resulting understanding is limited. Thus, separating the practices associated with Narasimha into two, classifying them as classical traditions and folk traditions juxtaposing them rather than studying them jointly, had led to spreading confusion on the subject of study. Therefore, in this book the first chapter devotes a considerable amount of space to discussing the lacunae of previous scholarship of Narasimha. Here, the study also turns to identifying the geography of Middle India, the symbolic nature of Narasimha, in addition to an examination of the previous scholarly work on Narasimha. The first chapter helps to establish the scope of the subject and the merits of studying the subject from all available sources rather than singular sources. Therefore, our examination of the subject, previous scholarship, and identifying the geographical base provide us the necessary springboard for the innovative study of Narasimha that follows in the subsequent chapters of this book.

Chapter 2: Classical Sources of Narasimha: Symbolism of the Middle

Examination of the subject of Narasimha begins with an examination of classical accounts of Narasimha from the Vedas, Puranas, and folk traditions. This chapter begins with applying the method of thematic understanding of Narasimha regardless of the nature of sources. Hence, the goal of this chapter is not to discuss each source separately, but to study each of the sources with regards to Narasimha and bring together the most common thread of all-encompassing features of Narasimha spread across the variety of sources regardless of the nature of the source, either classical or folk tradition. Interestingly, each of the sources provides us with unique information, which only provides part of the information on a special aspect of the sojourn of the avatara Narasimha. One needs to bring together information from all the available sources together to arrive at a comprehensive understanding of Narasimha. Like the parable of the elephant and blindmen, studying parts could only lead to partial understanding leading to mistaken assumptions. Hence, examination of complete set of varied sources is important than focusing on each source independently.

The Vedic texts provide cryptic verse on the nature of the deity, while the Vaishnava texts narrate the divine appearance of Narasimha, the Shaiva texts provide information on the withdrawal of the avatara, while the most crucial part of the story, the earthly sojourn, marriage, and life of Narasimha, is provided by the regional stories (Sthalapuranas) and popular tales (Mahatmyas). It is necessary to analyze all of these storied source texts together to help one arrive at the complete cultural context of Narasimha, since none of the sources, when studied individually, provide complete information to analyze and understand the mystical avatara of Narasimha.

The Vaishnava Puranas depict the austerities of Hiranyakashipu followed by his special boon, and his demonic rule overturning the world order. The texts also narrate the travails of Prahlada along with the appearance of avatara Narasimha and vanquishing of the demon Hiranyakashipu as well as returning the upturned universe (*trilokas*) back to its proper course of order restoring universal harmony and dharma. Although the Vaishnava Puranas provide ample information on the cosmology, theology, and Bhakti, they remain silent on the legend of the earthly sojourn of the deity Narasimha. These additional details are furnished by the Shaiva Puranas, Sthalapuranas, and popular tales preserved in the Telugu states in Middle India.

The Shaiva Puranas furnish the withdrawal of the Narasimha form by symbolically incorporating the Kala (Time) in the terrifying form of Shiva, the Bhairava. The appearance of Narasimha temples in association with Shiva temples or in major Shaiva kshetras needs to be understood in this context. Here, we also encounter the deeper symbolic association of Narasimha with the goddess, the Shaktis (Matrikas). Chapter 2 also surveys the close affiliation of Narasimha with Shiva and the goddesses (Matrikas), which provides context for understanding the representation of Narasimha in the state of Odisha.

The most interesting accounts of Narasimha are received in the form of Sthalapuranas and Mahatmyas of Narasimha. Narasimha's marriage, his yoga practices, and visits to sacred centers of significance are narrated in detail in the accounts preserved lovingly by the common folk through oral rendition before being committed to writing beginning in the early second millennium from the twelfth century CE. These unique events are also preserved in the special landmarks of middle India.

Therefore, it is very important to bring all these distinct resources together to chart out the journey of Narasimha, which is also important for understanding the religion of Middle India (Madhya Desha). The religion of Madhya Desha is deeply entwined with Narasimha as the region is depicted as the *leelasthali* (land of divine play) of the deity. Each of the rivers and major mountains which dot the region with numerous temples are identified with the *leela* of Narasimha.

Chapter 3: Historical Narasimha from Prehistory to Present

Notable early evidence of Narasimha is found in the Rigveda (datable between 4500 BCE and 2300 BCE), while the early excavations in Vidisa (600 BCE–400 BCE) reveal material evidence. Next evidence is noted from the Shatavahana era at Nasik caves. Even though the early material evidence for the god Narasimha are few and infrequent it successfully establishes the well-entrenched tradition of Narasimha in the first millennium BCE. Such parity in data could have been explained by loss beyond recovery, especially, the long timespan might have been a cause for natural destruction. However, textual resources abound for this period. The textual narrative of the Mahabharata and the Puranas are spread between 400 BCE and 1000 CE, indicating the growing influence of Narasimha on the religious mosaic of India. However, beginning with the early first millennium the material evidence also multiplies gradually in the form of coins, seals, and monuments. The earliest historical evidence for the practice of devotional traditions associated with Narasimha in central India is noted from the Gupta period onwards at the now destroyed and partially preserved Eran temple complex. Early monuments are also noted from Telangana datable to the Chalukyan era temples of Narasimha. The eastern part of the Madhya Desha preserved early sculptural and monumental evidence. The sculptural evidence of a Narasimha panel from Kondamotu and an image of Narasimha from Motadaka, recovered in excavations datable between 100 and 300 CE, indicate the prevalence of early Narasimha traditional practice of this region. Early temples datable to the regional Chalukya states are noted in Andhra Pradesh and Telangana. In the eastern region of Middle India, Odisha also has monuments preserved from 800 CE.

The Vakataka era temples of Maharashtra and Eastern Chalukya of Karnataka provide evidence of the widespread religious practice associated with Narasimha from 400 CE onwards. Even though the monumental and sculptural remains are not uniform, the availability of local stories in Middle India indicates the enduring practice based on the deity Narasimha.

Chapter 4: Narasimha in Middle India: From Rigveda to Oggukatha

The sacred geography of the middle region is reflected in the divine symbolism and the association of its unique landforms with Narasimha. It is important to understand the symbolism of the association of creation and the Earth with Vishnu to be able to analyze the symbolism of the middle and its representation in the avatara of Narasimha and also the land itself. The land reflects the god Narasimha identifying unique Shaktisthalas, which continue to extol Narasimha through temples, traditions, and practices. Vishnu is the partner of Bhumi, the goddess of the Earth, and the cosmogony and cosmology uniting the life on the Earth with the world of gods.

Chapter 5: Lakshmi in the Classical and Regional Tales of Narasimha: Gender and Family

Lakshmi plays the most important role in the universe as the feminine counterpart of Vishnu. The role of Lakshmi as Bhulakshmi/Bhudevi is noticed along with the Varaha incarnation, the previous incarnation of Vishnu. Lakshmi relates to Vishnu and the Earth as the prosperity and positive attributes of the world. Even though the Puranas are sparse about the incarnation of Lakshmi, local tales abound about her incarnation among the simple folk of Ahobilam, the Chenchus. The romantic tale of Chenchulakshmi and Narasimha's marriage and their life forms the basis for numerous narratives and folk songs in Andhra Pradesh. It is through the tales of arts narrating the stories of Chenchulakshmi and Narasimha that the divine *leela* and the incorporation of *leelasthali* into the popular memory of Middle India are noticed.

Chapter 6: Narasimha in the Eastern Region: Odisha and Andhra Pradesh

Devotional and religious practices associated with Narasimha in the states of Andhra Pradesh and Odisha form the subject of study in Chapter 6 of this book. The traditional religion and practices of Narasimha are centered in the state of Andhra Pradesh as the appearance of Narasimha is located in Ahobilam,

Andhra Pradesh. Similarly, early evidence from Kondamotu and Motadaka is also located in the state of Andhra Pradesh. Similar practices in association with Narasimha are noticed in the state of Odisha at the temples of Padampur. The unique tradition of Narasimha in the state of Odisha is the affiliation of Jagannatha with Narasimha and the goddesses. Narasimha traditions in the eastern region preserve unique tales of the feminine divine with the mother goddesses, the Matrikas, and multiple forms of Lakshmi, as Sri Lakshmi and Chenchu Lakshmi.

Examining the historical and sculptural resources this chapter studies the practices and performance traditions associated with Narasimha in the states of Odisha and Andhra Pradesh. Although many of the early sacred centers of Narasimha have been destroyed, early practices associated with Narasimha could be discovered from the sculptures excavated from Kondamotu and Motadaka indicating the devotional practices associated with Narasimha as early as the first century CE. The most important sacred center of Narasimha is located in the center of the middle region at Ahobilam. Even though most of the sacred centers of Narasimha were subjected to attacks, many survived, Ahobilam being one of those centers, which was revived despite repeated attacks and looting. This chapter helps elucidate the enduring traditions, performances, and practices associated with Narasimha through the study of regional sacred lore (Mahatmyas) and practices.

Chapter 7: Narasimha in the Central Region: Madhya Pradesh, Chhattisgarh, and Telangana

The central region of Middle India consists of the states of Madhya Pradesh, Chhattisgarh, and Telangana. The earliest evidence for the devotional practice of Narasimha comes from Madhya Pradesh in the form of a seal excavated at Bidisa datable between 600 and 400 BCE. This seal depicts a seated Narasimha (Kevala Narasimha), which is in line with numerous later depictions. Another massive image of Narasimha currently lies at the temple complex at Eran datable to the Gupta era, 300–400 CE. These images are coeval with the composition of the Mahabharata and the earliest Puranas, which establishes the well-established tradition of Narasimha in literary and devotional traditions well ahead of 600 BCE for it to be represented so emphatically in literary and sculptural representations by this period. Temples and traditions in the states of Telangana and Chhattisgarh also record temples of Narasimha from the first millennium CE onwards. Closer affiliations with yoga as well as health and healing form an important aspect of Narasimha traditions in this region.

Chapter 8: Narasimha in the Western Region: Maharashtra and Karnataka

Focusing on the states of Maharashtra and Karnataka, this chapter examines the early sources such as inscriptions and cave temples along with modern temples and legends. This region is unique for preserving early evidence of devotional practices associated with Narasimha as well as being noted for preserving some of the massive depictions of Narasimha, at Hampi, Ellora, and Badami. Early evidence is noted from Ramtek from the Vakataka inscriptions of Queen-Regent Prabhavati Gupta. Similarly, Chalukyan cave temples and depictions from Ellora and Badami also include images of Narasimha, which indicate a well-entrenched Narasimha tradition in this region before the early centuries of the first millennium CE. One of the interesting features noted in the Narasimha temples of the western region is the explicit depiction of a closer affiliation of Narasimha and Shiva. Even though early scholarly works hypothesized the appearance of Narasimha in a region of Shiva devotion as anathema it is in accordance within the established theological norms of Narasimha notable in the Puranas. The western region is notable for unique practices associated with Narasimha in the context of yoga and his association with Shiva.

Chapter 9: Narasimha in Popular Culture, Performing Arts, and Devotional Practice

Narasimha lives in the memory of the people through the performing arts and practices. This art is not merely an art, but imbued with spiritual and devotional essence every time it is performed in the temples or among the devotees. The rituals performed every day as well as special rituals performed during festivals of Narasimha connect the present generation of devotees with a profound ancestral lineage of rites and rituals performed millennia ago by the ancestors in the same manner in the same region. Therefore, popular culture is central to understanding the Narasimha tradition in Middle India since most of the information regarding the life of Narasimha is preserved in the Sthalapuranas and popular tales preserved in the songs and stories of the region.

Conclusion: Narasimha in Totality

The comprehensive examination of the Narasimha tradition undertaken in the previous chapters of the present book is noted in this chapter. The examination of texts, traditions, and practices associated with Narasimha revealed the religion and Hindu practice in Middle India. This study showed that a comprehensive examination of Narasimha helped us to understand Hinduism in practice in one of the crucial geographical locations of India. This study has also shown that the examination of disparate sources such as classical texts and popular traditions helps us to gain a deeper understanding of the religion and culture of a region in depth.

This book has examined the literary and oral literature as well as performance and practice together to describe the symbolic nature of the tradition and its representation in practice. In addition, this book has shown the futility of separating classical literary sources and regional tales (oral as well as performance traditions) as opposites, but shows the nature of all these sources as complementary. Scholarly preoccupation with Aryan invasion/migration theory rendered the primary evidence on hand inadequate for understanding the cultural and religious traditions of India. First, this preconceived view led to the perception that the Vedic and classical evidence of Narasimha was non-indigenous to India and somehow brought from outside of the subcontinent. Second, the regional tales and practices were considered only ancillary and later in origin, and not helpful for understanding the religion of India. In this overarching "invader vs. indigenous" framework, the Chenchus and other local communities who kept the oral stories and cared for and maintained the temples were seen as gullible communities passively receiving cultural influences from outsiders without questioning. However, it is not clear why the influences which came from northwestern India did not influence the northwestern or northern states before finally reaching Middle India to establish the Narasimha tradition. If this Aryan invasion theory was true, the Narasimha tradition should have shown gradual spread from northwestern India to Middle India to southern India. However, no such gradual expansion could be seen in the northern to the southern direction. On the contrary, the Narasimha tradition appears deeply entrenched in Middle India, especially in the Telugu region, the states of Telangana and Andhra Pradesh, spreading gradually in all directions.

Methodological Focus

Oral traditions did not receive their due within the field of the historical study of Indian religions. Even though some ethnographic studies were conducted previously in the western and eastern parts of Middle India, the focus had always been on retrofitting the subject under study with the Aryan invasion/migration theoretical frameworks. For example, an ethnographic study on the western part of Middle India of pastoralists ended up naming the deities as Pastoral Deities as though deities have caste and are restricted to a single social community (Sontheimer 1989). Similarly, ethnographic studies on the eastern part of Middle India, Odisha, called Narasimha a tribal god, "hill born" (Girija), again applying the Aryan invasion frameworks, even though the evidence pointed to the influence coming from the opposite direction, the south, from Andhra Pradesh.[1] Therefore, it is clear that the earlier scholarly studies gave primacy to the theoretical sources (Aryan invasion, etc.) that were not even part of the study, and relegated the primary evidence on hand to a secondary position. Hence, I suggest that the evidence of oral sources, performance tradition, and practice should be accorded primacy, while the classical references should be considered in conjunction to understand the cultural and social history. History and history of religions have relegated the oral sources to the background with perilous results. A change would help bring an authentic understanding of the history of religion to the fore.

Sometimes it almost seems that the understanding of a region is sacrificed in favor of imposing the preconceived theory of Aryan invasion or Hinduization. At least for Middle India, based on the evidence discussed in this book, this theory seems misconstrued, since no progressive spread from northern to southern India is noted, but evidence only indicates gradual evolution of religious practices here. For this Aryan invasion theory to work with regards to Narasimha, the earliest evidence must be encountered in northwestern India along with copious amounts of sacred centers and datasets located in northern India. Following that, only a small superimposed layer of information must be connected to Middle India, with even less information noticed in southern India.

Such gradual emergence of Narasimha could not be traced from northwestern India to southern India, but the greatest centers and practices are located in Middle India, with peripheral spread located in the northwestern and southern parts of India, which indicates that the traditions of Narasimha originated in the middle region of India. This also firmly contradicts the previous notions of Aryan invasions and spreading of culture and language into the peninsula and southern India. The performance traditions further support this theory of the indigenous development of religious traditions of India.

Methodological Concerns and the Future Course of Indological Studies

One of the major overarching frameworks applied to almost any subject of study concerning India is the Aryan invasion theory. Hinduism is considered to have been brought into India by some invaders although evidence for their arrival in India is scarce. Examination of the Narasimha story showed how certain aspects of the Narasimha story are isolated for applying this theory of invasions. The deity Narasimha's stories from classical texts and ethnographic/oral sources are studied separately representing Narasimha as not one, but two Narasimhas, the classical Narasimha, and the folk Narasimha. They also theorized that Narasimha became part of local tradition by being identified with hill or assuming female representation, Narasimhi (see Chapter 6). The most common hypothesis of such studies is the application of Aryan invasion theory arriving at a preconceived conclusion of Hinduization, another term for Aryanization or Sanskritization. It is hypothesized that the popular forms of Narasimha are localized at temples in various sacred centers of Odisha or Andhra Pradesh. The regional practices of Odisha were interpreted to show that the folk Narasimha of sacred centers (Padampur and others) may have originated as a folk deity of Khonds before he was assimilated into Hinduism (see Chapter 6).

The devotion of Prahlada, Chenchus, and others is interpreted to represent Aryan invasion and a machination of Brahmins to assimilate tribal groups into Hinduism (see Chapters 3, 6, 7, and 8). The devotion of Prahlada is interpreted to show that non-Aryan folk societies were assimilated into Hinduism.

Narasimha's marriage to Chenchulakshmi is interpreted to show that a folk deity/folk goddess was absorbed into Hinduism. This hypothesis also assumes that a lion-type of totemic god and a popular goddess might have been worshiped before their assimilation into Hinduism through marriage without adequate evidence. Marriage has been one of the aspects interpreted to show a non-Aryan folk society was assimilated into Hinduism (see Chapters 5, 6, and 8).

In their enthusiasm to show two Narasimhas, one an avatara of Vishnu and another a folk totemic deity of the tribals, scholars utilized select sources, ignoring contrary evidence. Theories are construed to show the existence of two Narasimhas as separate, but popular deities even though no concrete evidence for such existence of two distinct deities is available in any sources. This theory was only construed to support the invasion and occupation theories isolating elements of Narasimha traditions. However, our examination of classical as well as regional sources disproves such theories as all aspects associates with Narasimha show organic growth and symbolic representation within the land and culture of Middle India.

Therefore, the crucial events in the story of Narasimha are interpreted to support an overarching theory of Indology construed a century ago rather than applying current indigenous frameworks developed from examining the local stories and factors as sources for understanding Indian religion and society. The oral traditions such as the Yakshaganam, Oggukatha, or Bhagavatamela are studied as art forms but not authoritative sources contributing to the understanding of religion and society. Similarly, the oral and regional texts of temples take a back seat in favor of classical texts; popular oral versions of Chenchulakshmi story are ignored while the Sanskrit composition of this story, Vasantika Parinayam is examined to resulting in partial understanding of the culture. The practitioners of these forms of oral performances, as well the devotees are seen as passive receivers, but not as active participants of religion and culture. Their performances are considered secondary in the case of subject matter, while the Sanskrit texts are considered primary. The foregoing study on Narasimha in this book from a variety of sources showed that the affiliation of Narasimha with common folks and his association with the land are embedded in the personality of Vishnu (see Chapter 4). The symbolism of the middle and/or transitions embedded in the accounts of Vishnu plays a crucial role in Narasimha's association with common people on the margins and the forest-dwellers. This symbolism is also seen in the sacred centers, located on the hills or forest and identified with Narasimha. From the Vedas to classical stories and then on to the Sthalapuranas (local stories), and theatrical and devotional practices and oral tradition, are connected by a thin thread of symbolism, illuminating the multiple aspects associated with Narasimha in particular and indian religion in particular.

The position of the feminine divine is even more complicated as this aspect of Narasimha's story is also obfuscated through interpreting it within the framework of assimilating Aryans. Although the folk stories identify Chenchulakshmi as a form of Lakshmi, scholars, as well as traditional schools of Vaishnavism, thought to relegate her to the background by envisioning her as the second wife, and a simple forest-dweller, without individual choice or independent will. This type of interpretation also disregards the appearance of Lakshmi as a multi-form goddess in the Vedas and other early texts.

One way forward from this imbroglio for Indological studies is to give primacy to local practices and religion in comparison with the Sanskrit and classical texts. The regional texts and oral traditions must be included along with regional practices to understand the impact of a tradition in India. The regional texts and practices hold deeper meaning for the folk practicing them. Hence, relegating them to the secondary position prevents one from understanding a culture deeply. However, this should be done in a careful and considerate manner not completely divorced from classical texts as doing that might also lead to similar issues. A delicate balance between sanskritic and regional sources, and practices is necessary to achieve a fuller understanding of society and culture.

This book bridges the discrepancy between Indological studies based either on classical texts or on practice. Oral and local sources are used within this framework of previous Indological study, but only partially. This methodological practice of keeping classical texts and practice separate from folk practices has led to discrepancy and to a limited understanding of Indian religion. Early studies failed to comprehend the enormity of the practice centered on Narasimha in Middle India through their survey of the cryptic references of the Vedas and recollection of brief accounts of Narasimha's sojourn from the early Purana texts (Biardau; Hacker; Soifer; Swain). These early studies only understood Narasimha as a minor deity of Hinduism, theorizing that the "High" religion of Aryans might have assimilated Narasimha from folk traditions. Some of the early researchers even expresses bewilderment that a perceivably minor deity of the classical texts might have become a major deity in southern India. The only explanation they have assumed was that it should have been derived from a non-Aryan folk cult, and hence not represented fully in the texts as it was incorporated later. This not only demonstrates the issues with partial study of sources but in addition it shows the debacles of applying preconceived colonial theories to all aspects of Indological studies. By not focusing on peripheral elements of the story such as demonic mischief, while sidelining the central aspects of Narasimha such as his affiliation with the middle and/or transitions, his association with hills, caves, and any elements of land and culture, which incorporate these features, only a partial understanding of the subject is gained.

Another area of studies focusing on Narasimha is based on fieldwork at a single sacred center or a few sacred centers of Narasimha in Andhra Pradesh, Telangana, Maharashtra, Karnataka, and Odisha (Murty; Debicka-Borek; Madabhushini; Sontheimer; Eschmann; Vasantha; Adinarayana; Emigh; Guy). These studies to their credit used a variety of sources such as classical texts, inscriptions, and local stories, in addition to field studies of practice. However, they too fell short of grasping the immensity of the Narasimha tradition due to their focus on a single geographical spot/area or aspect of practice (art or performance). The practices, sacred centers, and local stories are tied by a simple thread of symbolism of Narasimha associated with his distinguishing features. Hence, the temples located at hills and caves, and the performances that do not show the performer, but only the masque depicting the deity, are part of the nature of Narasimha as the *leela* (divine play), which is only visible to the discerning eye and felt by the devoted. Any examination of religion in Middle India without an understanding of the overarching nature of Narasimha demonstrated symbolically fails to understand the true extent of practice associated with Narasimha and the religion of Middle India. The religion of Middle India is symbolically connected to Narasimha through all aspects of practice noticed here, which is not noted in the classical texts, which simply narrate the stories of Narasimha. Therefore, it is important to bring together all these aspects of practice associated with Narasimha to obtain a clear understanding of Hinduism in particular and the religion of India in general.

Glossary

antarala	This is a small hall/room in front of the garbhagriha/garbhagudi. This is where the devotees sit/stand to offer their sevas to the deity.
avatara	This is a concept associated with Vishnu.
Daitya	Demons, so called as a derivative of their mother's name, Diti.
garbagudi/garbhagriha	This is the sanctum sanctorum, the center of the temple in which the deity is seen.
Kala/Mahakala	The form of Shiva as Time, so named Kala, the Sanskrit word for time.
Kali	The divine feminine counterpart of Kala, called Kali or Mahakali.
Kalanta	The end of Time. The complete dissolution of the world. Similarly, life is measured in Time and Space. The end of Time results in the dissolution of Space/body. The end of an era (Yuga) is Yuganta; the end of an entire cycle of Time, Kalpa, is known as Kalpanta.
leela	Divine play, so designated since the incarnation of the deity lives among the common people, who remain unaware of his divinity.
leelasthali	The region touched by the divine play (*leela*) of the deity during his appearance on the Earth.
mandapa	This is a pillared hall. A temple might have a single or multiple mandapas. The first hall one enters while entering a temple is called mukhamandapa. The temple might have additional pillared halls called Rangamandapa, Adhyayanamandapa and so on.
rupa	Roughly translates as form, a representation of the deity.
Salagrama	Special sacred rocks collected from the river Gandaki considered as the representation of gods.
svayambhu	Translates as self-born. Most of the Narasimha temples are located in dense forests or hills and are considered to be self-expressed/self-born.
trikuta	Three temples located in a jointed stellar architectural pattern. This is a style of temple commonly seen in Middle India.

Vanavasi	This translates as residents of forest. This term is used to designate the tribal societies before the term tribe was adapted under the British administration.
Vyuha	This is another way in which the central deity Vishnu connects with the world through emanatory appearance.
Yatra/Jatra/Jatara	A week-long celebration held at the Narasimha temples during Narasimha Jayanti.
Yantra	Visual representation of a mantra in geometrical form. For Narasimha Yantra a circle is used. Therefore, Narasimha Yantra is a circle inscribed with sacred mantra from left to right. Yantra is the diagrammatic (geometrical) representation of mantra. Drawings inscribed with Narasimha mantra are used by devotees for mediation and puja (worship) and are installed for protection in the house.

Notes

Chapter 1: Introduction

1 Cave paintings at Bhimbedka are noted to be one of the earliest examples of prehistoric art. The cave shelters are 40 kilometers from Bhopal. There are about 750 rock shelters, of which around 400 contain paintings. However, only 20 cave shelters with paintings are open to visitors. The Bhimbedka shelters are included in the UNESCO World Heritage List.
2 Shankara traveled throughout India and brought universal practice regardless of caste. The life of Shankara includes an episode where Shiva assuming the form of Chandala meets Shankara, which acted as an epiphany for Shankara allowing him to develop an inclusive as well as a universalist monastic tradition (Pandey 1994).
3 Ramanuja is known to have accepted followers from many castes noting the universal message of Vishnu (Lipner 1986).
4 Basavanna is known for a universal message centered on Shiva regardless of caste or creed (Leslie 1998: 228–61; Chidananda Murthy 1991).
5 The Mahabharata includes numerous stories of admixture of jati in the Adiparva including the weddings of the progenitor of the Kurus Shantanu to Ganga and Satyavati (Mahabharata. Adiparva).
6 Acknowledged by Soifer on page 13 note 21 this term "loophole in the law" was coined by A. K. Ramanujan who had directed her on this aspect. Unfortunately, Ramanujan was a master of strange epithets with regard to the numerous terms he coined to understand/misunderstand Hindu deities. Another popular set of terms he coined are "breast goddesses" and "tooth goddesses," very misogynistic terms to classify the goddesses, dividing them as mother goddesses and fierce goddesses. He decided to call the mother goddesses "breast goddesses," as though calling a mother "breast woman" was normal.
7 Bhakti (devotion) is an integral part of Hinduism even though early colonial studies isolated it from mainstream Hinduism, calling it a distinct movement; for practicing Hindus Bhakti represents a way of connecting with the deity and forms an essential aspect of Hinduism, which is deeply practiced by monastic traditions constituting their spiritual practice.
8 An earlier version of this story is published in my paper: Vemsani (2016a): 147–61.

Chapter 3

1. Castes and tribes denote different lifestyles and practices rather than different religions. It is apparent in the practices associated with Narasimha that the religious practices once may have overlapped and diverged gradually. All the people of India might have had more shared culture and practice historically. Lion symbolism is preserved in the classical literary texts as well as popular and folk religion and practice. Apart from general practice of Hinduism, centered on temples and festivals, an individual and informal practice is also noticed in Hinduism. For example individual devotional practice is noticed in one's adherence to Family deity (ilavelpu), favorite deity (ishtadaivam), and clan deity (Kuladaivam) are also noticed in practice in addition to the major deities worshipped. Therefore, it is impossible to decide the nature of a social group based on the deities worshipped and vice versa.
2. Originally thought of as a representation of a female with a lion head, the final restoration completed in 2013 gave it the final shape. Museum (2013). The image certainly indicates deeper meaning than what could be gleaned from a first impression.
3. Simhādri Nrisimha Śatakamu of Gogulapati, Kurmanatha Kavi. Visakhapatnam: Simhāchalam Devasthanam, 1962.

Chapter 4

1. Atharva Veda X.XII.1. Hymn to Goddess Earth. Translator. Ralph. T.H. Griffith. 1895–96. Hymns of the Atharvaveda.
2. The translation is mine. However, the following works can be considered for earlier translations: *Sri Vishnupurana with Hindi Translation*. Translator Sri Munilal Gupta. Gorakhpur: Geetapress, 1990. *The Vishnu Purana: A System of Hindu Mythology and Tradition*. English Translation. H. H. Wilson. London: John Murray, 1840.
3. Glucklick (2008: 1–25) begins her examination of the history of Hindus noting the imprint of pada (footprint) of Vishnu in Gaya as she examines India, examining the classical stories in practice across space and time. Soifer examines the classical stories of Vamana in the classical texts including the Vedas and the Puranas. Kuiper (1962: 144–51) notes the ability of Vishnu to spread between the three worlds and indicates his typical madhyastha and his ability to unite opposing forces, the upper and lower world, the opposite ends of the world.
4. The Vishnu Purana alludes to the Vishwarupa Darshana (vision of Universal form) shown to Prahlada, although it is not clearly described. Later texts only indicate the appearance of Vishnu as Narasimha to Prahlada. The sacred tale of

the temple of Narasimha at Simhachalam notes that Prahlada founded the temple memorializing the appearance of Narasimha to protect Prahlada in another era, the Krita Yuga.

5 This is also described in almost all the Puranas in addition to the numerous independent theatrical and literary productions based on the childhood of Krishna.
6 Atharvaveda Book VII. Verse 3–4: 3. The earth upon which the sea, the rivers, and the waters, upon which food and the tribes of men have arisen, upon which this breathing, moving life exists, shall afford us a precedence in drinking! The earth whose are the four regions of space, upon which food and the tribes of men have arisen, which supports the manifold breathing, moving things, shall afford us cattle and other possessions also! The earth that holds treasures manifold in secret places, wealth, jewels, and gold shall she give to me; she that bestows wealth liberally, the kindly goddess, wealth shall she bestow upon us!
7 The Upper Paleolithic period is noted around 50,000 years ago at a number of archaeological sites. However, historians theorize that the Toba volcano eruption of about 74,000 years ago resulted in immense ash cover over the world, which resulted in the annihilation of most of the populations. The current population revived from the small population that survived this natural calamity. Hence, the genetic heritage is fairly uniform and continues to remain the same and does not show any sudden change for the period 2,900–2,500 years ago (1900–1500 BCE) indicating external invasions as theorized by colonial historians through the Aryan invasion theory.
8 Based on the author's field notes and personal communication.
9 Based on the author's field notes.

Chapter 5

1 The wedding of the god Surya's daughter Suryaa with Soma is noted in the Rigveda Book 10.85.1–10. Verse 7 of this section (85) notes that her treasure was the essence of Earth (Bhumi) when she married Soma. This also shows the identification of Bhumi with wealth, which is personified as Lakshmi.

Chapter 6

1 The story of Urvashi and Pururavas is one of the well-known legends of classical literature. See Vemsani 2021: 229–41.
2 The Mesolithic goddess temple excavated at Baghor indicates early worship of the goddess in India. Similarities with modern goddess worship are striking and may indicate origins of early settled life and agriculture (Kenoyer et al. 1983).

3. Lion is listed as one of the meanings. Monier Williams, *The Sanskrit-English Etymological Dictionary*.
4. The Venkateshwara of Tirupathi, a regional form of Vishnu, is commonly regarded as the most significant deity of Andhra Pradesh and Tirupathi as the most sacred pilgrimage center of South India. However, the temples of Narasimha are numerically greater and found commonly in a number of villages. Although Sardula could also mean tiger, using this term in conjunction with Nara indicates the popular deity Narasimha.
5. Narasimhamantra
6. The Venkateshwara of Tirupathi is commonly regarded as the most significant deity of Andhra Pradesh and Tirupathi as the most sacred pilgrimage center of South India. However, the temples of Narasimha are numerically greater and found commonly in a number of villages, which is the reason I have selected Narasimha for my study.
7. Ahobila Mahatmya: Sri Ahobila Mahatmyam (Brahmanda Puranam). *Sanskrit and Kannada Meanings in English*. M.V. Padmanabhachariyar Editor. Bengaluru. S.d No date.
8. Garuda, the eagle, is the mount of Vishnu. By indicating the name of the mountain as Garudadri, the relationship between Narasimha and Vishnu is invoked here, through noting the presence of Garuda.
9. Translation mine.
10. Srighatikacalamahatmyamu of Tenali, Ramakrishna. Hyderabad 1969.
11. See O. M. Starza for a discussion of Navakalevara rituals and the involved ritual participants and performers in connection with Jagannatha and their symbolism. O. M. Starza 1993: 88–90.

Chapter 7

1. Narasimha Tirtha is mentioned in classical texts (Vishnudharmottara I.167.19); Brahmapuarana Ch.149; Skandapurana (V. Avantikhanda 77.14–16) notes its location on the Sipra river. The efficacy and significance of the Narasimha Tirtha are mentioned in Brahma Purana (149.19) and Skanda Purana (V. 77.23-4).
2. Family lore preserved in my family narrates that my husband's grandmother Venkamma had the vision in her dream, which indicated the presence of the deity Narasimha on the hill. The next morning she walked to the hill from their village Astnagurthy, which is about 32 kilometers from Khammam, finding the cave temple, which is later renovated and the Narasimha temple is rebuilt there.

Chapter 8

1 Four stages of life are advised for a Hindu: Brahmacharya, Grihastha, Vanaprastha, and Sanyasa. Except for the grihastha stage of life one is advised to live simple life in the natural settings fo the forests practicing yoga, sustaining with minimal facilities.

Chapter 9

1 The Mahabharata is referred to as the Adikavyamu since that was the first literary text to be written in Telugu. The composition of Telugu Mahābhāratamu was completed in three stages. Nannayya (1023–63) could only complete two and a half parvas of the translation of the Mahabharata, and Tikkana (1205–88) completed parvas 4 to 18 in the thirteenth century. Tikkana is also credited with writing the Nirachanottara Ramayanamu, the second part of Ramayana. Errana completed the remainder of the third parva bringing the Mahābhāratamu to completion. Errana also composed the Narasimha Puranamu, bringing the Sthalapuranas into writing about the same time as the classical texts in Telugu. Known as Prabandha Yugam, the fourteenth to sixteenth century CE brought the translation of numerous texts into Telugu based on classical texts and Sanskrit literature. The term Prabandha Yugam is a misnomer for Telugu literature of this period, since more texts composed this period are derived from puranas, classical and local puranas, rather than Prabhandhas.
2 Jena, Siddheswar, pp. 299, 304. Jena notes another version of Narasimha Gayatri from other texts. However, this is the version noted in the Narasimha Purva Tapaniya Upanishad.

Chapter 10: Conclusion

1 Incidentally, Eschmann noted the influence from Andhra Pradesh in passing, although dismissing it rather than exploring it fully, instead of focusing on the Hinduization. The Padampur image of Narasimha bears an uncanny resemblance to the Narasimha image of the Kondamotu panel with slight differences in the facial features.

References

Primary Texts

Telugu

Andhra Pradesh District Gazetteers 1975. Ed. N. Ramesan. Hyderabad: Central Press, Government of Andhra Pradesh, 1979.
Korukonda Sarvaswa Sangrahamu. Gundu, Vighneswara Sastri. Rajahmundri, 1956.
Korukonda Sarvasva Sangrahamu. Gundu, Vigneswara Sastri. Rajamundry: Gollapudi Veeraswamy and Son, 1981.
Mangalagiri Ksetra Mahatmyamu. Kodali, Venkata Ratnamu Choudari. Guntur, 1967.
Mangalagiri Mahatmyamu. Nandiraju, Chalapathi Rao Pantulu. Eluru, 1947.
Mangalagiriksetra Mahatmyamu. Namburi, Sitaramaiah, Vinjamuru Viraraghavacharyulu. Guntur, 1911.
Simhagiri Vachanalu of Krishnamacharya. Ed. M. Kulasekhara Rao. Hyderabad: Telugu University, 1968.
Srighatikacala Mahatmyamu of Tenali Ramakrishna. Hyderabad: Telugu Sahitya Akademy, 1969.
Sri Simhadri Narasimha Satakamu. Gogulapati, Kurmanatha Kavi. Simhachalam: Simhachala Devasthanam, 1983.
Sri Totāchala Mahātmyamu Nambūri Sanjeevakavi Rachita. Ed., trans. Channapragada, Jayalakshmi. Mangalagiri: Sri Lakshminrisimhaswāmy Devasthānam, 2000.
Sri Yadagiri Ksetra Mahatmyamu. Sadhu Venkata Narayana Swamy. Yadagirigutta, 1968.
Vasantika Parinayam. A Play in Sanskrit and Prakrutam. By Sri Sathakopa Yatindra Mahadesikan. Trans. P. Desikan. PDF Available at: https://www.sadagopan.org/pdfuploads/Vasanthika%20Parinayam.pdf.
Yādagiri Kshetra Darśini. Govardhanam, Narasimhacharyulu. Yadagiri: Yadagiri Devasthanam, 1978.

Kannada

Kannada Narasimha Purana. Padmanabhacharya, N. V. Mysore: Sri Jayachamarajendra Granthamala, 1959.
Sri Ahobila Mahatmyam (Brahmanda Puranam). Sanskrit and Kannada Meanings in English. Ed. M. V. Padmanabhachariyar. Bangaluru.

Sanskrit

Agnipurāna. Ed. Dutt, Manmathanath. Varanasi: Chowkamba Sanskrit Series, 1967.
Atharvaveda. Trans. Maurice Bloomfield. Sacred Books of the East vol. 42. 1897.
Brahmāndapurāna. Ed. Sastry, J. L. New Delhi: Motilal Banarsidass, 1973.
Brahmā purāna. Ed, trans. Schreiner, Peter, Renate Sohnen. Wiesbaden: Otto Harrassowitz, 1987.
Bhagavatapurāna. Ed, trans. Tagare, Ganesh Vasdeo. New Delhi: Motilal Banarsidass, 1976-1978. Skandha VII. Chapters 1-10. 885-954.
Chaturvarga Chintamani of Hemadri. Vol. 1-4. Ed. Pandita Bharatachandra Shiromani. Calcutta: Asiatic Society of Bengal, 1871. Reprint. Kashi: Chowkambha Sanskrit Sansthan, 1985.
Garuda Purana. Ed. Srirama Sarma. Bareli: Samskriti Samsthana, 1968.
Goddess Lakshmi Purana. Ed. Narendranath Chaudhury. vol. IV. no.1. Varanasi.
Harivamsa. 2 vols. Ed. P. L. Vaidya. Pune: Bhandarkar Oriental Research Institute, 1969-1971.
Harivamśapurāna of Punnāta Jinasena. Edited with Hindi translation. Pannalal Jain. Jñapapīṭa Mūrtidevī Granthamāla, 27. Kashi: Bharatiya Jnanapitha Publications, 1962.
Krityakalpataru of Bhattta Lakshmidhara. Ed. Rangaswamy Aiyengar. Baroda: Baroda Oriental Institute, 1943.
Kurma Purana. Ed. English Trans. Anand Swarup Gupta. Varanasi: All India Kashiraj Trust, 1972.
Lakshmitantra: A Pancaratra Agama. Ed. Pandit V. Krishnamachayra. Madras: The Adyar Library and Research Center, 1959.
Linga Purana. Srirama Sarma. 2 vols. Bareli: Samskriti Samsthana, 1969.
Mahabharata. Critically Ed. V. S. Suktankar. Poona: Bhandarkar Oriental Research Institute, 1933-1940.
The Mahabharata, V. S. Suktankar. Critical Edition. vol. I, II. Poona: Bhandarkar Oriental Research Institute, 1927.
Mahabharata. Trans. Ganguly, Kishori Mohan/P. C. Roy. New Delhi: Mushiram Manoharlal, 2004 [1877].
Mahalakshmi Pujapaddhati. Ed, trans. Chandrashekhar Tripathi. Varanasi: Chowkamba Press, 1976.
Markandeya Purana. Trans. Eden Pargiter. Delhi: Indological Book House. Reprint 1969 [1904].
Mastyapurāna. Chandra, Vasu Srisa. Sacred Books of the Hindus 17.2. New York: AMS Press, 1974.
Narada Purana. Ed. Srirama Sarma. Bareli: Samskriti Samsthana, 1971.
The Narasimha Puranam: A Study. Ed, trans. Jena, Siddheswar. Delhi: Nag Publications, 1987.

Padma Purana. Anandasrama Sanskrit Series vol. 31. Poona, 1891.
Padmapurāna. Mora, Mansukharaya. Gurumandal Series no 18. Calcutta: Gurumandal, 1957.
Praise Poems to Vishnu and Sri: The Stotras of Ramanuja's Immediate Disciples. Ed, trans. Nancy Ann Nayar. Bombay: Ananthacharya Indological Research Institute, 1994.
The Rigveda, The Earliest Religious Poetry of India. Trans. Stephanie W. Jamison and Joel P. Breretson, vol. I–III. Oxford: Oxford University Press, 2014.
Shiva Purana. J. L. Sastry. Ancient Indian Tradition and Mythology. vols. 1–4. Delhi: Motilal Banarsidass, 1969.
Skandapurana. Ed. Bakker, Hans. Groningen: E. Forsten, 1998.
Sri Vishnu Purana. Ed. Hindi Trans. Sri Munilal Gupta. Gorakhpur: Gita Press, 1990.
Sri Vishnu Purana: A System of Hindu Mythology and Tradition. English Trans. H. H. Wilson. Calcutta: Punthi Pusthak, 1972 [1840].
Srimad Bhagavadgita, Gorakhpur: Gita Press, Reprint 2020 [1658].
The Texts of the White Yajur Veda. Trans. Ralph T. H. Griffith. Benares: E.J. Lazarus and Co, 1899.
Vamana Purana. Agrawala Vasudeva Sharana Trans. Varanasi: Prithvi Prakasan, 1964.
Varaha Purana. Sriram Sarma. Bareli: Samskriti Samsthana, 1973.
Vayupurāna. Part I & II. Tagare. Ed, trans. Ganesh Vasdeo. Dealh: Motilal Banarsidass,1988. Chapter 6. 511–21.
Vayupurāna. Ed, trans. Tagare, Ganesh Vasdeo. Dealh: Motilal Banarsidass, 187–8.
The Veda of the Black Yajus School. Entitled Taittiriya Samhita. Trans. Arthur Berrindale Kieth. Delhi: Motilal Banarsidass, 1966 [1914].
Visnudharmottarapurāna. Ed., trans. Grunendahl, Reinhold. Wiesbaden: Harrassowitz, 1983–1989.
The Vaishnava Upanishads. Ed. A. M. Sastri. Madras: Adyar Library, 1945.
Vishnu Dharma Sutra. The Institutes of Vishnu. Trans. Julius Jolly. Oxford: Clarendon Press, 1880.
Vishnudharma 1–3. Ed., trans. Reinhold Grunendahl. Wiesbaden: Otto Harrasowitz, 1983.

Secondary Texts

Adinarayāna, N. (1993). *Narasimha in Cuddapah District*. Tirumala Tirupati Devasthanam: Tirupati
Adinarayāna, N. (2006). "Iconography of Narasimha Temples in Kadapa District." *Saptagiri* 46: 1–4.
Adluri, Sucharita. (2019). "Viewing Telugu Inscriptions at Ahobila." *South Asian Studies* 35: 168–80.
Agrawala, R. C. (1970). "Harihara in National Museum." *East and West* 20 (3): 351–6.

Agrawala, R. C. (1976). "Baladeva and Lion-crowned Plough." *Journal of Oriental Institute, Baroda* XVII: 281.

Aravamuthan, T. G. (1969). "The Pancha-Viras. Archaeological Society of South India." *Transactions for the Years* 1962–65 (Madras): 63–79.

Badam, Giani Lal. and V. G. Sathe. (1991). "Animal Depictions in Rock Art and Palaeoecology – A Case Study at Bhimbetka, Madhya Pradesh, India." In S. A. Pager, B. K. Swatrz Jr., and A. R. Willcox (eds.), *Rock Art – The Way Ahead: South African Rock Art Research Association First International Conference Proceedings*, 196–208. Natal: Southern African Rock Art Research Association.

Bajpai, K. D. (1971). "Presidential Address." *Proceedings of the Indian History Congress* 33: 21–6. http://www.jstor.org/stable/44145299.

Bakker, Hans. (1989). "The Antiquities of Ramtek Hill, Maharashtra." *South Asian Studies* 5: 79–102.

Bakker, Hans. (1990). "Ramtek: An Ancient Centre of Viṣṇu Devotion in Maharashtra." In Hans Bakker (ed.), *The History of Sacred Places in India as Reflected in Traditional Literature*, 62–85. Leiden: E. J. Brill.

Bakker, Hans and H. Isaacson. (1993). "The Ramtek Inscriptions II: The Vākāṭaka Inscription in the Kevala-Narasiṃha Temple." *Bulletin of the School of Oriental and African Studies* 56 (1): 46–74. doi:10.1017/S0041977X0000166X

Balantrapu, Rajanikantha Rao. (2001). *Andhra Vāggeyakara Charitramu Vol I, II*. Hyderabad: Telugu University.

Banerjea. (1942). "The Holy Pañcavīras of the Vṛishṇis." *Journal of the Indian Society of Oriental Art (Calcutta)* X: 65–8.

Basu, Prabir Kumar., S. Biswas, and S. K. Acharyya. (1987). "Late Quaternary Ash Beds from Son and Narmada basins, Madhya Pradesh." *Indian Minerals* 41: 66–72.

Becker, Catherine. (2010). "Not Your Average Boar: The Colossal Varaha at Eran, I Iconographic Innovation." *Artibus Asiae* 70 (1), "To My Mind": Studies in South Asian Art History in Honor of Joanna Gottfried Williams. Part II: 123–49.

Behera, K. S. (1991). *The Cult of Jagannatha*. Calcutta: Firma K.C. Mukhopadhyaya.

Behera, Sujata. (2015). "Nrusimhanath: A Heritage Site." *Odisha Review II* (Feb-March): 114–20.

Bhandarkar, Ramkrishna Gopal. (1965 [1993]). *Vaishnavism, Shaivism, and Minor Religious Traditions*. Reprint. Varanasi: Indological Bookhouse. Collected works of R. G. Bhandarkar. Vol. 1. Pune: Bhandarkar Oriental Research Institute.

Bharadwaja, Krishna. (1981). *A Philosophical Study of the Concept of Vishnu in the Puranas*. New Delhi: Pitambar Publishing.

Biardeau, Madeline. (1975). "Narasimha." *Myth et Culte in Purusartha* 2: 31–48.

Biardeau, Madeline. (1976). "Etudes de Mythologie Hindoue: Bhakti and Avatara." *Bulletin d'Ecole Francaise d'Extreme Orient*, 63: 111–263.

Bose, Mandakranta. (2018). *Sri/Lakshmi: Goddess of Plenitude and Ideal Womanhood*. *The Oxford History of Hinduism*. Oxford: Oxford Scholarship Online.

Chalier-Visuvalingam, Elizabeth and Sunthar Visuvalingam (2006). *Bhairava in Banaras: Negotiating Sacred Space and Religious Identity*. Wiesbaden: Harrassowitz.

Chattopadhyaya, Rampada. (1992). *A Vaishnava Interpretation of the Brahmasutras Vedanta and Thiesm*. New York: E.J. Brill.

Chaudhuri, Narendra Nath. (1962). *Goddess Lakshmi Purana*. Varanasi: Chaukamba Press.

Chidananda Murthy, M. (1991 [1972]). *Basavanna*. Delhi: National Book Trust.

Coburn, Thomas. (1984). *Devi Mahatmya*. Delhi: Motilal Banarsidass.

Coomaraswamy, Ananda Kentish. (1929), "The Origin of the Buddha Image." *Art Bulletin* 9: 287–317.

Cunningham, Alexander. (1847). "Eran and Other Early Monuments." *Journal of the Asiatic Society of Bengal* CLXXXI.

Cunningham, Alexander. (1884). *Report of a Tour in the Central Provinces and Lower Gangetic Doab in 1881–1882*, vol. XVII, 17. New Delhi: Archaeological Survey of India.

Cunningham, Alexander. (1974–1975). *Eran*, vol. 7. Archaeological Survey of India.

Dasgupta, Mrinal. (1931). "Early Vishnuism and Narayana Worship." *Indian Historical Quarterly* 7: 93–116.

Debicka-Borek, Eva. (2016). "When a God Meets a Tribal Girl: Narasimha's Second Marriage in the Light of Vasantika Parinaya." *Cracow Indological Studies* 18: 301–39. https://doi.org//10.12797/CIS.18.2016.18.12.

Debicka-Borek, Eva. (2019). "From Kanchipuram to Ahobilam and Back: Narasimha Chasing the Demons in Kanchimhatmya 3." *Folia Orientalia* LVI: 159–85. https://doi.org//10.24425/for.2019.130708.

Dhal, Upendra Nath. (1978). *Goddess Lakshmi: Origin and Development*. New Delhi: Oriental Publishers & Distributors.

Donaldson, Thomas E. (1980). *Hindu Temple Art of Orissa*, vol. II. Leiden: E.J. Brill.

Donaldson, Thomas E. (1995). "Orissan Images of Varahi, Oddiyana, Marici and Related Sow-faced Goddesses." *Artibus Asiae* 55 (1–2): 155–83.

Duessen, Paul. (2010). (reprint). *The Sixty Upanishads of the Veda*. New Delhi: Motilal Banarsidass.

Eaton, Richard M. (1995). "Temple Desecration and Indo-Muslim States." *Comparative Studies in Society and History* 37: 59–71.

Emigh, John. (1984). "Dealing with the Demonic: Strategies for Containment in Hindu Iconography and Performance." *Asian Theatre Journal* 1 (1): 21–39. http://dx.doi.org/10.2307/1124364.

Eschmann, Annacharlotte. (1978). "The Vaishnava Typology of Hinduization and the Origin of Jagannatha." In Annacharlotte Eschmann, Kulke Hermann, and Gayacharan Tripathi (eds.), *The Cult of Jagannātha*, 97–114. New Delhi: Manohar.

Eschmann, Annacharlotte. (1978). "Hinduization of Tribal Deities in Orissa: The Sakta and Saiva Typology." In Annacharlotte Eschmann, Kulke Hermann, and Gayacharan Tripathi (eds.), *The Cult of Jagannatham*, 79–99. New Delhi: Manohar.

Fabri, Charles Luis. (1974). *History of the Art of Orissa*. London: Longman Group.

Feldhaus, Anne. (2003). *Connected Places: Region, Pilgrimage, and Geographical Imagination in India*. New York: Palgrave Macmillan.

Feldhaus, Anne. (1995). *Water and Womanhood: Religious Meanings of Rivers in Maharashtra*. New York, Oxford: Oxford University Press.

Fergusson, James and James Burgess. (2013 [1880]). *Cave Temples of India*. Cambridge: Cambridge University Press.

Fisher, Elaine. (2018). "Multiregional and Multi-Linguistic Virasaivism: Changes and Continuity in an in an Early Devotional Tradition." In Lavanya Vemsani (ed.), *Modern Hinduism in Text and Context*, 9–23. London and New York: Bloomsbury.

Gail, Adalbert. (1983). "On the Symbolism of Three and Four Faced Vishnu Images: A Reconsideration of Evidence." *Artibus Asiae* 44: 297–307.

Gail, Adalbert. (1990). "The Mythical Planets Rāhu and Ketu and Their Addition to the Navagrahas." *East and West* 40: 27–36. Ghantijogi, Somayaji. *Yaksaganamulu*. Vol. I. Waltair: 1955.

Ghosh, Niranjan. (1979). *Concept and Iconography of the Goddess of Abundance and Fortune in Three Religions of India*. Burdwan: University of Burdwan.

Glucklich, Ariel. (2008). *The Strides of Vishnu*. Oxford: Oxford University Press. OhioLINK EBC. Accessed on Web. September 7, 2020.

Gonda, Jan. (1970). *Aspects of Early Vishnuism and Sivaism: A Comparison*. London: Athlone Press.

Gopinatha Rao, T. A. (1971). *Elements of Hindu Iconography V.I. 1 and 2; V. 2. Part 1 and 2*. Delhi: Indological Book House.

Gupta, Vinay Kumar (2013). *Mathura: An Art and Archaeological Study*. Delhi: Manohar.

Guy, John. (2016). "Roaming the Land." *Orientations*, Vol. 47. No. 3: 33–42.

Hacker, Paul. (1959). *Pahlada: Werden Und Wandlungen, enier Ideal Gestalt*. Weisbaden: F. Stainer.

Hacker, Paul. (1978). "Zur Entwirklung der *avatāra* Lehre." In Lambert Schmithausen (ed.), *Kliene Schriften*, 404–83 Wiesbaden: Harrasowitz.

Hazra, R. C. (1958–1963). *Studies in Upapuranas*, vol. 1&2. Calcutta: Sanskrit College.

Heimendorf, F. Ch. (1982). *Tribes of India. The Struggle for Survival*. Berkeley: University of California.

Hiltebeitel, Alf. (1972). "The Mahabharata and Hindu Eschatology." *History of Religions* 12: 2.

Hiltebeitel, Alf. (1973). *Gods, Heroes, and Krishna: A Study of Indian and Indo-European Symbolisms*, i–xii. PhD. Dissertation. University of Chicago.

Hopkins, Thomas J. (1914). "The Epic Use of Bhagavata and Bhakit." *Journal of Royal Asiatic Society* 1914: 727–38.

Ingalls, H. H. Daniels. (1966). "Foreword." In Milton Singer (ed.), *Krishna: Myths, Rites, and Attitudes*, i–vii. Honolulu: East-West Center.

Inguva, Kartikeya Sarma. (2000). "Fresh Evidence on the Cult of Narasimha." In Inguva Kartikeya Sarma and Aaradikoppam Narasimha Murthy (eds.),

Narasimhapriya: Prof. A.V.N. Murthy Felicitation Volume, 301–2. New Delhi: Sundeep Prakasan.

Jaiswal, Suvira. (1967). *The Origin and Development of Vaishnavism*. New Delhi: Munshiram Manoharlal.

Jaiswal, Suvira. (1973). "Evolution of the Narasimha Legend and Its Possible Sources." *Proceedings of the Indian History Congress* XXXIV: 140–51.

Jamkhedkar, Arvind P. (1987 [1986]). "Vaiṣṇavism in the Vakataka Times." In R. Parimoo (ed.), *Vaiṣṇavism in Indian Arts and Culture*, 335–41. New Delhi: Manohar.

Jamkhedkar, A. P. (1987). "A Newly Discovered Vakataka Temple at Ramtek, Dist. Nagpur." In M. S. Nagaraja Rao (ed.), *Kusumāñjali: New Interpretation of Indian Art & Culture. Sh. C. Sivaramamurti Commemoration Volume*, vol. I, 217–23. Delhi: Mahohar.

Janaki, S. (1988). *Dwajasthambha*. Madras: Kuppuswami Sastri Research Institute, 1–13.

Jena, Mihir K. (2002). *Forest Tribes of Orissa: Lifestyle and Social Conditions of Selected Orissan Tribes*. New Delhi: D.K. Printworld.

Jogarao, S. V., ed. (1961). *Andhra Yaksagana Vangmaya Charitra*. Waltair: Andhra Univesity.

Joshi, A. (1961). "Newly Discovered Sculptures and Inscriptions of Lord Jagannath Temple." *Orissa Historical Research Journal* XXXV (1&2): 2–4.

Joshi, N. P. (1978). *Iconography of Balarama*. New Delhi: Abhinav Prakasan.

Kalidos, Raju. (1987). "Iconography and Symbolism of Panchamukha Narasimha." *East and West* 37 (1–4): 283–97.

Kenoyer, J. Mark., J. Clark, J. Pal, and G. Sharma (1983). "An Upper Palaeolithic Shrine in India?" *Antiquity* 57 (220): 88–94. doi:10.1017/S0003598X00055253.

Khan, Md. and Abdul Waheed. (1964). *An Early Sculpture of Narasimha*. Hyderabad: Department of Archaeology and Museums, Government of Andhra Pradesh.

Kinsely, David. (1986). *Hindu Goddesses*. Berkeley: University of California Press.

Knipe, David M. (2015). *Living Vedic Tradition of Taittiriya Samhita*. Oxford: Oxford University Press.

Kulasekhara Rao, M., ed. (1968). *Krishnamacharyuni Simhagiri Vachanālu*. Hyderabad: Telugu University.

Kulke, Herman. (1986). "Max Weber's Contribution to the Study of Hiduization in India and Indianization in Southeast Asia." In Detlef Kantovsky (ed.), *Recent Research on Max Weber's Studies on Hinduism*. Munchen: Weltforum Verlag.

Kuiper, F. P. J. (1962). "The Three Strides of Vishnu." In Ernest Bender (ed.), *Indological Studies in Honor of W. Norman Brown*, 137–151. New Haven: American Oriental Society.

Kumar, Pratap. (1997). *The Goddess Laksmi: The Divine Consort in South Indian Vaishnava Tradition*. Atlanta: Scholars Press.

Law, Bimala Charan. (1968). "Mountains of India in Ancient Literature." In *Mountains and Rivers of India*, 1–35. 21st International Geographical Congress. Calcutta: National Committee for Geography.

Leslie, Julia. (1998). "Understanding Basavanna: History, Hagiography, and a Modern Kannada Drama." *Bulletin of the School of Oriental and African Studies* 61 (2): 228–61.

Lipner, Julius. (1986). *The Face of Truth: A Study of the Meaning and Metaphysics in the Vedantic Theology of Ramanuja*. Albany: SUNY Press.

Lippe, Aschwin. (1969–1970). "Early Chalukya Temples." *Archives of Asian Art* XXIII: 6–24.

Lippe, Aschwin. (1972). "Early Chalukya Icons." *Artibus Asiae* 34: 273–331.

Madabhushini, Narasimhacharya. (1989a). *History of the Cult of Narasimha in Andhra Pradesh*. Hyderabad: Sri Malola Grantha Mala, Ahobalamath.

Madabhushini, Narasimhacharya. (1989b). *History of the Cult of Narasimha in Telangana*. Hyderabad: M. Radha & Sons.

Mahadeva, A. (1950). "Saubhagya-Lakshmi Upanishad." In *The Shakta Upanishads with the Commentary of Sri Upanishad Brahma Yogin, Adyar Library Series 10*. Madras.

Mahalik, N. (1984). *Sri Nrusimhanath-Tatwa, Mandira O Khetra Parichaya (Oriya)*. Padampur: Nrusimhanatha.

Marriott, McKim and Alan R. Beals. (1955). *Villege India: Studies in the Little Community*. Beloit: American Anthropological Association.

Meister, Michael. (1987). "Regional Variations in Matrika Conventions." *Artibus Asiae* 47: 97–112.

Michell, George (1998). *Architecture and Art of Southern India: Vijayanagara and the Successor States 1350–1750*. Cambridge: Cambridge University Press.

Miester, Micheal W. (1986). "Regional Variants in the Matrika Conventions." *Artibus Asiea* 47: 233–62.

Miester, Micheal W. (1996). "Man and Man-lion: The Philadelphia Narsimha." *Artibus Asiae* 56 (3–4): 291–301.

Misra, K. C. (1971). *The Cult of Jagannatha*. Calcutta: Firma K.C. Mukhopadhyaya.

Misra, Virendra Nath. (2001). "Prehistoric human colonization of India." *J Biosci* 26(4): 491–531. doi: 10.1007/BF02704749. PMID: 11779962.

Misra, Virendra Nath. and Y. Math Pal. (1979). "Rock Art of Bhimbetka Region, Central India." *Man and Environment* vi: 27–33.

Mitra, Debala. (1963). "Varāha Cave at Udayagiri – An Iconographic Study," *Journal of the Asiatic Society* 5: 99–103; J. C. Harle, *Gupta Sculpture*. (Oxford, 1974): figures 8–17.

Mohapatra, Rames Prasad. (1986). *Archaeology in Orissa (Sites and Monuments)*, vol. 1. New Delhi: Cosmo Publications.

Mohapatra, Ratnakar. (2016). "Narasimhanatha Temple at Nuasasan : A Study of Art and Architecture." *Odisha Review* vi: 96–9.

Mukunda Rao, N. (1987). *Simhachalam Temple Inscriptions*. Simhachalam: Simhachalam Devasthanam.

Murty, M. L. K. (1981). "Hunter-Gatherer Ecosystems and Archaeological Patterns of Subsistence Behaviour on the South-East Coast of India: An Ethnographic Model." *World Archaeology* 13 (1): 47–58.

Murty, M. L. K. (1994). "Forest People and Historical Traditions in the Eastern Ghats, South India." In Bridget Allchin (ed.), *Living Traditions: Studies in Ethnoarchaeology of South Asia*, 205–18. Delhi: Oxford and IBH Publishing Ltd.

Murty, M. L. K. (1997). "The God Narasimha in the Folk Religion of Andhra Pradesh, South India." *South Asian Studies* 13 (1): 179–88, doi:10.1080/02666030.1997.9628535

Murty, M. L. K. (2003). "Settlement and Subsistence Patterns of Palaeolithic and Mesolithic Periods." In M. L. K. Murty (ed.), *Pre and Protohistory of Andhra Pradesh*, 73–85. Hyderabad: Orient Longman.

Nagabhushana, Sarma M. (1995). *Folk and Performing Arts of Andhra Pradesh*. Hyderabad: Telugu University.

Nagappa, B. L. (1985). "Numismatics as a Source of Iconographic and Architectural Studies." *Journal of Indian History* LXIII A-D: 7–17.

Nagy, Gregory. (2001). "Orality and Literacy." In T. O. Sloane (ed.), *Encyclopedia of Rhetoric*, 532–8. New York: Oxford Publisher Press.

Narasimhacharya, P. V. (1978). *Korukonda Sri Lakshminarasimhaswāmi Vāri Purāna Gādha*. Korukonda: P.V. Narasimhacharya.

Neumayer, Eric. (1993). *Lines on Stone: The Prehistoric Rock Art of India*. New Delhi: Manohar.

Nigam, M. L. (2000–2001). "Identification of Vasudeva/Krishna Images in Early Indian Art." *Kalā (Guwahati)* VII: 109–16.

Ong, Walter J. (1982). *Orality and Literacy: The Technologizing of the Word*. London: Methuen.

Otto, Schrader. (1942). "Narasimha." *Vishwabharati Quarterly* I (II): 17.

Paidipati Venkata Nrisimha Kavi. Lakshmi Nrisimha Vilāsamu. MSS in the Tanjore Maharaja Serfoji's Saraswati Mahal Library. No. 733.

Pal, Pratapaditya. (1973–1974). "A Brahmanical Triad from Kashmir and Some Related Icons." *Archives of Asian Art* 27: 36–46.

Pande, Govind Chandra. (1994). *Life and thought of Sankaracarya*. Delhi: Motilal Banarsidass Publishers.

Petraglia, Michael and Ravi Korisettar. (2007). "Middle Paleolithic Assemblages from the Indian Subcontinent Before and After the Toba Super-Eruption." *Science* 317: 114–16.

Pidatala, Sitapati. (1982). *Sri Ahobala Narasimhaswāmy Temple*. Hyderabad: Department of Archaeology and Museums, Government of Andhra Pradesh.

Pidatala, Sitapati. (2001 [1933]). *Sri Venkateswara: Lord of Seven Hills, Tirupati*. Bombay: Bharatiya Vidya Bhavan.

Pradhan, Sadasiba., ed. (2006). *Art and Archaeology of Orissa, Recent Perspectives*. New Delhi: Mahohar.

Rajaguru, Satyanarayan. (1971). *Inscriptions of Orissa*. Vol. 2. Bhuvaneshwar: Orissa State Museum.

Rajajee, M. S. (2003). *Sri Narasimha Avatāra*. Hyderabad: Sri Ahobala Math.

Rama Rao, M. (1965). *Early Chālukyan Temples of Andhra Deśa*. Hyderabad: Govt. of Andhra Pradesh.
Ramesan, N. (1962). *Temples and Legends of Andhra Pradesh*. Bombay: Bharatiya Vidya Bhavan.
Rao, Narayana C. (1937). *Andhra Vaggeyakara Charitramu*, vol II. Madras: Ananda Press.
Reddy, H. M., dir. (1931). *Bhakta Prahlāda (Telugu film)*. Madras: H.M. Productions.
Rhodes, Constantina. (2011). *Invoking Lakshmi: The Goddess of Wealth in Song and Ceremony*. Albany, NY: State University of New York Press.
Sadhu Venkata Narayana Swamy. (1968). *Sri Yadagiri Ksetra Mahātmyamu*. Yadagirigutta: Yadagiri Devasthanam.
Sastry, B. V. S., ed. (2005). *Lakshminarasimha Stotramu*. Rajamundry: Gollapudi Veeraswamy and Son.
Satyanarayana Murthy, A. (1991). *Religion and Society: A Study of the Koyas*. New Delhi: Discovery Publishing House.
Sherwani, Haroon Khan. (1974). History of the Qutb Shahi Dynasty.
Sheshappa, Kavi. (1974). *Narasimha Satakamu*. Rajamundry: Gollapudi Veeraswamy & Son.
Shinde et al. (2019). "An Ancient Harappan Genome Lacks Ancestry from Steppe Pastoralists or Iranian Farmers." *Cell*, https://doi.org/10.1016/j.cell.2019.08.048.
Shreiner, Peter. (1997). *Narayaniya-Studien*. Wiesbaden: Harrasowitz.
Shulman, David Dean. (1980). *Tamil Temple Myths: Sacrifice and Divine Marriage in South Indian Saiva Tradition*. Princeton: Princeton University Press.
Singer, Milton. (1972). *When a Great Tradition Modernizes*. London, Chicago: University of Chicago Press.
Sinha, S. (1958). "Tribal Cultures of Peninsular India as a Dimension of Little Tradition in the Study of Indian Civilization: A Preliminary Statement." *The Journal of American Folklore* 71 (281): 504–18. https://doi.org/10.2307/538574
Sircar, Dinesh Chandra. (1982). "The Introduction of Balabhadra Worship in the Puri Temple." *Journal of Royal Asiatic Society* XXIV (1–4): 45–8.
Sitapathi, Pidatala. (1982). *Sri Ahobala Narasimhaswāmy Temple*. Hyderabad: Ahobalamutt.
Soifer, Deborah. (1991). *The Myths of Narasiṃha and Vāmana*. Albany: State University of New York Press.
Sontheimer, Gunther G. (1989 [1978]). *Pastoral Deities in Western India*, Translated by Anne Feldhaus. New York: Oxford University Press.
Sontheimer, Gunther D. (1985). "Folk Deities in the Vijayanagara Empire: Narasimha, and Mallanna/Mailar." In A. L. Dallapiccola and S. Zingel-Ave Lallemant (eds.), *Vijayanagara: City and Empire: New Currents on Research*, 124–52. Stuttgart: Stener Verlag Wiesbaden.
Sontheimer, Guther D. (1994). "The Vana and the kshetra: The Tribal Background of Some Famous Cults." In G. C. Tripathi and Harman Kulke (eds.), *Religion and*

Society in Eastern India: Eschmann Memorial Lectures, 117–64. Bhubaneswar: Eschmann Memorial Fund, Distributors: Manohar Publisher, New Delhi.

Sontheimer, Gunther D. (1997). "King Khandoba's Hunt and His Encouter with Banai, the Shepherdess." In Heidun Bruckner, Anne Feldhaus, and Aditya Malik (eds.), *Essays on Religion, Literature and Law*, 278–322. New Delhi: Manohar.

Srinivas, Mysore Narasimhachar. 1955. "A Note on Sanskritization and Westernization." *The Far Eastern Quarterly* XV: 481–96.

Srinivasachar, S. and T. S. Satyan. (1995). *Hampi: The Fabled Capital of the Vijayanagar Empire*. Bangalore: Directorate of Archaeology and Museums, Karnataka.

Srinivasan, Doris Meth. (1979). "Early Vaishnava Imagery: *Catu vyūha* and Variant Forms." *Archives of Asian Art* XXXII: 39–55.

Srinivasan, Doris Meth. (1981). "Early Kṛishṇa Icons: The Case at Mathurā." In Joanna G. Williams (ed.), *Kalādarśana: American Studies in the Art of India*, 127–36. New Delhi: American Institute of Indian Studies.

Srinivasan, Doris Meth. (1997). *Many Heads, Arms and Eyes*. Leiden: Brill.

Srinivasan, Doris Meth. (2010). "Sri-Lakshmi in Early Art: Incorporating the North-Western Evidence." *South Asian Studies* 26 (1): 77–95.

Sripathi, Pidatala. (1982). *Sri Ahobala Narasimhaswamy Temple*. Hyderabad: A. P. State Archaeolog and Museums.

Sriramachandracharya, T. P. (1991). *Simhāchaladarsini*. Simhāchalam: Simhachala Devasthanam.

Stadtner, Donald M. (2004). "Vidarbha and Kosala." In Hans T. Bakker (ed.), *The Vakataka Heritage: Indian Culture at the Crossroads*, 157–66. Groningen: Egbert Forsten.

Starza, O. M. (1993). *The Jagannatha Temple at Puri: Its Architecture, Art, and Cult*. New York, Leiden: E.J. Brill.

Stietoncron, Heinrich von. (1981). "Jagannatha-Narasimha: A Unique Syncretistic Stone Image Based on an Episode from the Skandapurana." *Journal of Orissa Research Society* 1: 3–7.

Stietencron, Henry von. (1978). "Early Temples of Jagannatha in Orissa." In Annacharlott Eschmann, Kulke Hermann, and Tripathi Gaya Charan (eds.), *The Cult of Jagannath and the Regional Tradition of Orissa*. New Delhi: Manohar.

Subbalaxmi, V. (1981). "Narasiṃha Images in Simhāchalam Temple." *Journal of Indian History* 59: 35–51.

Subba Rao, Aduri. (1958). Director. *Chenchulakshmi. Telugu Film. Vempati Sadasivabrahmam (Dialogues)*. Chennai: Subba Rao, A.

Sundaram, Kandarpa. (1969). *The Simhāchalam Temple*. Simhāchalam: Simhachala Devasthanam.

Swain. (1971). "A Study of the Man-Lion Myth in the Epics and Purana Texts." *Indian Antiquary* V: 87–113.

Thaplyal, Kiran Kumar. (1972). *Studies in Ancient Indian Seals: A Study of North Indian Seals and Sealings from Circa Third Century B.C. to Mid-Seventh Century A.D.* Lucknow: Akhila Bharatiya Sanskrit Parishad.

Ticku, Rohit, Anand Srivastava, and Sriya Iyer. (2019). *Economic Shocks and Temple Desecration in India. Online Publication*. Available at: https://economics.harvard.edu /files/economics/files/economic_shocks_and_temple_desecrations_in_medieval _india_april_2019.pdf.

Timmareddy. (1993). Mesolithic and Neolithic- Presidential Address, AP History Congress.

Trebold, L. Jeane. (1970). "A Chronology of Indian Sculpture: The Satavahana Chronology at Nasik." *Artibus Asiae* 32: 49–88.

Tripathi, Chandrasekhar, ed., trans. (1976). *Mahalakshmi Pujapaddati*. Varanasi: Chaukamba Press.

Tripathi, Gaya Charan. (1968). *Die Ursprung und Entwiklung der Vamana-legende in der Indische Literature*. Wiessbaden: Otto Harrosowitz.

Tripathi, Gaya Charan. (1974). "Das Navakalevara Ritual in Jagannatha Temple von Puri." *ZDMG Supplement* 2: 410–18.

Tripathi, Gaya Charan. (1978). "On the Concept of Purushottama in the Agamas." In A. C. Eschmann, Herman Kulke, G. C. Tripathi (eds.), *The Cult of Jagannatha and the Regional Tradition of Orissa*, 1–23. New Delhi: Manohar.

Tripathi, Gaya Charan. (1987). "The Ritual of Daily Puja in the Jagannatha Temple of Puri: An Analytical Approach." *Journal of the Asiatic Society* Vol. XXIX No. 2: 83–93.

Trivedi, R. D. 1972. "Vishnu and His Incarnation in the Works of Kalidasa," *East and West* 22 (1–2): 51–63.

Tyagarajaswami. (1986). *Prahlāda Bhakta Vijayamu*. Hyderabad: Telugu University.

Turner, Victor. (1969). "Liminality and Communitas." In *Ritual Process: Structure and Anti-Structure*. Chicago: Aldine Publishing.

Varadacharya, T., ed,, trans. (1969). *Sheshappa Kavi Narasimha Satakamu*. Chittiguduru: T. Varadacharya.

Varma, Brijendranath. (1970). "Vishnu Trivikrama in Literature, Art, and Epigraphs." *East and West* 18 (1–2): 323–34.

Vasantha, R. (1991). *Ahobilam Narasimha Swamy Temple*. Tirupati: Tirumala Tirupati Devasthanam.

Vasistha, Neelima. (1977). "Sculptural Representation of Narsimha Incarnation in the Temples of Post-Gupta Period in Rajasthan." *Journal of Oriental Institute, Baroda* XXVI: 444–8.

Vedagiri, Anu. (2004). *Five Narasimha Temples in Andhra Pradesh and Their Function as a Religious Collective*. Ph.D. Thesis. The Ohio State University. Available at: https:// etd.ohiolink.edu

Veluri, Sivaramasastry, ed. (1968). *Nrsimhapurānamu of Erra Pragada*. Madras: Vavilla Ramaswamy Sastrulu.

Vemsani, Lavanya. (2006). *Hindu and Jain Mythology of Balarāma*. 3 edition. Lewiston; Queenston; Lampeter: Edwin Mellen Press.

Vemsani, Lavanya. (2009). "Narasimha, the Supreme Deity of Andhra Pradesh: Tradition and Innovation in Hinduism -An Examination of Local Mythology, Folk Stories and Popular Culture." *Journal of Contemporary Religion* 24 (1): 35–52.

Vemsani, Lavanya. (2014). "Genetic Evidence Disproves Aryan Migration/Invasion Theories Light of Small-Statured Human Groups of the Indian Ocean Region." In Nalini Rao (ed.), *Sindhu Saraswathi Civilization: A Reappraisal*, 594–620. DK Print World and Nalanda International, LA, USA.

Vemsani, Lavanya. (2016). *Krishna in History, Thought, and Culture: Encyclopedia of the Hindu Lord of Many Names*. 2 Editions. Santa Barbara, CA: ABC-Clio.

Vemsani, Lavanya. (2016a). "Narasimha Mantra as a Connection between Classical, Regional, Devotional, Artistic, and Ritualistic Traditions." *Journal of Vaishnava Studies* 24 (2): 147–61.

Vemsani, Lavanya. (2016b). "Narasimha, Lord of Transitions, Transformations, and Theater Festivals: God and Evil in Hindu, Cosmology, Myth and Practice." *Journal of Hindu-Christian Studies* 29: 21–35.

Vemsani, Lavanya. (2017). "Narasimha, the Supreme Lord of the Middle: The Avatāra and Vyūha Correlation in the Purāṇas, Archaeology and Religious Practice." *International Journal of Indic Religions* 1 (1): Article 5. Available at: https://digitalcommons.shawnee.edu/indicreligions/vol1/iss1/5.

Vemsani, Lavanya. (2019). "Narasimha, the Supreme Lord of Telangana: Saiva and Sakta Correlation of the Avatara of Vishnu in Saiva Texts." In *Souvenir of 139th South Indian History Congress, Hyderabad*, 28–41. Hyderabad: Osmania University.

Vemsani, Lavanya. (2021). *Feminine Journeys of the Mahabharata: Hindu Women in History, Text, and Practice*. 3 Editions. New York: Palgrave Macmillan and Springer.

Vogel, J. Ph. (1929–1930). "Prakrit Inscriptions from a Buddhist Site at Nagarjunakonda." *Epigraphia Indica* 20: 1–36.

Warrier, A. G. Krishna, trans. (1931). *Saubhagya Lakshmi Upanishad*. Chennai: Theosophical Publishing House.

Younger, Paul. (2002). *Playing Host to Deity: Festival Religion in the South Indian Tradition*. Oxford: Oxford University Press.

Index

Ahobilam 6, 9, 15, 20, 21, 50, 51, 54, 55, 64, 69, 71, 73, 74, 77, 83, 92–4, 102, 105, 119, 120, 125, 127, 129, 131, 135, 137–40, 142, 149, 156, 158, 159, 161, 178, 187, 190, 192, 202, 207, 208
Aryan 9, 14, 17, 60, 82, 96, 98, 104, 113, 129, 169, 184, 203, 210–12, 218, 221
Aryanization 8, 14, 17, 19, 21, 34, 104, 129, 212
   pre-Aryan 113

Badami 71, 72, 76, 93, 134, 175, 176, 179, 181, 209
Baishakh Mela 145
Bhargava Narasimha 139
Bhulakshmi 87–9, 99, 102, 110, 116, 117, 179, 195, 207
   Bhuvaraha 179
Bhumi 84, 102, 110, 116, 117, 207, 221
Bidala Narasimha 70, 72, 77, 143, 145,
   see Marjala Narasimha
Brahmotsavam 191

Chenchulakshmi 7, 63, 102, 118, 119, 120, 121, 124, 126, 133, 135, 136, 139, 141, 149, 164, 174, 182, 192, 202, 207, 210, 212
   Chenchitha 25, 89, 99, 101, 102, 118–21, 124, 125, 131, 192, 193
Chenchus 5, 6, 8, 9, 64, 94, 96–9, 102, 103, 107–9, 117–19, 125, 127, 128, 135, 136, 149, 150, 160, 174, 182, 192, 193, 202, 207, 210, 212

Devarayanadurga 177
Devimahatmya 47, 115
Dharmapuri 44, 73, 78, 152, 153, 162–4, 178

Eran 71, 83, 154, 165, 206, 208
Errana 15, 137–9, 187

Gandhagiri 145
Gonds 98, 107, 118

Hampi 73, 90, 91, 173, 180, 182
Hinduization 8, 9, 14, 19–21, 34, 129, 211, 212, 223
Hiranyakashipu 1, 13, 15–17, 21, 35–7, 39, 41, 42, 44, 45, 49, 52, 53, 56, 63, 71, 76, 87, 89, 90, 102, 103, 120, 122, 136–8, 141, 143, 146, 156, 159
Hiranyaksha 15–17, 35, 39, 47, 71, 87, 88, 120, 136, 143

Inugurthi 158

Jatara 189, 191, 195, 218
Javagal 178
Jharni 179–81

Kakatiya 50, 73, 96, 159, 160, 163, 185, 192, 193
   Prataparudra 50, 73
Kala 22, 23, 26, 31, 40–2, 44–6, 48–50, 56, 62, 64, 86, 132
Karanja Narasimha 140, 141
Karumgad 177
Khammam 158, 159, 222
Khond 5, 96, 99, 107, 118, 145–7, 150, 194, 202, 212
Kondamotu 3, 67, 69, 128, 131, 139, 143, 147, 206, 208, 223
Konds 26, 128, 182
Koyilakonda 152, 161
Krita Yuga/Satya Yuga 49

Lakshmi 11, 25, 88, 89, 101–17, 119, 126, 164, 174, 189, 195, 207, 208, 214, 221
   Bhulakshmi 87, 88, 89, 99, 102, 116, 117, 120, 121, 122, 123, 124, 125, 126, 127, 141, 148, 179, 195 (*see* Chenchulakshmi)

Lakshmi Narasimha 75, 76, 105, 141, 149, 157–9, 161–4, 178, 180
Mahalakshmi 116, 179
Papilakshmi/Alakshmi, or Jyeshtha 112
Sri or Srilakshmi 110–12, 114, 116, 117, 124, 125
Yajurlakshmi 196
Langala Narasimha/simha-langala 70, 143, 170
leela 2, 5, 7, 22, 85, 86, 94–5, 101, 104, 136, 187, 188, 202, 206, 207, 215, 217
leelasthali 2, 4–7, 21, 54, 59, 81, 83, 94, 101, 109, 127, 136, 138, 139, 149, 150, 155, 167, 171, 188, 201, 202, 206, 207, 217

Mangalagiri 40, 94, 132, 139, 147, 198, 202, 203
Marjala Kesari/Marjala Narasimha 145
Matrikas 31, 32, 39, 45, 47, 56, 81
Mela
   Baisakh Mela 145
   Narasimha Mela 19
Melkote 177
Mushikasura 72, 145

Nallamala 92, 98, 107, 127, 136, 149, 187
Namuci 17, 30, 40, 203
Narasimha Jayanti 27, 95, 132, 187, 189, 191, 194, 198, 199
Narasimha mantra 12, 48, 77, 144, 148, 196, 197
Narsimlapalle 159, 164
Nasik 170–2, 181, 206
Nira Narasimhapur 172, 173
Nityapuja 189–91
Nrusimha 44, 70, 145
   Nrusimha Chaturdasi 145
   Nrusimha Shatakam 118
Nrusimmhanatha 47, 143–5, 194, *see* Bhuvaraha Narasima; Nrivaraha; Varaha and Narasimha; Varahanarasimha
Nuggehalli 180

Oggukatha 1, 9, 14, 15, 20, 25, 27, 81, 95, 118, 120, 164, 183, 184, 192, 194, 207, 212

Padampur 6, 67, 70, 72, 77, 99, 143, 144, 146, 155, 156, 194, 223
Paleolithic 9, 59, 62–7, 96, 98, 125, 129, 151
   Lower 64
   Middle 64
   Upper 3, 62, 64, 221
Panchamukha Narasimha 157, 159, 160
Penchalakona 105, 133, 139, 202
Prabhavati Gupta 70, 171, 172, 209
Prahlada 17, 18, 34, 35, 52–5, 57, 72, 76, 122, 124, 133, 134, 136–40, 156, 163, 172, 173, 178, 182, 186, 187, 194, 195, 202, 205, 212, 220, 221
   child devotee 16, 127
   devotion of 212
Prahlada Charitram 95
   Anugrahamurthy/ Prahladanugramurthy 76
Prahlada Varada Narasimhaswamy 105, 135
Prahlada Mettu 141, 142

Ramtek 70, 170–3, 179, 181, 193, 209
Rigveda 1, 14, 25, 30, 40, 81, 87, 95, 111–13, 116, 196, 201, 207

Sabara 5, 26, 97, 107, 117, 118, 128, 143, 192, 202
Sadasiva 180
Salagrama 132, 139, 147, 172, 177, 198
Samalai 144
Savara 96, 107, 118, 143
Shakti 21–3, 30, 32, 37, 41, 74, 131, 138, 149, 197, 205
shaktisthana/shaktipeetha 29, 85, 90, 197, 207
Shiva 10, 21, 22, 26, 30, 31, 33, 37, 39–51, 54–7, 73–5, 78, 81, 83, 85, 90, 98, 125, 127, 131, 134, 137, 143–5, 150, 158, 161, 163, 167, 170, 171, 173, 180, 181, 202, 205, 207, 209, 219
Shivalinga 50, 74, 180
Shiva Purana 36, 37, 46
Shiva temple, Shivalaya 157, 176, 181
Simhachalam 4, 20, 25, 39, 50, 71, 73, 75, 78, 83, 92, 146, 179, 189, 190, 220, 221
Simhika 143

sthambhadri 158, 159
Sudarsana Chakra 203
svayambhu 132, 146–7, 161, 167, 205, 208

Tirupati 12, 54, 55, 92, 100, 118, 173
Toba volcanic eruption 63–5, 79, 221
Treta Yuga 62
trikuta/trikutaka 179, 180, 217
triloka 35
tripundra 76, 158, 162
Trivikrama 88, 143, 198

Ugra Sthambham 141

vanavasi 5, 60, 63, 74, 91, 95–8, 108, 119, 125, 127, 129, 130, 149, 152, 165, 174, 182, 218
Varaha 35, 39, 40, 71, 77, 85, 87, 88, 102, 105, 116, 126, 155, 172, 175, 207
Varahanarasimha/Krodha 71, 76, 134, 140, 142, 143, 146, 190, 198
   Bhuvaraha Narasimha 179
   Nrivaraha 71, 154

Varaha and Narasimha 16, 35, 71, 76, 77, 134, 143, 171, 175
Vasantika Parinayam 74, 105, 108, 118, 120, 122–4, 213
Vedadri 8, 132
Vijayanagara 73, 74, 78, 96, 132, 142, 163, 172, 173, 180, 182, 192–4
   Saluva Narasimha Devaraya 73
Vishwarupa/Vaikuntha, 30, 38, 77, 87, 143, 164, 167, 187, 220
Vratas 195, 196, 198
   Narasimha Vrata 198
Vyuha 30, 38–41, 49, 56, 69, 70, 72, 130, 131, 143, 150, 170, 218

Yadagiri(gutta) 4, 77, 83, 94, 152, 153, 156, 157, 190
   Yadadri 26, 151, 156, 157
Yantra 196, 197, 218
Yelgandal 160
Yoga Narasimha 4, 8, 41, 43, 73, 75, 76, 91, 154, 157, 158, 164, 173, 176–82, 197
   Yogananda Narasimha 140, 157

www.ingramcontent.com/pod-product-compliance
Lightning Source LLC
Chambersburg PA
CBHW062138300426
44115CB00012BA/1976